MAKE

AMERICA

SAVED

AGAIN

Dr. Randall Mooney

CROSSOVERPUBLICATIONS.COM

OTHER BOOKS BY:
RANDALL M. MOONEY TH.D.

FINDING HOPE
IN THE WORDS OF JOHN

THE HOMELESS CHURCH
A VIEW FROM OUTSIDE OF THE WALLS

PROPHETS AND POETS

ROBBING GOD

WOGBOOK

CROSSOVERPUBLICATIONS.COM

MAKE

AMERICA

SAVED

AGAIN

Dr. Randall Mooney

CROSSOVERPUBLICATIONS.COM

PRINTED IN THE USA

MAKE AMERICA SAVED AGAIN

RANDALL M. MOONEY TH.D.

PUBLISHED BY: CROSSOVER PUBLICATIONS, HOUSTON, TEXAS USA
ALL RIGHTS RESERVED

All Scripture quotations, unless otherwise indicated are taken from: The KING JAMES VERSION of the Bible (KJV)

The Bible text designated (NKJV) is from THE NEW KING JAMES VERSION, Copyright © 1982, Thomas Nelson, Inc. All rights reserved.

Scripture quotations marked (NLT) are taken from the Holy Bible, New Living Translation, copyright © 1996, 2004. Used by permission of Tyndale House Publishers, Inc., Wheaton, Illinois 60189. All rights reserved.

The Bible text designated (CEV) is from CONTEMPORARY ENGLISH VERSION ® Copyright © 1995 American Bible Society. All rights reserved.

The Bible text designated (NIV) is from HOLY BIBLE, NEW INTERNATIONAL VERSION ® Copyright © 1973, 1978, 1984 by International Bible Society Used by permission of Zondervan Publishing House. All rights reserved.

The Bible text designated (ESV) is from THE HOLY BIBLE, ENGLISH STANDARD VERSION™ Copyright © 2000, 2001 by Crossway Bibles, A Division of Good News Publishers, 1300 Crescent Street, Wheaton, Illinois 60187, USA. All rights reserved. This edition published by arrangement with Crossway Bibles, a Division of Good News Publishers. The Holy Bible, English Standard Version™ is adapted from the Revised Standard Version of the Bible, copyright Division of Christian Education of the National Council of the Churches of Christ in the USA. All rights reserved.

ISBN 978-1-949620-03-0

Library of Congress Control Number: 2020941727

Cover design: Matthew Mooney & Randall Mooney
Interior design: Randall Mooney
Cover photo: Adobe Stock

CROSSOVERPUBLICATIONS.COM

DEDICATIONS

TO MY WIFE DEIDRE: MY BEST FRIEND AND THE LOVE OF MY LIFE – MY ROCK AND MY COMPANION – MY INSPIRATION AND MY JOY. I CELEBRATE YOUR ROAD TRIP AND YOUR HEALING.

TO EVA MOONEY: FOR YOUR LOVE, YOUR PRAYERS, AND FOR INTRODUCING ME TO THE ANGELS. MAY I ALWAYS HEAR THEIR SONG.

TO MATT MOONEY: MY MOST CREATIVE WORK – TIRELESS AND LOYAL – GOD GIVE YOU DOUBLE ALL YOU HAVE GIVEN.

TO MY FAMILY AND THEIR FAMILIES: MAY GOD'S LOVE KEEP YOU FOR A THOUSAND GENERATIONS.

TO RICK LYONS: FOR HELPING ME REMEMBER WHO I AM.

FOR JEFF AND LYNN WYLIE: HE CAN'T HELP HIMSELF.

FOR THE MEN'S GROUP: ALWAYS FRESH AND INSPIRING.

FOR THE HUNDREDS OF PEOPLE WHO BRING ME JOY JUST THINKING ABOUT YOU. GOD KNOWS WHO YOU ARE.

THANK YOU, JESUS: I LOOK TO AN ETERNITY OF SEEING YOU AS YOU ARE. I NEVER TIRE OF YOUR GAZE.

TABLE OF CONTENTS

Chapter One

God has a Plan

God always has a plan for you, and it doesn't matter which part of your world just crashed and fell apart. His plan for you has not ended. You are not alone. God is with you through every loss and tragedy. He is there to comfort and guide you. He is there to heal and restore you. His peace is there to help you catch your breath. All the running to escape the trials that have tried to paralyze your life have left you exhausted and speechless. But do not fear, God understands the slightest groan of your heart when you cry out to Him. Yes, God has a plan for your life – even now.

All of us have experienced seasons or situations at one time or another when we watched everything crumble before our eyes and we felt as if we would never recover. For some it may be the loss of a dear loved one, a spouse, a mother or father, a sister or brother, or God forbid, a child. For others it may be a fire, a tornado, a flood, or sudden destruction that leaves nothing behind, not even a photo for an endearing memory during the most painful of times. And for some it may be an unexpected diagnosis. A moment in time when everything grinds to slow motion and the words become faint and barely legible as the doctor apologizes for having to tell you of a disease or illness that is about to take all your attention away from everything you thought was important. Your focus has suddenly been turned to survival because of an invisible enemy that has emerged with little regard for what you considered necessary or important. But God, still has a plan for your life – even now.

I remember when a young man in his late twenties found himself sitting on a bed in a motel room in Newburgh, New York. He sat painfully alone, wondering what had just happened to all of his dreams. He stared at the wall trying to understand where it went wrong and could it ever be recovered. Everything he had planned for was now uncertain, and thanks to the free will and actions of someone else he was left to rebuild his life. What if he did rebuild it only to have it collapse again? What was the point of working so hard to build a life worth having only to have it taken away against his will? How was a young man with three small children, the youngest only ten months old, going to survive the simple rigor of being responsible for these new circumstances alone. But God still had a plan for his life – even then.

It was in that lonely and desperate moment he cried out in prayer. He asked a question of God he thought he understood but was now unsure of what to trust. With an anxious need to know he cried, "God, what are your plans for me?" His question was the only sound he heard in the room. What did he expect? Would God answer him in an audible voice? Maybe God would shatter the quietness of this dimly lit room and spell it out for him. It really didn't matter how the answer would come. He wanted to understand that despite life having dramatically changed from what he had known, he still needed to feel he had a future. After waiting a while for a word, he decided to pick up the Bible lying next to him on the bed hoping for something inspirational. When he opened the Bible, these words jumped off the page into his view.

"For I know the plans I have for you," declares the Lord, "plans to prosper you and not to harm you, plans to give you hope and a future." (Jeremiah 29:11 NIV).

Wow, he wanted an answer! There are over 31,000 verses in the Bible and in that moment, he just happened on the one that would answer his question. Some coincidence, right? However, despite God not spelling out all those plans for him, it was enough to know on that painful day that God knew the plans He had for him. If God had spelled it all out, he would more than likely attempt to do it on his own and get it wrong.

That's why we need to trust God, because He always gets it right. Sometimes it may not feel right, and it may not look right, but it is always better to trust and rely wholly on God for the direction of our lives. Remember, God always has a plan for us – even now.

"For I know the plans I have for you," declares the Lord, "plans to prosper you and not to harm you, plans to give you hope and a future. Then you will call upon me and come and pray to me, and I will listen to you. You will seek me and find me when you seek me with all your heart. I will be found by

you," declares the Lord, "and will bring you back from captivity. I will gather you from all the nations and places where I have banished you," declares the Lord, "and will bring you back to the place from which I carried you into exile." (Jeremiah 29:11-14 NIV) (1).

These are wonderful words in Jeremiah, and God used the first portion of verse eleven to encourage a young man needing hope and direction. Many others have also found comfort in these same verses. But when you put the words in historical context you get a much different picture. These words were written to a nation that had been suddenly brought to a screeching halt and conquered and taken into captivity to another land. I assure you that was not in their plans. But it was in God's plan. His words are comforting and assuring. They provide hope that this is not the end and that they have a future. However, the captivity lasted seventy years as God said it would. He wanted to teach them because they were His children and that is what a good father does. And this lesson needed seventy years to learn.

Our culture can't stomach a seven-minute wait. We want it now, and if we don't get it someone is going to hear from us. Doesn't God know we have plans and we don't have all day? I assure you my friends, God loves us all very much, but has little concern for our time frame. He knows when we were born, and He knows when we will die – we don't.

Proverbs 19:21 reads, *Many are the plans in a man's heart, but it is the Lord's purpose that prevails.* (NIV) (2).

There is nothing wrong with making plans. Plans are a good thing. Plans help us reach goals. But all too often our plans provide little room for God to get in a word that will help us with our plans. And when that happens, our plans fall apart. It is curious how we then give God the blame.

Realistically, it's insane how often we blame God when our plans don't work. Another verse in the same chapter of Proverbs points this out.

People ruin their lives by their own foolishness and then are angry at the Lord. (Proverbs 19:3 NLT) (3).

Interestingly enough we also like to blame the devil. For some, it makes no difference who we blame, just so we don't blame ourselves. You might know someone like that. You may be someone like that. Proverbs 21:2 reads, *Every way of a man is right in his own eyes, but the Lord weighs the hearts.* (NKJV) (4).

I learned a long time ago not to argue with someone who is right in their own eyes. It's impossible to find common ground with someone like that. Maybe that's why God doesn't waste time arguing with us. If we genuinely want to do God's will then we must submit to His plan.

In the Book of Numbers, chapter 22 through 24 (5), there is an interesting account of an Old Testament prophet named Balaam. The story revolves around a ruler of a nation who was extremely afraid because the people of God, that had come out of Egypt, had quite a reputation and were now at his doorstep. The ruler thought he would gain some advantage by having the local prophet come out and curse the people of God. So, he called for Balaam. Now Balaam was not the most noble character, but he did insist that he could only speak what God put in his mouth to say. On the second attempt by the princes, to get him to come see the ruler, God told him if they asked for him to come again in the morning, he was to go with them but only speak the words He put in his mouth. However, Balaam got up the next morning and saddled his donkey and headed out to Moab on his own without waiting to be asked. God wasn't happy about it and sent the Angel of the Lord to intercept Balaam and the donkey. Unfortunately, only the donkey could see the angel, while Balaam remained clueless of his presence. Three times the Angel of the Lord blocked the donkey's path and three times Balaam beat the donkey for refusing to go. The donkey was saving his life.

How many times has God put what appeared to be a stubborn donkey in our way in order to save our lives? Maybe more than we know. I've always been fascinated by the fact that the donkey began speaking to Balaam, but Balaam never questioned how a donkey could speak. I've learned throughout my life that God speaks to me in a variety of ways. And I always pay attention if it looks like a donkey. The point to all this is simple. Many of us want to hear from God about something to do, but spend little time waiting to hear how to do His will. We confess we can't do it on our own, but still press on to do it our own way. We read earlier that God always gets it right, but He wants us to get it right also. That's why He has given us His Word and His Spirit, to help us navigate the plan for our lives. He hasn't abandoned us to our own devices without a hope and a prayer that things work out. And depending on our level of stubbornness or ignorance from time to time, we may even need a talking donkey to steer us from danger.

There are many people who claim to know what God's plan is for America. Oddly enough, these same people appear to know very little about God's plan for their own lives. So, what makes them the experts at telling the rest of us how to live. God is not playing a game of hide-and-seek with any of us. He desires that we know Him, and He really desires that we learn to do His will.

While some people are content to let life hit them in the

face, there are others that long for their lives to be intentional. They feel deep in their souls that they are on this earth for a reason. They even feel that the reason has eternal value and therefore they must do what they are called to accomplish. Most all of us have had those feelings. We have often said to ourselves there must be a reason for us to be alive at this point in time. The reason we feel this is because God has invited us to participate in His eternal purpose. Read what God revealed to the apostle Paul centuries ago and what he shared with us in his letter to the Ephesians.

In Him we have redemption through His blood, the forgiveness of sins, according to the riches of His grace which He made to abound toward us in all wisdom and prudence, having made known to us the mystery of His will, according to His good pleasure which He purposed in Himself, that in the dispensation of the fullness of the times He might gather together in one all things in Christ, both which are in heaven and which are on earth — in Him. (Ephesians 1:7-11 NKJV) (6).

Let me say it again, God is not playing a guessing game with us. He has made known to us the "mystery" of His will, and that mystery is found in Christ. God did not leave us in the dark. He sent His Son, the light of the world, to light our way. That doesn't mean we won't stumble a few times, but it does mean we can find the right path for our lives as He has planned for us. No more wasted detours and side-streets. Less wasted time and unnecessary confusion. God has a specific plan for each and every one of us and He simply wants us to enjoy the life He has laid out for us all.

God also has a plan for America, but that plan is linked directly to His people. Abraham's descendants were people of promise. The benefits they enjoyed as "the people of God" were the result of God keeping His promise to Abraham. In fact, multiple nations and peoples are still benefiting from the promises God made to Abraham, and America is no exception. America has blessed the children of Israel and has therefore been blessed. Balaam's prophecy included words that disturbed Balak very much because Balak, felt that he needed an edge over the people of God, thus requesting the local prophet to come and curse them. But Balaam repeatedly told Balak he could only say what God gave him to say. And God said: *"Blessed is he who blesses you and cursed is he who curses you."* (Numbers 24:9 NKJV) (7). Of course, he was referring to the chosen people of God, Abraham's descendants.

With that in mind, America has not only blessed the children of Abraham in tremendous ways, America has been a blessing to the entire world and every nation upon it. God has blessed America with abundance beyond measure. We feed the world. We educate and advance the world through creativity and invention. And we carry the gospel of the Kingdom of God to every corner of the world through our people who have answered the call of God to share the message of hope and love in Christ. No wonder people have lined up to curse and destroy this country in much the same way they lined up to destroy Israel. The enemies of God vehemently hate what God blesses and America is a land that has truly been blessed by God.

America has stood in the way of wicked and perverse leaders of corrupt governments around the world that have destroyed their own people to promote a devilish agenda. America has provided food and clean drinking water to many nations and peoples incapable of doing it for themselves or ruled by leaders that refused to do it for them.

America has sacrificed its young men and women to defend other nations under attack from within and without. America has provided medicine and expertise in all of her available medical fields in order to bring healing, health and hope to the sick and injured around the planet. And being paid for her services was the last thing on her mind.

Whether you believe God has a plan or design for America or not, it is still hard to deny that America, like no other nation on earth, has occupied itself with fulfilling what the scriptures teach as the plan of God for the duration of her existence. Sure, America is not without fault. Absolutely, America has done things none should be proud of. And yes, this country is not perfect, and she may never meet your expectations of perfection. But I believe America has God's attention when it comes to being a blessing for the rest of the world. And with that said I acknowledge America has many enemies, within and without, foreign and domestic, that want nothing more than her total transformation and total destruction, if necessary, to accomplish their goal of world domination and control.

But, is that God's plan? Does God hate America? Does God want to damn America, as some of her very own preachers have proclaimed? I think not! God continues to demonstrate His love everyday through His care and protection of the people that make up this country from East to West and North to South. Are we perfect people? No! Are we caring people? Yes! Are we loving people? Absolutely! Do we have enemies that despise us no matter what we do? Yes, we do.

But God, who is rich in mercy, because of His great love with which He loved us, even when we were dead in trespasses, made us alive together with Christ (by grace you have been saved), and raised us up together, and made us sit together in the heavenly places in Christ Jesus, that in the ages to come He might show the exceeding riches of His grace in His kindness toward us in Christ Jesus. For by grace you have been saved through faith, and that not of yourselves; it is the gift of God, not of works, lest anyone should boast. For we are His workmanship, created in Christ Jesus for good works, which God prepared beforehand that we should walk in them. (Ephesians 2:4-10 NKJV) (8).

God has a plan for you. But, it's His plan. And He is the one we must go to in order to discover what the plan is. God has a plan for America. But, it's His plan. And we as a people must go to God to continue our discovery of what that plan is. If we neglect such a great gift as this, we will have no one to blame but ourselves.

Let's pray: Lord Jesus, we thank You for all You have done for us. We acknowledge that we fully understand we cannot do it on our own. Lord, we thank You for the plans You have for us. Plans to forgive and save us. Plans to bless and empower us. Plans to fill us with Your love and use us for Your kingdom work. Help us to re-focus and see You clearly beyond the smoke and mirrors. Help us to look past the hate and distractions and cause us to love one another as You instructed us to do. Help us to love our neighbor as we love ourselves. Help us to understand and walk in the plans You have for each and every one of us daily. We ask this in Jesus name! Amen.

Chapter Two

When the Church Doors Closed

Sunday, March 15, 2020: Churches across America and many others around the world, experienced something only previously endured by local churches in oppressive societies. The government forced them to vacate their buildings. For many, church in the box was all they knew. For some, the new media via the internet, seemed to be the only way to reach the faithful. Which may have been part of the problem with church in America. Reaching the faithful had become more necessary than reaching the lost. The faithful were what was needed to pay for the buildings, and the buildings seemed to get bigger and bigger, while a heart for the lost and hurting diminished year by year.

At first, everyone thought it would only take a couple of weeks to flatten the curve. At lease that was what we were led to believe. For those without a strong media capability, the faithful just hunkered down in their homes and waited it out. Where was God in all this? Was church in the building the only way the Body of Christ could find identity?

In America, identity appears to be found in all kinds of ways. A car, a job, a business, a home, clothes, money, or even a fancy church building. If any of that gets taken away some suddenly feel a loss of who they are. The Church is supposed to find its identity in Christ and in Him alone. And there are two things we better learn in a hurry. The people are the Church, and the building is not.

In reality, despite there being much focus on the buildings constructed as houses of worship over the centuries, the Body of Christ has continued to fulfill the call of God and the great commission without much fanfare. And while some of us were maintaining our buildings, God's faithful were preaching the gospel of the kingdom, reaching the lost, healing the sick and feeding the poor. These unseen soldiers of the heavens have not been shaken by the lack of building identity, because they understand that Christ is the head and they are His Body. And they also understand they were sent to do His will, which left little time for staying at the building.

On March 29, 2020, we marked the third week of the Covid-19 exile from our much-loved church buildings. We were still having fun honing our multi-media skills and were still excited about developing more creative ways to have church with the faithful over the internet. We were also still thinking we would get the all-clear just any day now and get to go back to church as we knew it before the plague.

However, we didn't quite realize that despite using their systems for good reasons, the giants of the web were not friends of the gospel. Try to preach or write something they deem offensive and you'll soon discover their mission is different from yours. Unfortunately, the land of the free, is now more edited, regulated and monitored than ever before, and it's only going to get worse. Sadly enough, the masses are still playing along instead of pushing back.

As we continued experiencing what many were hoping would not become the new norm for the Church, millions were longing for the day we would get to return to business as usual for thousands of congregations. But the opportunity appeared to be pushed out even further as the President extended the exile to April 30th, eroding our dreams of Easter Sunday services.

When did we decide that buildings defined church? Buildings are places for gathering. From churches to football stadiums, the buildings serve a purpose. The building is not the purpose. Football stadiums don't play football, players do. Church buildings don't worship God, people do. If the only way to maintain your relationship with God is in a building, then you only have a relationship with the building rather than with God.

In the book of Matthew, we read, *Then Jesus went out and departed from the temple, and His disciples came up to show Him the buildings of the temple. And Jesus said to them, "Do you not see all these things? Assuredly, I say to you, not one stone shall be left here upon another, that shall not be thrown down."* (Matthew 24:1-2 NKJV) (9).

That building did in fact get leveled in 70 AD, by the same Romans that permitted it to be upgraded and expanded by King Herod of Judea, beginning in 20 BC, and completed in 4 BC. This was the second temple, which Cyrus the Great, a Persian emperor, allowed the Jews to rebuild from 538 BC to 515 BC, after Solomon's temple, built in the tenth century, was completely destroyed by the army of Nebuchadnezzar in 586 BC.

Interestingly enough, since its total destruction in 586 BC, the exact location of the first temple is not known, nor had any artifacts from the first temple ever been unearthed by archaeologists. However, in 1999, people began noticing an underground construction project on the Temple Mount in Jerusalem, and witnessed trucks carrying debris away from the site. A group of people founded the Temple Mount Sifting Project and claim to be finding evidence of many artifacts while sifting through the dust and rubble.

Back to Matthew 24. Why didn't Jesus appear to be upset when He predicted this dismal future of the temple? Why didn't He tell His disciples to fast and pray for God to intervene and prevent it from happening? It was obviously upsetting to some Jews, because they brought up some of his comments about the temple at the crucifixion. Could it be because He knew the building would no longer be the temple that we would need in order to worship God? He did know that after His sacrifice there would no longer need to be a blood sacrifice in the temple. Which triggers another thought, have our buildings become places of unnecessary financial sacrifice rather than places filled with the Glory of God, carried in by His people? While we're anxiously waiting for the day we get to go back to the building and continue having church as usual, have we learned anything God wants us to learn during this exile? This is not the first time God has exiled His own people in order to teach them a lesson.

So, what is our lesson? What is a church? The Jews, and many Christians have been preoccupied for centuries with the rebuilding of the temple. Jews have longed for it to be rebuilt since its destruction in 70 AD. To what end and purpose? Do they want to resume the yearly sacrifice even after the perfect sacrifice said it was finished while He was still upon the cross? Is their ancient building irrelevant to the purpose of God? Are our modern buildings just as irrelevant? There are church congregations all over the world that have never had a building dedicated to the purpose of gathering. It is particularly prevalent in the USA, that buildings have taken on value over substance. Can the American Church learn to thrive without structure and structures?

So, without trying to confuse you with Greek, the original text of Jesus' words offers something to seriously think about. When he said, *"not one stone shall be left here upon another, that shall not be thrown down,"* the implication was a dissolution, to come to naught, a breaking up of a journey. So, seriously, have we come to the end of our journey as pertains to our ways of doing God's work? If so, what does He want from his Church going forward?

On Sunday, April 5, 2020, week three drifted into week four and still no distinct sign of being allowed to return to our buildings. Don't they know that our biggest Sunday of the year is almost here, and we need to be in our buildings to get the most out of it? Sadly, we marked the fourth Sunday since we began the exile from our church buildings having to continue from home.

What have we learned so far? I remember when John 3:16 was the most recognized verse in the Bible? That verse told us things like, *"God so loved the world, that he gave his*

Son." Those words have effectively changed untold millions of lives over the last two thousand years. It also said, *"whosoever believes in Him should not perish, but have everlasting life."* This verse is made up of three very important points; 1) the action, 2) the expectation, and 3) the result.

What is the action? God gave! It wouldn't have mattered if anyone other than God did the giving. He made the sacrifice, not us. And it was His only Son that was given, because nothing else would have been sufficient. And that gift was required for one simple reason – we fell from God's will, purpose and plan through disobedience. Apparently, the disobedience was so detrimental to the big picture and overall plan of *"thy will being done on earth as it is in heaven,"* that God knew the death of his own Son was required to restore the loss. There was no greater price available or adequate enough for our redemption than the blood sacrifice of the Son.

What is the expectation? That we believe! The word believe in this verse comes from the Greek word, "pisteuo." It directs us to have faith in, upon, or with respect to a person or thing. It further instructs us to entrust, especially one's spiritual well-being to Christ. The expectation is far more than just to acknowledge Jesus. You must take your response to a deeper level and entrust your whole life to Him. You must make your own sacrifice of believing that He is trustworthy of your surrender and that He will not fail to have your spiritual and physical well-being in His heart and mind. Is that how you believe?

What is the result? That we will not perish but have everlasting life! Eternal life is not something we purchase at the church building. We go to the grocery store for groceries.

We go to the gas station for gas. But we do not go to the church building for eternal life, we go to God. Please don't misunderstand my statement. There is much to receive from the church building, but only if it is filled with the people of God. It is in those people that God has entrusted His Word and provisions to minister to a needy world. But, if those people are only interested in serving themselves, then what is the point of going to their building?

As previously stated, millions of the faithful are longing for the day when they are able to return to business as usual. But is that what God is trying to teach us at this time? Is He trying to teach us how to maintain our buildings or how to be the Church? Remember what I said earlier, if the only way to maintain your relationship with God is in a building, then you only have a relationship with the building rather than with God.

So, what is the Church to do if the buildings continue to be off limits? The answer is simple. Be the Church. When Jesus and His disciples miraculously fed thousands, it was not in a building. When Jesus healed people of various afflictions and diseases, it was not in a building. When He was crucified for our sins and provided a way for our salvation, it was not in a building.

However, He did turn some money tables over one time, at a building. When the disciples witnessed His ascension into heaven, it was not in a building. When Peter preached his first sermon and three thousand souls gave their hearts to the Lord Jesus, it was not in a building. When the gospel message was spread out to the whole world, buildings were optional and only rarely available, nonetheless, the gospel was spread. And the Church at large in many countries around the world is forced to have church without specialized buildings in order to avoid giving away their locations and facing certain persecution if discovered. The Church has never needed a building to fulfill its great commission to be the Church and reach the world with the gospel message of Jesus. It is simple by design and everything we've done to complicate it has now proven unreliable.

I would like to point out a verse of scripture that has recently become as popular to quote as John 3:16 (10). The new verse of the season appears to be 2 Chronicles 7:14 (11). This verse often rises to the surface in believers' minds when things aren't going well. While this is in fact a great verse with much promise, it is impossible to appreciate the full value of this verse without including the other verses connected to its message. Remember how we looked at the action, expectation and result, of John 3:16? Let's put this 2 Chronicles verse to the same test.

What is the action? The action, once again, by God, is found in verse 13, where He says, *"When I shut up heaven and there is no rain, or command the locusts to devour the land, or send pestilence among My people."* Whoa, wait a minute. Would a God of love do such a thing? Yes, and He has many times. His ways are higher than ours and we can't explain everything He does. Furthermore, He's God and we're not. In John 3:16, we saw what God was willing to do because of the disobedience of the human race. That includes all of us. Once again, He's God and we're not. He's expecting us to obey Him, He doesn't have an obligation to think like us, or obey us.

What is the expectation? That we humble ourselves, pray, seek His face, and turn from our wicked ways. Hey, I don't have any wicked ways…Jesus took care of that on the cross. I'm good to go! Right? If you really believe in that carnal and simplistic understanding of the gospel, including the price that Jesus paid for each of us, then it is definitely time to humble, pray and repent. The price was paid for us to have everlasting life as a believer, not to continue to live as we please while following a concept that his sacrifice came without requirement. We're not talking about law, judgement and condemnation – we're talking about a more abundant life made possible because of God's gift to man, his Son; and fully experienced when we surrender our will and our desires to God.

What is the result? God will hear from heaven and will forgive our sin and heal our land. God's eyes will be opened to us, and His ears will hear our prayers. Our turning away from sin, rebellion and disobedience, will move God to turn to us, our plight, and our need for deliverance. The word of God is filled with many verses demonstrating God's willingness to turn to those who turn to Him. The gospel needs to be preached and partaken of in its fullness, rather than being reduced to catch phrases and slogans that offer hope without instructions. Many are asking God what we must do at this time, and this is the right place to start. The results we need will come from Him as we humbly submit to Him for His will to be done.

God has given us the opportunity to look beyond our buildings and processes, to look at what He intends His Bride to be. The future of the Church, as we should know, is her destiny to become the Bride of Christ.

And I heard, as it were, the voice of a great multitude, as the sound of many waters and as the sound of mighty thunderings, saying, "Alleluia! For the Lord God Omnipotent reigns! Let us be glad and rejoice and give Him glory, for the marriage of the Lamb has come, and His wife has made herself ready." And to her it was granted to be arrayed in fine linen, clean and bright, for the fine linen is the righteous acts of the saints. (Revelation 19:6-8 NKJV) (12).

Are we ready for this future honor? Is the Church willing to accept this calling and put forth the effort to "make Herself ready?"

Easter Sunday, April 12, 2020. The day arrived for the Church in America to celebrate Easter in Her buildings, but once again She was not allowed to enter. That marked the fifth Sunday since the exile from our buildings. But that was not just any Sunday. That was Easter Sunday; a day that was usually the most attended day of the year at church buildings worldwide. But at that time, continued to be off limits to the faithful and hopeful because of fear of an unseen enemy. Politicians at every level, with doctors and medical experts in tow, all collaborated in the name of protecting us from their worse-case models, pushed aside our civil rights and welfare in the name of trying to save the world from a pandemic.

While millions died daily for a multitude of reasons, our leaders used their authority to cripple an economy that was once the lifeblood of the whole planet. From the largest to the smallest, untold thousands, that never faced this unseen enemy within their bodies, would never recover from the financial toll the alleged cure had on their businesses. What have we learned so far? What do we have to celebrate?

It had only been a few days earlier when enraged, jealous, religious leaders, had an innocent man dragged from his prayer time in a garden through the dark streets to a judgement hall, their building. It only took a few hundred guards and soldiers with torches and swords to capture one man. A man that did not resist, a man guilty of healing the sick, feeding the poor and encouraging the broken hearted. A man that simply claimed to have a close relationship with the God those religious leaders claimed to worship. As far as they were concerned, He had crossed the line and needed to be destroyed. Despite their own laws preventing them from having Him killed for His crimes, they manipulated their enemy and captors into carrying out their desire for Jesus' destruction. Their own scriptures, which they claimed to know better than any, left them blind and foolish to the outcome of their actions.

It wasn't enough for them to murder this man. They had Him publicly stripped and humiliated, battered and beaten beyond recognition, and forced Him to carry His death sentence up the hill until He could no longer hold up under the weight, then grabbed a bystander from the crowd to carry it for Him. They drove nails into His feet and hands, leaving scars that would never be forgotten. They raised His body between heaven and earth for all to see. Only His Father, also hated by the zealots, refused to look at the sins of the world, that His only begotten Son chose to carry to His death. Jesus would literally go to hell and back to deliver the sins of us all to a proper and lasting judgement. A sentence He didn't earn but by the will of His Father owned.

He had told them privately of things to come, and also told them of His resurrection. Nevertheless, they went back to their homes feeling afraid and rejected because their friend, one they had hoped was the Messiah, was gone. Starting over after losing everything you've invested in, is a horribly painful experience. They had invested their lives into this man's vision of a new kingdom. Now He was gone. Some would go back to the life they had before, but others had nothing to return to. What now?

On the morning of His resurrection, Jesus' return was met with the same skepticism of who He was, just like before His death. The women who first encountered the risen Lord, were treated as foolish and unbelievable by those who had also followed Him when He was alive. They had not listened. They had not believed. What they failed to grasp more than anything was that Jesus had foretold them of His ability to raise up the temple of His body only three days after it was destroyed. From then to now, the buildings of His Church are all too often mistaken as the temple of His body. It is not our building He longs to dwell in, it's our bodies, the real temple of God.

And for me, this is the real goal for my writing. The Body of Christ, the Church at large, the Bride of Christ, has abdicated Her place in the kingdom of God, to the brick and mortar. Buildings, built by men, and even dedicated to God, fall short in appeal to God and man. And when we failed to draw the masses with our fancy architecture, we resorted to audio and video equipment, light and laser shows, and all the internet and multimedia we could develop. Don't misinterpret my sarcasm. I have used every tool available during the course of my nearly fifty years in ministry, to spread the gospel. However, the power of God to change lives is found in the Holy Spirit and in the power of God's Word, and not in the tools we use to make it available.

So, there we sat, buildings large and small, equipment vast and simple, teams ready and willing, but were left unable to use the tools we had become accustomed to using. What now? How about a resurrection. Maybe Easter should be used to celebrate the resurrection of the Body of Christ. What if we could celebrate a Church that returned to Her first love. We could celebrate a Church that picks up Her Bibles and returns to the words that first changed Her world. Let's rejoice in a Church that falls to Her knees in humility and contrition before a Holy God. Let's be a Church that loves neighbors and friends and can't wait for the opportunity to serve others as we serve ourselves. Let's celebrate a Church that loves the world and the lost and doesn't consider the loss of a facility as a hindrance to fulfilling Her commission to take the gospel to the utter ends of the earth. Let's be a resurrected Church, filled with the power and love of God, fearless at any challenge, because we know Christ is in us, the hope of glory.

So, as previously asked, what is the Church to do if the buildings continue to be off limits? Simple. Be the Church. Feed thousands, heal the sick, preach the gospel message, and do all these things before we go to the buildings. Never forget, the Church has never needed a building to fulfill its great commission to be the Church and reach the world with the gospel message of Jesus. It is simple by design and everything we do to complicate it continues to prove unreliable.

What have we learned so far? Many of us have learned to fear. Or should I say we've learned how much fear we already have. What does fear look like? It has many different looks for each of us. Fear comes with torment. *"There is no fear in love; but perfect love casts out fear, because fear involves torment. But he who fears has not been made perfect in love.* (1 John 4:18 NKJV) (13). And we should also know, *"God has not given us a spirit of fear, but of power and of love and of sound mind."* (2 Tim 1:7 NKJV) (14). Fear cripples the mind and body. When we surrender to fear we cease to function the way God intended – in love and with a sound mind.

The Saturday before that Easter Sunday in 2020, I left my house to go help a friend with some home repairs. It was 9:30 am, in Houston, Texas. Normally an extremely busy time of the week. As I drove the empty highway, it literally made me feel uneasy because there were so few cars on the road with me. I almost felt like I was doing something wrong by being there. I also saw most every business was closed, and all the parking lots were empty. It was like the world had disappeared. It reminded me of some Twilight Zone episode. How could the fourth largest city in America be this still? Where did all the people go? Why are they missing? I literally said aloud to myself, "This is what fear looks like!" Then I started to think, what did the streets of Jerusalem look like the morning after Jesus was crucified.

Jesus' crucifixion had not been a typical execution. Even the Roman leader facilitating the sham believed the man was innocent, whether he believed Him to be a king or not. I'm sure his wife's warning words to steer clear of this murder of an innocent man, haunted him for days to come. Joseph had gotten the body off the cross before the beginning of the Sabbath, and into his own personal tomb. Despite being the Sabbath, the same Jewish leaders which insisted on his sentence, ventured back to the Romans to request that guards be placed at the tomb for preventive measures. Of what? Theft or resurrection? They feared both. While many of the Jewish faithful kept the Sabbath, the streets still had plenty of traffic as a result of all the others in the city conducting business as usual. I'm sure there was much chatter and anxiousness on the lips and hearts of those thinking about the day before and the events leading to Jesus' death.

The disciples had gone into hiding. I'm fairly certain

they were afraid for their safety and their lives. What if the Jewish leaders and Roman soldiers came after them next? Many of them had given up everything they owned to follow Jesus. What were they to do now? For some bystanders, the so-called believers of the Way, were just a cult, following a fake Messiah that would need to be dealt with later.

Mary Magdalene and the other Mary had stayed close to the sepulcher. Their hearts were broken over the tragic loss of their Savior. He had to be the one. They had bet their lives on it. The chief priests had secured the guards they wanted for the next three days. Did they believe there just might be something to his claim? Why would they be afraid of someone they claimed not to believe? Now talk about fear. When the angel of the Lord descended from heaven, rolled back the stone and sat on it, there was a great earthquake. The guards were shaken to their core and fell to the ground like dead men. How could the guards, having witnessed such power, still be bribed not to tell? Obviously, they told someone.

The angel told the women not to be afraid as they looked in the tomb for their friend. *Then he proclaimed to them, "He is not here because He is risen. Go quickly and tell his disciples that He is risen from the dead." And they departed quickly from the sepulcher with fear and great joy; and ran to bring His disciples word of His resurrection.* (Matthew 28:7,8 NKJV) (15). As they ran to report the news, people were fearfully looking around the city for signs of physical damage and to see if any were injured from the great earthquake.

Jesus' disciples had often come to Him with questions. But Jesus had a way of answering the questions they should have been asking. We also live in a time with many questions in mind. But are we asking the right questions? What will happen to me if I lose my job? What will happen if I get the virus? What will happen if the economy collapses? When will I get to go back to work? When will I be able to go back to church? When can we go out to eat, or go to a game, or travel? When will everything get back to normal?

Here's the problem with wrong questions. What if everything had gone back to normal after Jesus died on the cross and was buried in the ground? What if He failed to raise from the dead and ascend to the Father? Then all of us would still be dead in our sins without hope of redemption. Likewise, the question is not, why a God of love would allow something like a virus to bring the entire world to a screeching halt. The question is, why the human race of a loving God would not cry out to Him for healing, salvation and protection, from an attack that is clearly out of their control to overcome. The fact is that regardless of the situation and its effect on us, God does make a way.

And God is faithful. He will not allow the temptation to be more than you can stand. When you are tempted, he will show you a way out so that you can endure. (1 Corinthians 10:13 NKJV) (16).

I keep asking what we have learned so far. There are many great things happening as a result of the global pause. Creative ways to stay in touch with the faithful via internet and electronic means, demonstrates commitments to stay in fellowship with one another. More people profess to praying than ever before. Many are quoting verses in the Bible. But are the prayers and the verses producing the kind of fruit that shows our hearts are broken and contrite before God? We read the scriptures about turning from our wicked ways, but have we really turned from our wicked ways? Worse yet, do we even believe we have any wicked ways to turn from, or have we forgotten that all have sinned and fallen short. God not only provided the way; He lovingly waits for us to turn to Him in sincere repentance so He can change our lives forever. The right question is, "Lord Jesus, will You forgive my sins and come into my heart?" His answer is undoubtedly, "Yes, I have, and I will."

If you are ready pray this prayer: Dear Lord Jesus, forgive me of my sins and my shameful condition. Cleanse my heart with Your word and change my life forever. I believe You are the Lord of all, and I receive You into my heart and life. Fill me with Your love and joy, and I will follow You for the rest of my life. Thank You for the hope I find in Your words. I pray this in the name of Jesus. Amen.

Chapter Three

Is God Calling You

Is God calling you? Have you ever felt deep in your heart and soul that He has something for you to do? How many times as a child were you asked what you wanted to be when you grew up? Does it ever occur to you that the life you have lived might be much different than the life God may have chosen for you? Many of us have wrestled with the choices we made, and with understanding God's will in those choices. The first thing to realize is that God is not in the habit of playing hide and seek with us when it comes to knowing His will. Secondly, He has prewired us or designed us, if you please, for exactly what He wants to do with us. He didn't make it difficult. The hard part is usually us being able to see ourselves as God sees us.

Jeremiah must have wrestled with similar thoughts before God spoke to him. *"Before I formed you in the womb, I knew you; before you were born, I sanctified you; I ordained you a prophet to the nations."* (Jeremiah 1:5 NKJV) (17).

What did God tell him? I formed you; I knew you; I sanctified you; and I ordained you. What was his task? Jeremiah was to be a prophet to the nations. Did he fulfill his calling? He must have, because the nations of the world have been able to read his prophecies for over 2,500 years. He was able to fulfill his calling because the same God that called him, also equipped him.

What is God saying to us? I formed you; I know you; I set you apart for Me; and I have ordained you. Pardon me for changing the subject for a second. This is the real tragedy of the unborn. How many of those that never made it out of the womb alive, were equipped to find cures, save economies, be great leaders, and become people of character, integrity and inspiration, destined to change the world for the good of us all? We may never know.

Paul wrote to the Philippians declaring, *"Brethren, I count not myself to have apprehended: but this one thing I do, forgetting those things which are behind, and reaching forth unto those things which are before, I press toward the mark for the prize of the high calling of God in Christ Jesus."* (Philippians 3:13-14 KJV) (18).

Basically, he was saying I haven't arrived, and because of that I'm willing to leave the past in the past and press on to actually finish the race that is in front of me. There is a mark, a finish line; and there is a prize – *"the high calling of God in Christ Jesus."* Interesting words, high calling. High comes from the Greek, ano, which means, upward on the top. Calling comes from, klesis, which is an invitation. Simply stated, we have an invitation from the top.

Why is this important to know? Because an invitation elevates us beyond qualification and worth; and permits us access based on the will of the ones doing the inviting. Why is that relevant to us? Because the calling is of God and the qualification is found in Christ Jesus. We don't have to beg God to make us worthy to be called or used by Him. We also don't have to work our way into acceptability to be used by God; we have approval in Christ Jesus. Let's sum it up this way. God formed us, knew us, chose us and ordained us before we were born or capable of doing anything to deserve His calling. Some may have a past that isn't always one to be proud of, but God calls us anyway and equips us in His Son. Therefore, we can confidently race toward Him without fear of condemnation or rejection. Christ is our ticket and the door to boldly go where we have been invited.

Next question. Is it possible for me to be disqualified from the call of God because of something I've done in the past? Remember, you were never qualified. The answer is always in Christ. God planned it for us before the womb and Christ arranged it for eternity. If we really want to see the big picture, we will need to devote ourselves to seeking God and searching the scriptures. Because it is in the Word that we begin to see that our lives are more than what we experience between birth and death. Our real lives are found in Christ before the foundation of the world, and the womb; and it spans throughout eternity as an invitation from the top.

Some people have left the ministry because of sins or mistakes. Some have been forced out of the ministry by denominations because of divorce or other moral failures. But remember this, divorce is not the unpardonable sin. The denominations didn't call you into the ministry, God did. And especially remember this. *"For the gifts and the calling of God are irrevocable."* (Romans 11:29 NKJV) (19).

Simply put, God will not take back the gifts he has placed in you or revoke His calling on you because of your failure. He is always ready to forgive, reactivate and place you in His service when you humbly come to Him for restoration. As we anxiously wait for the church as we have known it to resume, I have to ask another question. Will any of us hear the call of God again, or for the first time, in order to fulfill His will and become the Church we were intended to be? I'm sure God is speaking. Who among us will hear His voice?

In 1st Samuel 1:1 thru 4:1 (20), there is a great story about a boy that heard the voice of God calling him. Not only did he hear God's voice, he grew up to become God's voice to generations. Please read the whole account.

For now, we'll hit a few highlights. Samuel was the first-born son of a woman named Hannah. She desperately wanted to have children, but her inability to conceive left her very upset. On her annual visit to the Tabernacle, to make the yearly sacrifice with her husband, she wept in anguish and prayed this prayer to the Lord, *"O Lord of hosts, if You will indeed look on the affliction of Your maidservant and remember me, and not forget Your maidservant, but will give Your maidservant a male child, then I will give him to the Lord all the days of his life, and no razor shall come upon his head."* (1:11). *Eli the priest, after noticing her praying and discussing her request said, "Go in peace, and the God of Israel grant your petition which you have asked of Him."* (1:17). *And Hannah said, "Let your maidservant find favor in your sight."* (1:18) *So Hannah, being sad no longer, went away believing God had heard her pray and vow.*

Soon Hannah conceived and had a son and named him Samuel. The next year when her husband gathered all his house to go offer the yearly sacrifice to the Lord, Hannah did not go but said to her husband, *"Not until the child is weaned; then I will take him, that he may appear before the Lord and remain there forever."* (1:22). Her husband said to her, *"Do what seems best to you; wait until you have weaned him. Only let the Lord establish His word."* (1:23). What, no argument from her husband?

This is an amazing story. A woman can't have children and prays to the Lord and has a child. Then she tells the father of the child she has dedicated him to the Lord, and after he's weaned, she's giving him to the Temple. And the father says, *"Do what seems best to you."* What is really going on here? Do you remember what we learned about Jeremiah's word from the Lord? God also knew Samuel before he was in his mother's womb and had a plan for his life. God had formed him, known him, set him apart, and ordained him for his calling. We are not mistakes. We are *fearfully and wonderfully made.* (Psalms 139:14) (21).

God has invested so much in us that it is a total shame when we fail to hear His voice. Do you think we will ever allow ourselves to get quiet enough to hear God's voice clearly again? A young man recently asked me how to hear the voice of God. I asked him if he read the Bible. He said no. I asked him how he was going to learn to hear from God unless he read the stories in the Bible of how other people learned to hear from God. Samuel is one of those stories. When he first heard God's voice, he didn't even know it was God speaking to him.

When Hannah finished weaning Samuel, she loaded up and took him to the house of the Lord in Shiloh. She brought her child to Eli, and said, *"I am the woman who stood by you here, praying to the Lord. For this child I prayed, and the Lord has granted me my petition which I asked of Him. Therefore, I also have lent him to the Lord; as long as he lives, he shall be lent to the Lord." So they worshiped the Lord there.* (1:26 – 28).

Hannah was very clear in her instructions to Eli. She made two specific points. 1) I have loaned him to the Lord. 2) As long as he lives, he shall be on loan to the Lord. In other words, this is my child, not yours, and there are no time limits to him being my child. I'm loaning him to God, because I'm fulfilling my vow.

I've seen a few baby dedications during the course of my life. One thing I remember about them all was from which perspective the babies were dedicated. The parents always took the position that God was loaning the children to them, to trust and raise in the ways of the Lord. There's nothing wrong with that concept. However, as I researched and wrote about Hannah, I saw the relationship between God the Father, and a mother and child, in a much different way. No doubt Hannah had been unable to have children, and no doubt God had blessed her with the birth of Samuel. God continued to bless her during the rest of her life with five other children after she loaned her first born to God. But Hannah was making it clear that God had given her a son, and true to her word she was loaning him back to God. She was demonstrating in her baby dedication that she was trusting God to take care of Samuel and to raise him up in the ways of the Lord. She would come up yearly not only for the sacrifice but also to see how God was doing with her son.

On a personal note, my grandmother raised me from the time I was born through the first grade. My mother was young and single when she had me. During the summer after finishing the first grade, the time seemed right for me to go live with my mother. After leaving my grandmother, life became very painful for me. Without my grandmother's love and Godly guidance, I became angry and very rebellious, almost destroying my life during my teenage years. One summer day while in Ann Arbor, Michigan, I had a dream that simply showed me to go home or go to hell. Two weeks later I was at my grandmother's front door in Mississippi, and it was not hell. I'm thinking the reason I'm the man I am today is because my grandmother loaned me to God. And on that September day in 1971, she reminded heaven and hell that this child was hers and then loaned me back to God.

I understand the calling of God on my life. Samuel understood the calling of God on his life. Do you understand the calling of God on your life? It's not as hard to discover as you may think. God's voice and God's call is unmistakable. Maybe it's time to give it another listen. You will be amazed how simple it is to recognize.

For you see your calling, brethren, that not many wise according to the flesh, not many mighty, not many noble, are called. But God has chosen the foolish things of the world to put to shame the wise, and God has chosen the weak things of the world to put to shame the things which are mighty;

and the base things of the world and the things which are despised God has chosen, and the things which are not, to bring to nothing the things that are, that no flesh should glory in His presence. But of Him you are in Christ Jesus, who became for us wisdom from God — and righteousness and sanctification and redemption — that, as it is written, "He who glories, let him glory in the Lord." (1 Corinthians 1:26-31 NKJV) (22).

What have we learned so far? Hopefully we've learned that God formed us, knows us, sanctified us, ordained us, and has called us. He did this because He loves us and wants us to hear His voice and accept His invitation. He wants us to hear what He has to say about His plans and direction for our lives. He wants us to get it right!

We also know this came with a price which He paid for in Christ Jesus. However, even that which is free comes with a commitment. A gift might be given to meet a need or fulfill a purpose. If you needed a car and I gave you a new one for free, I would assume you'd drive the car. I doubt you would park it in the driveway and continue to look for a ride. Nevertheless, you will have to do a few things to use the gift. It will need gas, insurance and maintenance, to keep it in good running order. That's what I mean by free with commitment. God has in fact freely given us all things in Christ, but with the gift comes the responsibility to engage on our part to do God's work. It's a great partnership. He pays the bills and we get the work done.

Lord Jesus, help us to see Your call and Your will clearly. Give us a heart to follow after You obediently and learn to enjoy and appreciate all You have called us to do. Amen.

Chapter Four

The Mission Hasn't Changed

The Church in America has more resources to carry out its mission than most churches in any nation of the world. But the real question is, does the Church in America still understand Her mission? On my recent mission trips to distribute Bibles and *Finding Hope* in other countries, I would meet with many pastors who informed me they paid close attention to the way churches in America conducted their services via the internet. But when they told me they tried very hard to copy American churches, I said please don't do that. Then I explained to them that I had interacted with church plants in America that were so good at the mechanics of church planting, that they needed very little help from God to build a church.

Let me explain. When we planted churches in remote villages of Africa, we first looked for a person that felt they had the call of God on their life to plant a church. Then we put a team of ten to fifty believers together and began to pray for God to show us a village that needed a church. Then the scout team would visit various villages in an area and pray for God to show them if they were in the right village. Some villages already had a church, so we moved on to the next village. Once we found a village that did not have a thriving church in place, we prayed for the Holy Spirit to show us if it was where the Lord wanted us to work. We would also make sure our church planting pastor felt God's peace and call to the area. Then we would ask for a meeting with the elders and chiefs of the village to discuss our plans.

At the meeting we would ask the village leaders what they needed the most and what we could do to help. In just about every case the greatest need was clean drinking water. Then we would offer to put water wells in the village at the locations they provided and that our desire was to be allowed have a crusade in the village, passing out Bibles and books, and praying for the people of their village. In some cases, the village leaders were Muslim, and we were asking them to let us come in and preach the gospel of Jesus Christ. And we would also ask them for a location to plant a church. In one village the king let us use the palace to meet, but usually we would meet in an open field, sometimes near a school. But regardless of having a building or not, we were there to provide the water of life in earthly and heavenly fashion.

Once the water wells were in, the whole village, with the leaders and our team, would meet for the dedication of the well. The water was always sweet, and all were so excited to taste and see. Then we would gather for singing and hearing the gospel message together. It didn't matter who did the preaching or what the conditions were, rain or shine, hot or cold. It mattered if the Holy Spirit came and changed lives. Hundreds would come to receive Christ, then we would give away the books and Bibles. The pastor of the new local church plant would begin meeting the people on the days to follow and the mission continued as a church was born. Some would plant, some watered, but God gave the increase. The mission is not complicated, nor should it be.

Now what does a church plant look like for many in America. You'll need a good building and just the right location. It needs to be in an area that is financially prosperous so the people attending can afford to give. There needs to be the availability of skilled and talented people that can help with building programs, children's ministry, and all the other functions of having church. You must have a great worship leader and musicians that are the best money can buy. And that means you need a good sound system, light equipment, and multi-media equipment. Then you need the right people to run all that equipment. Don't forget, you've got to have a good children's church and youth pastor so the parents can enjoy the adult service. And you need a good preacher that can keep everyone's attention. And he needs to be a little funny and a bit entertaining, and he needs to know when to stop so the parents can go pick up their kids from children's church.

Are you starting to get the point? We just read about being called by God. There was a time when the anointing and the calling of God was the most important part of church planting. That's why it's called "planting." The idea of planting something implies that you are expecting it to grow. But church growth is more than just numbers of people. Growth means something living is growing from seed that is planted. We plant and we water, but it is God that gives the increase.

I understand the numbers game. That's what happens when a church has to pay bills and keep the lights on. And some need multiple services to pay bills and salaries in order to keep the "work of the Lord" going. But that always brings up another question for me. If we have three Sunday morning services with the same songs, the same sermons and the same everything, which service will God decide to show up in and will He know that we have a schedule to maintain? I have news for you – God is not interested in fitting into our schedule. God is still looking for us to surrender to His will. And church on His terms happens with or without buildings and programs.

On April 29, 2020, a very wise pastor in Houston, Texas, invited me to be a guest on his radio program. He is one of my favorite ministers of the gospel. With over sixty years in pastoral work and broadcasting, Pastor David Schultz, has no confusion about his calling or the mission. He was staring at ninety and I always called him my hero, because I wanted to be just like him when I grow up. Our topic of discussion was, "Has the mission of the Church changed because of the current pandemic?"

Once we started the interview I said, "Before we talk about the mission of the Church, let's look at the condition of the Church."

The condition of the Church in America with the onset of the pandemic, was not a pretty sight to behold. For the first time in almost fifty years of ministry, I was looking at a fearful Church. And fear is not the way I had grown to see the Church. I know the disciples were afraid when the mob took Jesus to be crucified, but we weren't being threatened with crucifixion (yet). We were just being told to leave our buildings for a couple of weeks in order to "flatten the curve." We never saw the "months later" coming until it was too late, and by then many of the believers were afraid to return to church. But more than that the "new norm" showed few signs of allowing any of us to get back to the way church used to be before the virus.

The year became a breakout year for America and the American Church. But it was not the breakout moment many Christians had often prayed for. The voices of reason faded away as the voice of fear took over. Politicians, surrounded by so-called experts and charts, convinced millions to stay home for fear of the pandemic. Business owners closed their doors for a season, but the season never ended for some. Schools closed, but don't worry the kids could be home-schooled by unemployed parents or retired grandparents. And now that everyone was shut up in their homes, they could watch the various news networks point out to everyone what horrible and bad people we are. Every hour of programming was filled with hate and hopelessness. When you got tired of 24-hour strife and turmoil, you could still turn to fifty-year-old reruns.

And if the pandemic wasn't enough, hate filled the streets with protestors, looters and crime. Police were bad, criminals were good. The whole of society was being turned on its head. But the Church sat silent and afraid, and all for the good of the community, positions were compromised, and belief systems were discarded. The foundations were crumbling before our very eyes, and far too many Americans sat in disbelief and fear, especially Christian Americans. They were the ones that claimed to have all the answers, but now had little to say and nothing to do because they were seemingly evicted from their buildings. If the Church needs a building to function and fulfill its mission, and can no longer perform that mission without a building, then it is no longer a church. It is just another business that has had to shut its doors because of a government mandate.

The really sad part of this new norm is that the world is watching and also wondering where the Church is during the current pandemic. There are thriving, unseen churches all around the world, worshipping silently, and working in silence, because they lack the freedom to carry out the mission openly. They don't do this because they are afraid. They simply do whatever it takes to keep the mission alive. Buildings or not and freedom or not. If we wait for the circumstances to improve to reactivate our calling, then we will never fulfill that calling.

No, the mission hasn't changed, but the frame of mind and the condition of heart of those called to perform the mission has changed. What are we supposed to do? Do we run out into the streets and destroy everything and everyone that doesn't believe like us? Of course not. We look again at the mission we were given, and we look to the commander of the mission, and we take our direction from Him. When Jesus gave these instructions to His disciples, they had already watched Him die and be resurrected. They had already been filled with fear, but now the time had come to be filled with the power of God and the Holy Ghost, because there was still much work to do.

And Jesus came and spoke to them, saying, "All authority has been given to Me in heaven and on earth. Go therefore and make disciples of all the nations, baptizing them in the name of the Father and of the Son and of the Holy Spirit, teaching them to observe all things that I have commanded you; and lo, I am with you always, even to the end of the age." (Matthew 28:18-20 NKJV) (23).

This is not a mission for the faint hearted. This is a mission for those fully committed to walking in obedience to God. This mission is to all the nations, but fear not because all the authority in heaven and on earth has been given to Jesus. The authority is all His. It does not belong to rulers and dictators, it does not belong to Presidents, Senators and Congressmen. The authority belongs to Christ and we have been instructed to walk in His authority and get the job done. And He will be with us to the end of the age.

When I first witnessed the fear on the Church at the beginning of the so-called pandemic, I couldn't help but think of certain scriptures and wondered why they were not being quoted.

For God hath not given us the spirit of fear; but of power, and of love, and of a sound mind. (2 Timothy 1:7 KJV) (24).

Why were they afraid? Where was the power, the love, and the sound mind? These characteristics are required for soldiers of the cross, fully engaged in spiritual warfare. There is no room for crippling and uncontrolled fear on the battlefield. That's how people get killed. How is the world supposed to find hope during the battles of life when the Church fails to be the light on the hill sending hope to the world? The mission has not changed. In fact, it is now more important than ever.

What about verses like Matthew 10:28, *And fear not them which kill the body, but are not able to kill the soul: but rather fear him which is able to destroy both soul and body in hell.* (KJV) (25).

God is not expecting us to be terrified of Him. He loves us! And He has also provided us with His peace and power, so we don't have to be afraid of the mob. My times are in His hands. I have a calling and a mission to complete. I, and the Church with me, must trust God and our lives to Him, and only Him, and we cannot complete our mission by being afraid of the mob.

No one ever faced a mob like the one Jesus faced. You want to talk about hate speech? There has never been a mob so hateful, with speech as hateful, as the mob that repeatedly cried out for Him to be crucified. That is hate speech.

So, let's change gears. Does the Church in America have the right to be spared from hard things? Thank God for America. Thank God for those who have gone before us securing our freedom and our safety. Thank God for a constitution and a Bill of Rights, that has provided the Church with levels of religious freedom unparalleled in the world. But, while our constitution provides us with rights and protections, does that same constitution guarantee it will stop trials and tribulations from coming our way? Is the Church guaranteed that the protections of the American government will always be there for Her? I'm afraid to tell you the answer could be no.

Today, it's the buildings and the right to gather together in a reasonable manner. Tomorrow, when the mobs tire of political figures, they'll be going after crosses, statues of Jesus, and church buildings. And strange as it appears and as hard as it is to believe, the politicians we elected to serve have little stomach to protect us. My guess is, and may happen before this book is actually released, that the Church will soon learn how little of a friend they have in social media. What's next? The gospel of Jesus Christ will be treated as hate speech and will no longer be permitted in the new normal. Then what will the Church do? I suppose it may have to return to preaching the gospel one on one and to small gatherings. Jesus sent them out by two. The mission did not rely on buildings or large crowds. The ministers of the gospel relied on the power of the Holy Spirit to change the world. Are we ready to change it again?

So, if we lose our buildings to the pandemic and the new normal; and if we lose our ability to stream the gospel to the corners of the earth; will we take all that extra free time to present the gospel to our neighbor across the street? The mission of the Church during the pandemic has not changed. But maybe we should. Maybe all the things we thought we needed to do a good job for God were mere distractions that kept us from allowing God to do a good job on us.

Paul wrote a great letter to the Church in Rome. The first chapter points out the behavior and the culture of the Romans, with strong advise for the Christians in Rome to be careful about adopting the culture or its ways. But even more interesting than the condition of the culture, he gave the Church a long list of things that they could be doing in Rome, despite the actions and the behaviors of the locals.

The variety of culture and behavior in America today also provides much opportunity for Christians to become diluted and watered down in their thinking and their walk with God. Paul started out his letter to the Church in Rome, by warning them about the culture and admonishing them not to conform to the nation's sinfulness. He finished that letter by telling them how to behave like the Church and the disciples of the Church, regardless of the culture. The current culture we live in offers plenty of ways to dilute the Church and distract Her from Her calling and mission. The following are highlights of Paul's instructions to the Church in Romans chapters 12 – 16. Next time you question what God wants you to do, consider Paul's bullet list below.

- ➢ Give your bodies to God.
- ➢ Be a living and holy sacrifice.
- ➢ Do not copy the behavior and customs of this world.
- ➢ Let God transform you into a new person.
- ➢ Change the way you think.
- ➢ Know God's will for you.
- ➢ Do not think you are better than you really are.
- ➢ Be honest in your evaluation of yourselves.
- ➢ Measure yourselves by the faith God has given you.
- ➢ We are many parts of one Body, and we all belong to each other.
- ➢ God has given us different gifts for doing certain things well.
- ➢ If God has given you the ability to prophesy, speak with much faith.
- ➢ If your gift is serving others, serve them well.
- ➢ If you are a teacher, teach well.
- ➢ If your gift is to encourage others, be encouraging.
- ➢ If it is giving, give generously.
- ➢ If God has given you leadership ability, take it seriously.
- ➢ If you have a gift for showing kindness to others, do it gladly.
- ➢ Do not pretend to love others. Really love them.
- ➢ Hate what is wrong. Hold tightly to what is good.
- ➢ Love each other with genuine affection.
- ➢ Take delight in honoring each other.
- ➢ Never be lazy but work hard and serve the Lord enthusiastically.
- ➢ Rejoice in our confident hope.

➤ Be patient in trouble and keep on praying.

➤ When people are in need, be ready to help them.

➤ Always be eager to practice hospitality.

➤ Bless those who persecute you.

➤ Be happy with those who are happy.

➤ Weep with those who weep.

➤ Live in harmony with each other.

➤ Do not be too proud to enjoy the company of ordinary people.

➤ Do not think you know it all!

➤ Never pay back evil with more evil.

➤ Do things in such a way that everyone can see you are honorable.

➤ Do all that you can to live in peace with everyone.

➤ Never take revenge.

➤ If your enemies are hungry, feed them.

➤ If they are thirsty, give them something to drink.

➤ Do not let evil conquer you but conquer evil by doing good.

➤ Submit to governing authorities. For all authority comes from God.

➤ Pay your taxes.

➤ Give to everyone what you owe them.

➤ Give respect and honor to those who are in authority.

➤ Owe nothing to anyone except for your obligation to love one another.

➤ Love your neighbor as yourself.

➤ Wake up, for our salvation is nearer now than when we first believed.

➤ Remove your dark deeds and put on the shining armor of right living.

➤ Live decent lives for all to see.

➤ Do not participate in darkness and immoral living.

➤ Clothe yourself with the presence of the Lord Jesus Christ.

➤ Do not let yourself think about ways to indulge your

evil desires.

> Accept other believers who are weak in faith.
> Stop condemning each other.
> Live in such a way that you will not cause another believer to stumble.
> Aim for harmony in the Church and try to build each other up.
> Do not tear apart the work of God.
> We who are strong must be considerate of those who are sensitive.
> We must not just please ourselves.
> We should help others do what is right and build them up in the Lord.
> Wait patiently for God's promises to be fulfilled.
> Accept each other just as Christ has accepted you.
> Overflow with confident hope through the power of the Holy Spirit.
> Watch out for people who cause divisions and upset people's faith.
> Be wise in doing right and stay innocent of any wrong. (Romans 12:1 – 16:27 NLT) (26).

Paul sure had a lot to say to the Church at Rome in those last few chapters. And we, the Church at large, have a lot to hear and even more to do.

Let's pray: Dear Lord Jesus. We have more to do and less to make excuses about than we ever imagined. Thank You for Your power and gift of the Holy Spirit. Thank You for Your word and Your guidance. Fill us now with the courage to answer Your call to ministry and give us the strength to step out and get busy in Your kingdom. Help us realize more than ever no one will ever be able to take Your words from our hearts. We love You and ask for Your forgiveness and passion for the kingdom work ahead. In Jesus name. Amen!

Chapter Five

Remember the Cross

What is the gospel of Jesus Christ, and what is my mission with that gospel? While I certainly don't consider myself the most qualified person to write on this subject, I have certainly had enough time to come to understand the difference between qualified and called. And I particularly recognize the need and the timing to put forth the effort. For you see, it has not been the repeated attempts to eliminate the depth and meaning of the cross that has resulted in the most damage to its preciousness, it has been the dilution of this sacred symbol which has resulted in the hardening of even the most sensitive heart.

The cross has always presented a message of death. Jesus was not the first person to die on a cross, nor was He the last person to suffer its shame. He was not even the only person to die on the cross that dreadful day, still held in remembrance and celebrated to this very day. Despite being the most famous of all who would suffer crucifixion, the Romans did not abolish the practice after crucifying the Son of God. And you can be relatively certain He was not the first and only innocent man to be hung on a cross. The Romans ruled Jerusalem and the surrounding area for nearly four-hundred years. And it is reported historically that they adopted crucifixion from Alexander the Great and put the practice to use around the time Jesus was born. So, it is most likely Jesus had witnessed more than his share of crucifixions before finding Himself as a victim of this brutal form of execution.

As far as the Romans were concerned, the timing and the event of Jesus' crucifixion was not some special thing. Two other criminals had been tried, convicted, and crucified on either side of Him. But it was not his innocence that forever changed the meaning of this deadly symbol, it was his sinlessness. From that day until now there has never been a less deserving person to be placed on a cross. This man, Jesus, willingly submitted to a cross He had not earned. He was the same man who had taught others the need to carry the cross they would be appointed, and while the Jews and the Romans thought it was their idea, it was actually the Father of Jesus that required this heinous act to be performed. An act designed to benefit the very ones that placed Him there. And unlike every other victim of its torture, this victim had the power to summon the angels of heaven above to remove Him from its nails. But for us, He opted to endure its price.

The Romans had littered the landscape with crosses and thought nothing of leaving the remains of the dead hanging upon them as warnings to those passing by to be witnesses of Roman power and ruthlessness. Pilate marveled that Jesus had died so soon upon the cross. It could easily take days for some to die. Nevertheless, as it often is when it involves the human heart, even the witnesses of these barbaric executions were so accustomed to the horrible images and the smell of death, they were actually capable of making their journeys from one place to the next without paying much attention to the plight or condition of those hanging there.

It was not uncommon to place crosses along often used travel routes rather than on a selected hill like, Golgotha. The cross was a form of death reserved for murderers and thieves. But it was particularly favored to use on those responsible for rebellions and insurrections against the Roman Empire. In any case, it was designed to punish the guilty and to provoke the people they wanted to control in order to keep them in line. Unlike many nations today, the history of the Roman Empire revealed a nation that was not concerned with political correctness, sensitivity training, or worries over what anyone thought about unfair and brutal executions on display in the public arena. And the public at large clearly demonstrated, during that time period, an enormous thirst for the open humiliation and destruction of their fellow humans. A thirst that has yet to be quenched.

The use of a cross was not considered strange for the public to witness during that time period. But, the execution of Jesus by crucifixion, at the behest of religious Jewish leaders, was something to watch. It was highly unusual for those Jewish religious leaders to demand seeing Jesus crucified, because crucifixion was not an acceptable form of capital punishment under Jewish law. This mob of haters cried out repeatedly for the Roman authorities to have this man killed. When Pilate asked the crowd what they would have him do with Jesus, they were the first to suggest crucifixion, not the Roman ruler. Their determination to have Jesus executed on a cross, a punishment reserved for the guiltiest among them, provided great theatre for the world to remember and relive to this present day. Even Pilate's attempt to have Jesus acquitted, a man he found no fault in, led him to wash his hands of the matter. And against the advice of his own wife, Pilate granted this self-righteous mob, a mob which insisted that the blood of this innocent man be on them, the desire of their hearts. That desire being the illegal and despicable death of the most innocent man to have ever walked the earth.

How did such an illegal act on behalf of the Jews and a brutal and grotesque practice by the Romans, become the rallying symbol of worship for the followers of Jesus unto this present day? Why is the symbol of the cross as capable of uniting believers as it is for the dividing of unbelievers? Why are there so many battles waged to stamp out the image of the cross? A cross, not only revered by those that agonize over the thought of their savior dying on it, but a symbol also celebrated by those that were glad to see a man claiming to be God's Son, get murdered thereon. Is this symbol a victory or a distraction? That depends on who you are.

Once again, God takes the common and the ordinary, even the absurd, and forces all of humanity to focus on what He has done. Much like a father pointing out the obvious and often overlooked things done by even the most observant child, history had demonstrated for generations before the cross that people were looking for an event that would come and change everything. Now over two-thousand years later they still look back to the event that occurred in order to find comfort and strength.

But consider this, Jesus only spent a few hours on that cross and only three days in a borrowed grave, and it changed everything forever. And thank God it did. Yet, if our focus is forever fixed on the temporary use of another man's grave, what benefit from that moment are we possibly overlooking? The story did not end at the cross, it began there. For those of us that cherish and reverence this sacrifice, it's not that we've necessarily forgotten the cross in and of itself. However, it is quite possible that we have failed to remember or even recognize the whole event we refer to as Calvary, the event that changed everything. And with that in mind, we often fail to move away from the grave in order to witness the resurrection, the ascension, and the promise He made to return again.

The disciples walked away from his death feeling defeated. Some went fishing and others prepared to return to their old lives. They were confused, dismayed and disillusioned. They had forsaken all to follow this man. They invested everything and now He was gone. The women that had wept at his feet now waited at the tomb. And when one of the women witnessed his resurrected body and tried to tell his closest disciples she had seen the Lord; they brushed her report off as crazy. For those men, the ones that were the eyewitnesses of his miracles, the cross spelled the end of all they hoped for, not the beginning.

The women however, and as they most often do, reacted differently to the cross than the men. While at his feet, they managed to live in the moment and accept his death. But later at the tomb easily accepted his resurrection. The women must have been listening better than the men, because some of them refused to accept the cross as the end of the story. The women that were close to Jesus, had welcomed the seed of the new kingdom He had spoken about. But Peter, who was complemented at one time for understanding his words, was later told to put down his sword because he failed to recognize God's timing. Timing that men continue to misunderstand to this very day.

Jesus was very open about His death to those that walked with Him. On one occasion while in route to Jerusalem He clearly declared, *"The Son of man shall be betrayed unto the chief priests and unto the scribes, and they shall condemn him to death, and shall deliver him to the Gentiles to mock, and to scourge, and to crucify him: and the third day he shall rise again."* (Matthew 20:18-19 KJV) (27).

This was one of many things He said to prepare them for what was to come at the appointed time. But after this statement, the mother of the two Zebedee boys could only ask if her sons could sit on His right hand and left hand when He came into His kingdom. Those two boys, hand-picked by Jesus to be disciples, must have been hiding behind their mother's skirt when He addressed them after she posed that question.

But Jesus answered and said, "Ye know not what ye ask. Are ye able to drink of the cup that I shall drink of, and to be baptized with the baptism that I am baptized with?"

They say unto him, "We are able." (Matthew 20:22 KJV) (28).

The only problem was they weren't listening. They knew He was different. They hoped He was the Messiah, the King, come to free Israel. But their desire to have the best seats at the table kept them from really hearing the *mocked, scourged and crucify* part. They also had no idea whose time it was. Theirs would come soon enough.

What prompted Jesus to bring this up on the road to Jerusalem? Is it possible He and His entourage were walking past some of those victims placed on crosses in plain view by Roman soldiers? Could this common sight have been a constant reminder to Jesus of why He had come at such a time as this? If his initial appearance had not taken place during the time of the Roman Empire, and their use of the cross as a form of execution, what would the price of our salvation have looked like?

And he saith unto them, "Ye shall drink indeed of my cup, and be baptized with the baptism that I am baptized with: but to sit on my right hand, and on my left, is not mine to give, but it shall be given to them for whom it is prepared of my Father." (Matthew 20:23 KJV) (29).

All too often I've missed the most important part of this statement. I've given plenty of thought to the cup and the baptism. I've even thought about the arrogance of the Zebedee family for thinking their boys actually qualified for the best seats. And I bet the rest of the disciples got pretty irritated at the two of them for assuming they were better than the rest of them. But Jesus had a far more important focus than the suffering of the cross or the reward of the Kingdom. Jesus was always aware of understanding and doing the will of His Father – first and foremost. He knew His place within the timeframe of His own earthly life. He was committed to fulfilling the will of His Father. And He knew what His was to give and what was not. But most of all He understood that we all shared the opportunity to live the life that was prepared for us by the Father and would be given to us by Him. That grasp of God and God's timing is necessary to endure even the most difficult of times. And Jesus was aware that His most difficult time (*prepared for him by his Father*), had arrived.

The Bible is filled with stories and statements from Genesis to Revelation that magnifies the importance of recognizing the timing of God. We only have to look back across the connected stories and experiences of our own lives to bear witness to the fact that there were often undeniable moments that could have only happened within the realm of perfect timing, timing that we clearly had nothing to do with arranging. Those moments in time provided us with everything we needed to grow our faith and strengthen our resolve and increase our awareness that our lives were not without meaning. The times of trouble and refreshing reminds us most of all that we are not alone and there must be something unseen and supernatural working beyond our comprehension and awareness. Equipped with this understanding we discover that "God" timing gives us the greatest "*aha*" moments of our lives. The most famous of these verses is found in the third chapter of Ecclesiastes.

To everything there is a season, and a time to every purpose under the heaven: A time to be born, and a time to die; a time to plant, and a time to pluck up that which is planted; a time to kill, and a time to heal; a time to break down, and a time to build up; a time to weep, and a time to laugh; a time to mourn, and a time to dance; a time to cast away stones, and a time to gather stones together; a time to embrace, and a time to refrain from embracing; a time to get, and a time to lose; a time to keep, and a time to cast away; a time to rend, and a time to sew; a time to keep silence, and a time to speak; a time to love, and a time to hate; a time of war, and a time of peace. (1-8) (30).

He hath made everything beautiful in his time: Also, he hath set the world in their heart, so that no man can find out the work that God makes from the beginning to the end. I know that there is no good in them, but for a man to rejoice, and to do good in his life. And also, that every man should eat and drink, and enjoy the good of all his labor, it is the gift of God. (11-13) (30).

I know that, whatsoever God doeth, it shall be forever: Nothing can be put to it, nor any thing taken from it: And God doeth it, that men should fear before him. That which hath been is now; and that which is to be hath already been; and God requires that which is past. And moreover, I saw under the sun the place of judgment, that wickedness was there; and the place of righteousness, that iniquity was there. I said in mine heart, "God shall judge the righteous and the wicked: for there is a time there for every purpose and for every work." (14-17) (30).

I said in mine heart concerning the estate of the sons of men, that God might manifest them, and that they might see that they themselves are beasts. For that which befalls the sons of men befalls beasts; even one thing befalls them: As the one dies, so dies the other; yes, they have all one breath; so that a man hath no preeminence above a beast: For all is vanity. All go unto one place; all are of the dust, and all turn to dust again. Who knows the spirit of man that goes upward, and the spirit of the beast that goes downward to the earth?

Wherefore I perceive that there is nothing better, than that a man should rejoice in his own works; for that is his portion: for who shall bring him to see what shall be after him? (18-22) (30).

These immortal words were penned by a king in Israel many years ago. A man gifted as one of the richest and wisest of all men on the earth. I have always marveled that a man, which literally had everything the heart could desire, concluded in several places in his writings, there is nothing better under the sun than to enjoy the work of our hands and the wife of our youth. Two simple gifts of life that we overlook more often than we appreciate.

For all the times I have felt personally driven to accomplish some great task, I have to return to these verses and the most basic and fulfilling portion of my own life. If I can't get this right, enjoying the work that I do every day with the talent, skills and abilities that God has gifted me with, then I have failed to enjoy my greatest gifts. If I fail to hold on to, appreciate, and love more than myself, the wife that God has brought to me at the perfect time to share life with, then I have wasted the most precious gift God has provided in order to enable me to truly enjoy the times of my life.

Often, God gets the blame for our failure to understand and recognize his timing. Life is not always easy, nor is it always hard. It changes – a lot. Apart from trusting God, there is very little hope that we can successfully navigate the many routes that make up our journey. Instead of blaming God for the path we've taken, we must learn to follow God down the path He has prepared.

When Jesus invited his disciples to watch and pray with Him in the garden, He was preparing Himself and them for the path God had prepared. Jesus prayed. They slept. Just as with timing, there is a time to sleep, to rest and refresh, but there are also times when prayer is essential to prepare and strengthen what is lacking for the trail ahead. Just as Jesus submitted to and prepared for the will of the Father, we must learn the time to sleep and the time to pray in order to move through the times of life prepared for us.

Many of us pray for God's will to be done, but we often fail to prepare ourselves to do God's will. Successful athletes understand that training is useless if it fails to get them in shape for the events ahead. Many of us proclaim we are ready for God to accomplish His will. But, are we in shape for God's will to be carried out in our lives?

Carrying a cross will get us in shape. Blaming and complaining because of the things we face will not. Jesus understood His time had come. From His childhood; to His baptism; to the temptations in the wilderness; to the miracles, the sermons, His disciples and friends; and to the betrayal; all the disciplined obedience to the will of the Father had shaped Him for this darkest moment to come. But most of all, He knew it was not just obeying God's will that was at stake, it was the salvation of the world that depended on Him finishing this course to the hill ahead with a cross waiting for His timely arrival.

This was not a random event that happened at a random time. God had a plan that began at the foundation of the world. Jesus knew the plans for Himself long before His conception in Mary's womb. We know what this event looked like historically, but what did this event look like from heaven? What did the heavens, that we read declare the glory of God, see, and how did they react? Were there reasons that would result in more than the salvation of the human race? What were the thousands of angels prepared to do if Jesus would have called on them to deliver Him from the hands of Pilate?

How does our current culture reconcile itself to the shame of the cross while wearing its image on the seat of their pants, tatted on their skin and displayed around their necks? How do we find the truth that even Pilate questioned in a world where every form of available media and communication has rendered abominable opinions? What is the relevance of our message? Stay the course with us as we try to expand our perspective and heavenly view of the most significant event to have ever happened for mankind.

What hope does America have if she forsakes the message that is responsible for her greatness? Despite every attempt to rewrite Her history, it is the message of the cross that inspires and equips this nation and the world at large for their final future. And that future finishes with all standing before Almighty God and giving account of every word and action. Are they ready for that? Are we ready for that? Perhaps now, the timing may be right for us to learn the depth of the event, and height of the price, to secure a future with eternal promise.

Lord we thank You for the cross. We thank You for paying the price for our sin. We thank You for the hope and the future that is only possible with a life lived in faith in Your faithful Son, Jesus. We ask You to have mercy on us and our nation. We ask You to finish the work You started in us and pray that Your will be done. Amen.

Chapter Six

The Price of Disobedience

W as this depth of brutality really necessary? Why beat an innocent man beyond recognition when you're planning to kill him anyway? Tormentors at this level must really enjoy their job. They operate with complete indifference to the human suffering they inflict. Besides, he's just doing his job. Right?

The Romans were known for making examples out of criminals like this for others to see, but this man was no criminal. The real criminals were standing in the courtyard demanding death. Pilate had already tried to rid himself of being a part of this decision by sending Him to Herod Antipas. Herod found no reason to condemn Him and sent

Him back to Pilate. Pilate even attempted to have Jesus released, but to no avail. The crowd had demanded the ultimate punishment by asking for crucifixion. Were the thorns, the assault, and the added humiliation truly necessary to punish a man whose main offense seemed to be his claim that God was His Father? And if God was His Father, what kind of father could stand back and do nothing as these puny humans made sport of His Son? God with infinite power pushed mountains from the earth into their places and made the stars. How much restraint did it take for this all-powerful Father to stand watching without lifting a finger, while the offspring of His own creation mutilated His only begotten Son?

Jesus' path to the cross did not start in Jerusalem a few days before He arrived to meet His death. It started before the foundation of the world; *the Lamb slain from the foundation of the world* (Revelation 13:8 KJV) (31) and continued to manifest in Jerusalem while He was about to be born in Bethlehem. The battle to stop this man from becoming the final sacrifice for our sinful and fallen condition began long before the cross. Herod the Great, in an effort to have Jesus killed as a child, ordered the unthinkable by having all the male children two and under in Bethlehem and the surrounding coastal areas murdered.

Now when Jesus was born in Bethlehem of Judaea in the days of Herod the king, behold, there came wise men from the east to Jerusalem, saying, "Where is he that is born King of the Jews? For we have seen his star in the east and are come to worship him."

When Herod the king had heard these things, he was troubled, and all Jerusalem with him. And when he had gathered all the chief priests and scribes of the people together, he demanded of them where Christ should be born.

And they said unto him, "In Bethlehem of Judaea: for thus it is written by the prophet, 'And thou Bethlehem, in the land of Juda, art not the least among the princes of Juda: for out of thee shall come a Governor, that shall rule my people Israel.'"

Then Herod, when he had privately called the wise men, inquired of them diligently what time the star appeared. And he sent them to Bethlehem, and said, "Go and search diligently for the young child; and when ye have found him, bring me word again, that I may come and worship him also."

When they had heard the king, they departed; and, lo, the star, which they saw in the east, went before them, till it came and stood over where the young child was. When they saw the star, they rejoiced with exceeding great joy. And when they were come into the house, they saw the young child with Mary his mother, and fell down, and worshipped him: and when they had opened their treasures, they presented unto him gifts; gold, and frankincense, and myrrh.

And being warned of God in a dream that they should not return to Herod, they departed into their own country another way.

And when they were departed, behold, the angel of the Lord appeared to Joseph in a dream, saying, "Arise, and take the young child and his mother, and flee into Egypt, and be thou there until I bring thee word: for Herod will seek the young child to destroy him."

When he arose, he took the young child and his mother by night, and departed into Egypt: And was there until the death of Herod: that it might be fulfilled which was spoken of the Lord by the prophet, saying, "Out of Egypt have I called my son."

Then Herod, when he saw that he was mocked of the wise men, was exceeding wroth, and sent forth, and slew all the children that were in Bethlehem, and in all the coasts thereof, from two years old and under, according to the time which he had diligently inquired of the wise men. Then was fulfilled that which was spoken by Jeremiah the prophet. (Matthew 2:1-17 KJV) (32).

We are not told exactly how many babies and young children were killed. But it is clear that killing babies is one of the most commonly used methods the devil employs (still to this day), in his attempt to stop the gifts of God from manifesting through the hands of men and women; and from ever touching the world created to receive those gifts. People love to blame God for cancers, diseases and poverty. They raise their fist to the God of heaven demanding He do something about what lacks in the world and their lives. One day they will face the God they accuse and learn that He did do something. He sent human beings, gifted even before conception, with the talents to be great doctors, engineers, scientists, preachers, educators, and financial experts. They were carrying in their souls the abilities to discover cures, produce wealth, and provide answers for every need and malady the earth contained. But their solutions never arrived because they were murdered by the devil and his more than willing human accomplices before they could be born or grow to their appointed time to change the world with their individual gifts to man from a loving God. We all too often fail to understand God's greatest gifts and our greatest roles to be the carriers of what the world needs to experience; the love of God manifested in those loving human gifts.

How could the soldiers instructed to carry out the atrocity for this mad-man, Herod, even obey such a command? Didn't some of these soldiers have children of their own? Unfortunately, they have not acted alone. History haunts us with one mad man after another, carrying out the will of their father, Satan, with the murder of millions and millions of souls. And all too willing soldiers have carried out those orders from hell. Even doctors and nurses with the talents and gifts to save lives, have acted no less heinously than the Herod's and their soldiers of the world, by destroying untold millions of unborn babies. All of those individuals have acted like they did the world a favor by carrying out unspeakable atrocities, but they are, as Jesus pointed out, of their father the devil and are murderers from the beginning.

But, that's how the devil works. Without any regard to the life of these children or their families, the destruction of the ultimate and conclusive sacrifice for the sins of the world had to be accomplished before it was too late for the devil. The most accomplished murderer from the beginning of time was consumed and possessed by the desire to kill the greatest gift ever offered from God. His only begotten Son.

Jesus was very aware of who his real enemy was, and he plainly revealed it in a conversation with some religious Jews in the book of John, chapter eight.

"You are of your father the devil, and the lusts of your father you will do. He was a murderer from the beginning, and abode not in the truth, because there is no truth in him. When he speaks a lie, he speaks of his own: for he is a liar, and the father of it. And because I tell you the truth, you believe me not. Which of you convinces me of sin? And if I say the truth, why do you not believe me? He that is of God

hears God's words: you therefore hear them not, because you are not of God."

Then answered the Jews, and said unto him, "Say we not well that thou art a Samaritan, and hast a devil?"

Jesus answered, "I have not a devil; but I honor my Father, and you do dishonor me. And I seek not my own glory: there is one that seeks and judges. Truly, I say unto you, if a man keeps my saying, he shall never see death."

Then said the Jews unto him, "Now we know that thou hast a devil." (John 8:44-52 KJV) (33).

Do you understand what you just read? Jesus exposed the devil at his most basic nature: he was a murderer and a liar from the beginning. Everything he does is motivated by what he is – a murderer and a liar. He is not some fictional, red skinned, and horned character, holding a pitchfork. He is a murderer and a liar and has been one from the beginning.

What did Jesus mean when He said the devil was from the beginning? If Jesus was a mere man like the rest of us, how could He understand who and what was from the *beginning*? He understood because He was not a mere man. He was also from the beginning. And this is the primary reason people fail to recognize Jesus. Because in many cases, even the most religious among us fail to see that Jesus is the Son of God, simply because they are not of God. Being religious at any level doesn't automatically entitle us to *be of our Father, God.* Some may actually be of their father the liar and murderer. The opening statement of John's Gospel couldn't make it any clearer.

In the beginning was the Word, and the Word was with God, and the Word was God. The same was in the beginning with God. All things were made by him; and without him was not anything made that was made. In him was life; and the life was the light of men. And the light shined in darkness; and the darkness comprehended it not.

There was a man sent from God, whose name was John. The same came for a witness, to bear witness of the Light, that all men through him might believe. He was not that Light but was sent to bear witness of that Light. That was the true Light, which lights every man that comes into the world.

He was in the world, and the world was made by him, and the world knew him not. He came unto his own, and his own received him not. But as many as received him, to them gave He power to become the sons of God, even to them that believe on His name: Which were born, not of blood, nor of the will of the flesh, nor of the will of man, but of God. And the Word was made flesh, and dwelt among us, (and we beheld His glory, the glory as of the only begotten of the Father,) full of grace and truth. (John 1:1-14 KJV) (34).

Jesus was not just another religious man seeking approval or trying to develop a following. He was not another man that used his followers to establish a new religion. He was not the next self-proclaimed prophet or political leader who thought the world needed him. He was in fact, the Son of God, and He came to fulfill the will and the purpose of his Father *from the beginning.* And, He was the one individual that would set the stage for the defeat of that liar and murderer, who had also been *from the beginning.*

The Jews, who often confronted Jesus, were religious men which believed they clearly had a good understanding of God and prophecy. Even Herod sought advice from the Jewish scholars when the wise men from the east brought the news of a coming birth; a birth they suspected could be that of the promised Messiah. Oddly enough, these religious leaders and biblical scholars, if you please, were *troubled* by this news – news they had supposedly longed to hear for centuries. Wasn't this supposed to be the good news they had discussed, debated and taught so often? Instead, it was troubling to them on many levels. One of which could have been that it meant their exposure as liars and murderers. Not only was this birth going to fulfill prophecy, it was going to bring the true *light* of God into the world; a light that would expose all the darkness. And just as they were troubled and afraid at the birth of Jesus, men's hearts will fail with fear at the return of Jesus. For this very reason we must pay close attention to the instructions the apostle Paul gave Timothy and prepare to carefully abide by those instructions to the very end.

I charge thee therefore before God, and the Lord Jesus Christ, who shall judge the quick and the dead at his appearing and his kingdom; Preach the word; be instant in season, out of season; reprove, rebuke, exhort with all longsuffering and doctrine.

For the time will come when they will not endure sound doctrine; but after their own lusts shall they heap to themselves teachers, having itching ears; And they shall turn away their ears from the truth, and shall be turned unto fables. (2 Timothy 4:1-4 KJV) (35).

At the beginning of this chapter I asked the question: *Was this level of brutality necessary?* What is the answer? It may be simpler than we think, yet far more difficult to grasp. It is because of disobedience. It's because of us. It's because we disobeyed God. Jesus did not disobey God, we did. Jesus resisted unto blood in order to obey God. We have not.

For consider him that endured such contradiction of sinners against himself, lest ye be wearied and faint in your minds. Ye have not yet resisted unto blood, striving against sin. (Hebrews 12:3-4 KJV) (36).

Satan disobeyed God and rebelled against Him, and in the process of his disobedience his own spirit of deception deceived a third of the angels in heaven into disobeying God as well, and that same spirit of deception works to this day.

And war broke out in heaven: Michael and his angels fought with the dragon; and the dragon and his angels fought, but they did not prevail, nor was a place found for them in heaven any longer. So, the great dragon was cast out, that serpent of old, called the Devil and Satan, who deceives the whole world; he was cast to the earth, and his angels were cast out with him. (Revelations 12:7-9, NKJV) (37).

Eve disobeyed God. Adam disobeyed with her and established a pattern of living apart from God for all the generations of the earth to continue after them.

Kings and saints; preachers and priests; and you and I, have all disobeyed God. And this very disobedience to God was so destructive that hundreds of years of animal sacrifices proved insufficient to provide full restitution. But, at the right time, the ultimate sacrifice, God's own Son, was offered as the final sacrifice for the fall of all that God held precious.

Why would our disobedience demand such an outrageous price? Are we really worth such a price to be redeemed? All too often we're so comfortable *with* disobedience that it sounds too simple to just say, it's because we have disobeyed God. But look at the repercussions and consequences of our disobedience. Even further, we complicate the importance of choosing to obey God, even more, by thinking God's grace is some sort of antidote to the need for obedience whatsoever. Grace does not relieve us from obedience. It delivers us from the consequences of having disobeyed.

Pay close attention to this statement: Disobedience paves the way for sin. Sin separates from God. Disobeying God leads us down the path of painful separation from our creator.

Does this hurt us alone? No! Read carefully – sin not only separates us from God, it separates God from us, and while we may be able to adapt and learn to be comfortable with being separated from God, God never desires to be separated from us. His love for His own creation is beyond anything we can imagine or comprehend.

Therefore, how much are we worth? The value of most anything is determined by the price one is willing to pay. God paid the maximum available price to provide a way to end His separation from us. God paid the bill with His own Son; a Son that never deserved to pay the required price. A Son, by whom all things were made. A Son from the beginning with the Father at creation. A Son, willing to sacrifice all to satisfy the will of the Father. What is required of us? That we make the *choice* to enter into this provision.

So once again, how destructive is disobedience? Disobedience in the heavens resulted in the rebellion of a high-ranking angel, a liar and a murderer, an angel that thought he deserved the place of human creation above the place God designed for the angels as ministering spirits to the heirs of salvation. An angel, deceiving himself as if he were an equal decision maker with God, who also used his spirit of deception to deceive a third of the angels in heaven. These angels, all falling while exercising their gift of freewill, blindly following the one spearheading their fall from God, and the heavenly kingdom.

Disobedience on the part of Adam and Eve, handmade creations of God, also gifted with freewill, followed the lead of *that* disobedient liar and murderer, only to find themselves evicted from a garden paradise, a place where God could walk and talk with them at will. Their disobedience resulted in a cursed earth and a mortal existence for themselves and multiple generations after them. Disobedience altered everything that had been produced to bless heaven and earth. Never take disobedience lightly. For the world that we see to this day continues to shake because of continued daily disobedience to God, by the free will choice of the very people that hold to, or reject, the Lamb of God slain for them.

We must cleanse ourselves of this flippant attitude towards disobedience and commit ourselves more than ever to obey God; the same God that thought no price was too high to recover that which was lost. If good works are not enough, *and they are not*, where do we turn in order to secure this pursuit of purity?

See how very much our Father loves us, for he calls us his children, and that is what we are! But the people who belong to this world don't recognize that we are God's children because they don't know him. Dear friends, we are already God's children, but he has not yet shown us what we will be like when Christ appears. But we do know that we will be like him, for we will see him as he really is. And all who have this eager expectation will keep themselves pure, just as He is pure.

Everyone who sins is breaking God's law, for all sin is contrary to the law of God. And you know that Jesus came to take away our sins, and there is no sin in Him. Anyone who continues to live in Him will not sin. But anyone who keeps on sinning does not know Him or understand who He is.

Dear children, don't let anyone deceive you about this: When people do what is right, it shows that they are righteous, even as Christ is righteous. But when people keep on sinning, it shows that they belong to the devil, who has been sinning since the beginning. But the Son of God came to destroy the works of the devil. Those who have been born into God's family do not make a practice of sinning, because God's life is in them. So they can't keep on sinning, because they are children of God. So now we can tell who are children of God and who are children of the devil. Anyone who does not live righteously and does not love other believers does not belong to God. (1 John 3:1-10 NLT) (38).

Dear Lord Jesus. Have mercy upon us and forgive us of our disobedience. We truly want to follow You and be Your disciples in every expected way. We acknowledge that You paid the highest price, and with that payment enabled us to walk in Your ways. Deliver and cleanse us from any flippant attitude we may have towards disobedience and draw us more than ever to obey You. Amen.

Chapter Seven

Understanding Temptation

Many of us fail to understand temptation. First of all, temptation does not equal sin. Contrary to what the devil wants you to believe, the act of being tempted does not translate into failure. In fact, I am of the strong opinion that the lack of temptation, or the lack of recognizing temptation, should give us the most concern.

If temptation is sin then Jesus Christ, the Son of the Living God, was the greatest sinner to ever walk the earth. Because, no one has ever been tempted to the extent that He was tempted. We have never been tempted to the degree He was tempted and never will be. And while it may be said that He relates to us and our temptation, let it be fully understood that He did not surrender to sin in the same manner as we often do. He did, however, take our sin upon Himself to the grave, but He did not participate in or commit our sin. He earned the right to be the perfect and final sacrifice for sin because He did not sin.

So then, since we have a great High Priest who has entered heaven, Jesus the Son of God, let us hold firmly to what we believe. This High Priest of ours understands our weaknesses, for he faced all of the same testings we do, yet He did not sin. So, let us come boldly to the throne of our gracious God. There we will receive his mercy, and we will find grace to help us when we need it most. (Hebrews 4:14-16 NLT) (39).

He understands our weakness and has provided a way for us to rest and rely on His strength and ability to overcome these weaknesses. But He also provided access to the throne of God, which we didn't have before, because of our sin. Don't underestimate this provision. Access to the throne of God through Jesus Christ, is one of the greatest gifts God has bestowed upon us. Because without Jesus, there is no access.

The world loves to declare there are many ways to God, and we should all be more tolerant and accepting of other religions. But tolerance is not what enables us to resist temptation and overcome sin. Obedience and sacrifice, particularly the obedience and sacrifice of Christ, is what empowers us to experience life as overcomers.

The world loves to cheer on winners, but how many understand what is really involved to be an overcomer? At what point does temptation result in sin and whose fault is it? Well, let's look at that. It's easy and sometimes cute to say, "The devil made me do it!" Or we blame a brother or a sister. Sometimes we may even blame God for our failure to resist temptation. But what is the real bottom line reason that we give into temptation and take it to the next level? We want to, and we choose to; be honest, it's that simple.

God blesses those who patiently endure testing and temptation. Afterward they will receive the crown of life that God has promised to those who love him. And remember, when you are being tempted, do not say, "God is tempting me." God is never tempted to do wrong, and he never tempts anyone else.

Temptation comes from our own desires, which entice us and drag us away. These desires give birth to sinful actions. And when sin is allowed to grow, it gives birth to death.

So, don't be misled, my dear brothers and sisters. Whatever is good and perfect comes down to us from God our Father, who created all the lights in the heavens. He never changes or casts a shifting shadow. He chose to give birth to us by giving us his true word. And we, out of all creation, became his prized possession. (James 1:12-18 NLT) (40).

Why would God pay the ultimate price for us to have access to Himself only to toy with us by tempting us with opportunities to fail? He would not. This work belongs to the liar and enemy of our souls, not to God.

Pay attention to what this word teaches us. Temptation comes from "our" desires. What does that mean? The devil doesn't make me do it? It's not God's fault? Precisely! Temptation originates with us. We are the root cause and reason for our own failures. Just because we think of it, doesn't mean we have to do it. We have the choice. We have the will to freely make the choice not to participate. If temptation comes from our desires, then the strength of that desire is what we mostly have to battle against. Especially since we have desires in our flesh that our heart and mind have a God-given conflict with. The ability to discern between good and evil desires and choices, supports the evidence of the existence of God, considering we can feel these inherent differences without even being taught. We instinctively feel that it is wrong to lie or steal what is not ours. We know it's wrong to take someone else's life. God did not have to tell Adam and Eve what they did wrong. Look at the exchange between God and them after they chose to disobey.

And when the woman saw that the tree was good for food, and that it was pleasant to the eyes, and a tree to be desired to make one wise, she took of the fruit thereof, and did eat, and gave also unto her husband with her; and he did eat. And the eyes of them both were opened, and they knew that they were naked; and they sewed fig leaves together and made themselves aprons.

And they heard the voice of the Lord God walking in the garden in the cool of the day: and Adam and his wife hid themselves from the presence of the Lord God among the trees of the garden.

And the Lord God called unto Adam, and said unto him, "Where are you?"

And he said, "I heard your voice in the garden, and I was afraid, because I was naked; and I hid myself."

And he said, "Who told you that you were naked? Have you eaten of the tree, that I commanded you that you should not eat?"

And the man said, "The woman whom you gave to be with me, she gave me of the tree, and I did eat."

And the Lord God said unto the woman, "What is this that you have done?"

And the woman said, "The serpent beguiled me, and I did eat." (Genesis 3:6-13 KJV) (41).

Once Eve gave into her desire and her temptation to disobey and eat the fruit that was forbidden, she immediately offered it to her husband. He in turn gave into his desire and his temptation to go along with their act of disobedience and ate the fruit also. Then the man, who previously enjoyed access to God, by walking and talking with Him in the garden, hid from God, when He came to the garden looking for him.

God did not accuse and condemn. He already knew what they had done. He wanted to know if they knew. Where are you? How did you know? Who told you? What have you done? And the man who enjoyed walks and talks with God, could now only offer blame and excuses instead of taking responsibility for his actions. Actions that would result in dire consequences for all the generations of the world to come.

Desire for what we can't have, and temptation to have it anyway, leads to disobedience and sin, because we disregard what we know just to do what we want. The blame is clearly at our feet. But, despite our blame, Jesus willingly took the blame and the consequences of disobedience to restore the lost access to Father God. This separation has been endured by thousands of generations since that fateful day in the garden.

So, if Jesus endured all the same testings as we do without giving into sin, what does that look like for us? First of all, when we think of the scriptures which tell the story of His temptation, we tend to think He spent forty days fasting in the wilderness, got hungry, then endured three particular temptations at the hands of the devil. I assure you that it was much more involved than that.

After Jesus was baptized by John, the Spirit lead Him to go into the wilderness to be tempted by the devil. And the devil, who knew whom Jesus really was, was being given a forty-day free pass to throw everything at the Son of God, he had to throw. The devil intended to make the best of this opportunity.

Do you know the story of Job? The devil accused God of restricting access to Job, then accused Job of not being true to God.

So Satan answered the Lord and said, "Does Job fear God for nothing? Have You not made a hedge around him, around his household, and around all that he has on every side? You have blessed the work of his hands, and his possessions have increased in the land. But now, stretch out Your hand and touch all that he has, and he will surely curse You to Your face!"

And the Lord said to Satan, "Behold, all that he has is in your power; only do not lay a hand on his person." (Job 1:9-12 NKJV) (42).

Not only was Satan's access to Job limited to certain parameters, it had a time limit. And when that didn't work the devil scoffed and dared God to give him more access. That failed to work also. God was right. The devil was wrong. Nevertheless, Job, a righteous man, endured a great deal of suffering from the attack and was a much different man as a result of his encounter with God and the devil. But a faithful and gracious God did not forget Job.

So the Lord blessed Job in the second half of his life even more than in the beginning. (Job 42:12 NLT) (43).

Job's story clearly demonstrates how wicked and corrupt the devil actually is. When given access to this righteous man, a man that didn't deserve to go through any of the things he had to endure; the liar and thief – the murderer from the beginning, did not hesitate to use this opportunity and access to steal everything Job had, and to kill all of his children and employees in the process.

Now the Spirit was leading Jesus, not just a righteous man, but a man without sin, to face all the evil this fallen disgrace of heaven had to offer. This wicked serpent, that thought nothing of destroying anything and anybody in God's creation, was going to be granted unrestricted access to the Father's own Son – now in the form of a human man. For forty days and nights, he would do his best to stop God's plan to redeem that which he had deceived. This would not be a walk in the park, it would be warfare at the highest level. Not only did Jesus take the sin of the whole world on Himself at the cross of Calvary, he was about to take on the temptations of the whole world in this wilderness where he would face the same devil that so often attacks us.

But was in all points tempted like as we are, yet without sin. (Hebrews 4:15 KJV) (44).

Then Jesus, full of the Holy Spirit, returned from the Jordan River. He was led by the Spirit in the wilderness, where he was tempted by the devil for forty days. Jesus ate nothing all that time and became very hungry. (Luke 4:1-2 NLT) (45).

Day after day for forty days, the devil hammered Jesus with every conceivable temptation known to man. We only think we've experienced temptation. Jesus was experiencing the temptations of thousands of generations.

Then the devil said to him, "If you are the Son of God, change this stone into a loaf of bread."

But Jesus told him, "No! The Scriptures say, 'People do not live by bread alone.'" (Luke 4:3-4 NLT) (46).

The devil once got a man to sell his birthright for a bowl of beans. He was used to planning his attack on the hungry and the weak. Jesus became hungry and weak in the flesh for us and resisted and prevailed against temptation while in that condition. The devil would not win this battle. And furthermore, the devil knew this was no ordinary man, this was the Son of God. And his accusing question, *"If you are the Son of God?"* was an effort to get Jesus to show doubt in Himself or to prove He was the Son of God by taking the devil's challenging dare.

Then the devil took him up and revealed to him all the kingdoms of the world in a moment of time. "I will give you the glory of these kingdoms and authority over them," the devil said, "because they are mine to give to anyone I please. I will give it all to you if you will worship me."

Jesus replied, "The Scriptures say, 'You must worship the Lord your God and serve only him.'" (Luke 4:5-8 NLT) (47).

We must worship God and Him alone. Nothing else and no one else is worthy of our worship. Jesus knew this and the devil knew this. The devil's power and kingdom are only temporary and anything the devil could have given Jesus would be temporary as well. Jesus knew his Father had an eternal kingdom and an eternal throne waiting for Him. All He had to do was endure the temptation, suffer the shame, and conquer the flesh. The devil's days were numbered. It was winning over sin in the flesh and restoring God's greatest creation that was at the center of Jesus' purpose.

Then the devil took him to Jerusalem, to the highest point of the Temple, and said, "If you are the Son of God, jump off! For the Scriptures say, 'He will order his angels to protect and guard you. And they will hold you up with their hands so you won't even hurt your foot on a stone.'"

Jesus responded, "The Scriptures also say, 'You must not test the Lord your God.'" (Luke 4:9-12 NLT) (48).

Jesus knew He was the Son of God. He did not need to prove it to the devil (who also knew Jesus was the Son of God). Jesus also knew the angels would come as soon as He called on them for help. He would later tell a worldly ruler in the face of his own death that He could call thousands of angels to rescue Him. But He was not the one that needed rescuing, we were.

When the devil had finished tempting Jesus, he left him until the next opportunity came. (Luke 4:13 NLT) (49).

This last verse states, *he left him until the next opportunity.* The devil could do no more to Him until additional access would be granted by the Father. The sooner we recognize this and get it deep in our souls, the sooner we will quit blaming God, the devil, and anyone else for the things that come our way to temp and try us. God works all things to our good, and every temptation, challenge and trial can serve as a great opportunity for God to work something into our lives with eternal benefit. We must learn to see temptation as an opportunity to overcome and not as a reason to fail.

We started this chapter by proclaiming that temptation in and of itself is not sin. Let's look a little deeper. There are three things the enemy consistently tries to use against us for the sole purpose of getting us to take temptation to the next level, which is sin. Condemnation. Confusion. Fear. All of these are tactics the great deceiver uses to take us away from our race for Christ. He will get us so accustomed to experiencing these three items, that he will soon have us using them on ourselves and believing it is somehow originating from God.

What does the scriptures teach us about condemnation?

There is therefore now no condemnation for those who are in Christ Jesus. For the law of the Spirit of life has set you free in Christ Jesus from the law of sin and death.

For God has done what the law, weakened by the flesh, could not do. By sending his own Son in the likeness of sinful flesh and for sin, he condemned sin in the flesh, in order that the righteous requirement of the law might be fulfilled in us, who walk not according to the flesh but according to the Spirit.

For those who live according to the flesh set their minds on the things of the flesh, but those who live according to the Spirit set their minds on the things of the Spirit. (Romans 8:1-5 ESV) (50).

Contrary to popular thought, God does not use condemnation to reprove and correct us when we have sinned. He uses love and the Holy Spirit uses conviction, which is designed to turn our attention back to God's love. God's heart is always wanting to draw us back to Himself when we fail. It is not His desire to push us away, even when we have turned away from Him by our very own choice. It is our heart that condemns us, not God.

And hereby we know that we are of the truth and shall assure our hearts before him. For if our heart condemns us, God is greater than our heart, and knows all things. Beloved, if our heart condemns us not, then have we confidence toward God. (1 John 3:19-21 KJV) (51).

It is hard to approach God while the hammer of condemnation is pounding us for sin and failure, either real or imagined. The devil uses this tool to pry us away from having any confidence to approach God. Remember, it is God who eagerly waits for us to approach Him through the access provided by Christ. Look closer at the previous verse from Romans.

By sending his own Son in the likeness of sinful flesh and for sin, he condemned sin in the flesh, in order that the righteous requirement of the law might be fulfilled in us.

God's Son in the *likeness of sinful flesh condemned sin in the flesh.* He did not condemn our flesh. He did not condemn us. He condemned sin in the flesh. Sin that was there in the flesh as a result of the fall. He did that so the *righteous requirement of the law might be fulfilled in us.* By taking our sin on Himself and condemning it there, in Himself, He did not have to allow us to be condemned with the sin in our flesh. Again, He did that so the *righteous requirement of the law might be fulfilled in us.* That righteous fulfillment never relies on us for it to be satisfied. It's not about our works. It never has been, and it never will be. Relax and stop feeling condemned.

Now what about confusion? *For God is not the author of confusion, but of peace, as in all churches of the saints.* (1 Corinthians 14:33 KJV) (52).

For where envying and strife is, there is confusion and every evil work. But the wisdom that is from above is first pure, then peaceable, gentle, and easy to be entreated, full of mercy and good fruits, without partiality, and without hypocrisy. And the fruit of righteousness is sown in peace of them that make peace. (James 3:16 – 18 KJV) (53).

Confusion, simply put, is designed to produce doubt. And the purpose of doubt is to destabilize faith. And *without faith it is impossible to please God.* (Hebrews 11:6 KJV) (54). That said, we need to clearly understand the devastation a little confusion can have on our heart, soul and mind. Confusion causes us to pause or cease altogether from our intended journey in Christ. Confusion begs us to question even the most basic facts and truths that we have built our lives on. Confusion is used to undermine the very foundation of our walk with God. Confusion is extremely dangerous to the believer in Christ, which is exactly why the devil cherishes this effective tool.

There will always be things in life that confuse us. And with a little effort to get the facts we can refuse to allow those things to become stumbling blocks. But, when confusion is used as a weapon to attack and deceive us from our core beliefs in the gospel of Christ, we must respond as Jesus did in the wilderness of temptation. We must be effective with prayer and efficient with the word of God.

We now turn to what effects all of us on a regular basis. Fear. *For God hath not given us the spirit of fear; but of power, and of love, and of a sound mind. Be not thou therefore ashamed of the testimony of our Lord, nor of me his prisoner: but be thou partaker of the afflictions of the gospel according to the power of God; who hath saved us, and called us with an holy calling, not according to our works, but according to his own purpose and grace, which was given us in Christ Jesus before the world began.* (2 Timothy 1:7-9 KJV) (55).

There is no fear in love; but perfect love casteth out fear: because fear hath torment. He that feareth is not made perfect in love. (1 John 4:18 KJV) (56).

Fear is an emotion we love to hate. Some of us deliberately watch scary movies for the sole purpose of getting frightened out of our mind. Fear awakens our senses and puts us on edge. For some, fear is a stimulate. Why do you think roller coasters and amusement parks are so popular? But these experiences with fear are controlled. We know they will end and when we can expect to walk away.

But fear in the hands of the enemy of our soul is a weapon. And he is a master at using this weapon on those he hates, and he hates everyone. Remember, he is a murderer from the beginning and the tools he uses are designed and intended for no other purpose than to kill. He is not playing. His warfare is for real.

He uses fear primarily to paralyze his victims. Fear makes you freeze, stop dead in your tracks, or runaway to hide. It puts you in a state of mind that eliminates your ability to adequately defend yourself. It cripples your will to fight back. It distorts reality and makes you believe you are helpless in the situation or the moment. It leaves you feeling alone and there is no one to help or rescue you. Not even God.

And that is the point of this being a weapon of choice for the devil. He wants you to believe in that moment that it's between you and him and you have no chance to survive or overcome. It is the tactic of the wolf to separate a sheep from the flock in order to devour it as prey. The devil knows if he can separate you emotionally from your family, the Body of Christ, or the Spirit of God, then he has you where he needs you to be for no other reason than to destroy you.

Fear can also be used to warn and preserve you. It is used to keep a child from touching something that is hot. It provides a healthy source of guidance to steer you away from things that can harm you. It is healthy to have the fear of God, but God's love doesn't use fear to keep us in line. He uses love to keep us in Him.

The fear of the Lord is the beginning of wisdom: and the knowledge of the holy is understanding. For by me thy days shall be multiplied, and the years of thy life shall be increased. (Proverbs 9:10 – 11 KJV) (57).

Having therefore these promises, dearly beloved, let us cleanse ourselves from all filthiness of the flesh and spirit, perfecting holiness in the fear of God. (2 Corinthians 7:1 KJV) (58).

We have an enemy, but that enemy is not God. The cross was the price required to bring us to God. But Calvary provides us with the ability to abide in the power of the resurrected Son of the living God in order to share in the defeat of our real enemy, the devil.

A final word: Be strong in the Lord and in his mighty power. Put on all of God's armor so that you will be able to stand firm against all strategies of the devil. For we are not fighting against flesh-and-blood enemies, but against evil rulers and authorities of the unseen world, against mighty powers in this dark world, and against evil spirits in the heavenly places. (Ephesians 6:10 – 12 NLT) (59).

Oh Lord, deliver us from temptation. Protect us from the enemy and ourselves. Help us to walk free from condemnation. Keep our hearts and minds clear of confusion. And teach us to overcome all our fears in order to live life as an overcomer in Your kingdom. Amen.

Chapter Eight

Prayer Language

Effective communication is one of the most important skills we need to navigate the course of our lives. The lack of good communication has led to wars, resulted in divorce, been responsible for lifelong rifts between family and friends, and divided nations from within. Even knowing the same language as someone else does not insure communication will be effective. Not only will some misunderstand what you say, they will misunderstand your motives and the intent of what you say. Some will be offended by your speech whether you say anything or not. Others will be angry over what they think you would say if you were to say anything at all. Some will take a few of your words and twist them to imply you said just the opposite of what you were actually communicating. We are witnessing a world tearing itself apart on a daily basis, because it is simply failing to communicate.

The art of communication requires the ability and the willingness to listen as well as speak. Listening doesn't require the same beliefs and ideology for it to be beneficial. We can all hear what someone has to say when we choose to listen, whether we agree with them or not. We've all had conversations with people that clearly weren't listening to what we were saying. We see their eyes and their body language as we are speaking and it's obvious, they're not hearing a word we're saying. It's easy to spot that they are thinking about what they're planning to say next rather than considering anything we're saying. I often enjoy throwing in something completely irrelevant to the conversation at hand just to see if someone is paying attention. Sometimes, they snap out of it, most of the time they never catch the curve ball I've thrown them. The apostle James wrote about communication in his book.

Understand this, my dear brothers and sisters: You must all be quick to listen, slow to speak, and slow to get angry. Human anger does not produce the righteousness God desires. So, get rid of all the filth and evil in your lives, and humbly accept the word God has planted in your hearts, for it has the power to save your souls. (James 1:19 – 21 NLT) (60).

The need for skilled communication is equally important to understanding yourself and others. Breakdown in communication can often be the result of mounting frustration over a lack of feeling that the conversation is accomplishing what is intended or needed. Communicating is not limited to words. You can use all the right words with the correct usage and still fail to communicate. Communication involves more than words, it enlists our feelings, comprehension, understanding, listening, emotions, eye contact, body expressions and much more. Some people connect with you right away, while other encounters may never result in a serious connection. Very often, connecting with someone requires more effort than we are willing to give. If we only open our lives to those who make it easy to communicate with, we will discover we have far less friends than we may have desired.

We are now living in a world that would rather text and email than talk. These methods are convenient for transmitting information, but they are completely inept for effectual communication. If we are this challenged (and we truly are), when it comes to communicating with those around us on a daily basis, then how can we ever expect to effectively communicate with God?

First of all, I do realize, God can understand all of us regardless of language or communication abilities. But, keep in mind the all-important emotional side of effective communication. Do we feel like God is hearing and understanding us? Because, if we don't, we will shut down the conversation between us and God when we feel He is distant and not listening or understanding what we are saying. We may not blame God for the breakdown, but we do tend to avoid further conversations with Him until we feel better about talking to Him. Why? Because we never enjoy speaking to anyone for any length of time when we lack some level of connection with them – even God.

Would it be utter foolishness to propose the idea that we need to learn the language of God in order to effectively speak with Him? Maybe we need to learn to speak to God, if we would really like to understand when He is speaking to us. So, what does the language of God sound like? First off, whether you are aware of it or not, there are over six-thousand different languages in use on planet earth. That's a lot of potential miscommunication and confusion. Many of us have experienced the frustration of encountering someone that speaks a different language than our own. We raise our voice when we talk to them, as if they can't hear us in addition to not understanding us. We may even adopt their accent with our words as though that will help them understand our language. Then when all attempts with words fail, we start talking with our hands and our faces. We point and smile and try anything necessary to help them understand exactly what we are trying to convey to them.

Now I realize God understands all the languages on earth, including sign language, but how much effort are we willing to put forth to make sure God understands us? Our frustration with the stranger and his different language is rooted in our need to believe that He understands us. So, with God, our frustration in prayer is the need to believe that God hears us and understands us as we pray. Therefore, what is the language of God and how important is it for us to learn his language? Prayer is the language of God and it is all important that we learn to communicate with Him through prayer. Not for his good, but for ours.

Trust me, God understands me even when I'm face down on the floor and in so much anguish that all I can do is groan. I've been there and I knew He heard me and understood me. But it was not my manner of speech that I found most effective in that moment of desperate need – it was the cry from my heart for God to turn to me. Many of us have hit times of desperation when we cried out to God from the depths of our souls for help and we didn't care what it looked or sounded like. We just needed some relief, somehow, some way; and we knew at that moment our only hope was God. And for those of us that have never experienced such a moment, give it some time.

Are any of you suffering hardships? You should pray. Are any of you happy? You should sing praises. Are any of you sick? You should call for the elders of the church to come and pray over you, anointing you with oil in the name of the Lord. Such a prayer offered in faith will heal the sick, and the Lord will make you well. And if you have committed any sins, you will be forgiven.

Confess your sins to each other and pray for each other so that you may be healed. The earnest prayer of a righteous person has great power and produces wonderful results. Elijah was as human as we are, and yet when he prayed earnestly that no rain would fall, none fell for three and a half years! Then, when he prayed again, the sky sent down rain and the earth began to yield its crops. (James 5:13–18, NLT) (61).

Hardship, suffering, sickness and desperate times, will teach us the language of God. The need to understand and be understood, and the need to hear and be heard, becomes paramount in our most desperate times. In those seasons we learn to speak to God in a language He understands – the language of faith!

Hardship is a quick study. I know a person that decided to learn to speak Spanish. She knew nothing about the language. She opted not to take it in school and attempted no formal training with the language. Instead she moved to a Spanish speaking country for six months and placed herself in a situation that forced her to learn the language. How often has God allowed us to be put in situations that taught us the language of prayer? Think back on the times in your life when prayer was all you had. You learned. You grew. And you trusted you would never have to go through such things again after God carried you through to the other side.

But what about the times when you are not desperate? How do you talk to God during those times? Is He only available when you need Him the most? Remember Calvary. Remember the cross. Jesus Christ restored our access to the Father at the cross and it is the work of Calvary in our lives that helps us maintain access on a daily basis.

I have become good friends with the people in which I have endured tough times together. And when the tough times passed, we enjoyed our friendship even more. Likewise, I became a good friend with God during some of the most desperate times of my life. But I have also maintained that friendship in thought and in prayer when times are good. God is not just a fair-weather friend or a storm-chaser. He is a friend at all times, and in the language of prayer you can approach Him whenever you desire or need His touch and communion.

Don't worry about anything; instead, pray about everything. Tell God what you need and thank him for all he has done. Then you will experience God's peace, which exceeds anything we can understand. His peace will guard your hearts and minds as you live in Christ Jesus. (Philippians 4:6–7, NLT) (62).

Prayer produces peace with God and fills you with the peace of God. Prayer also increases love, love for God and love for others. All the more reason to learn the language of God through prayer. Connection with God produces joy and love, and results in tremendous spiritual growth throughout your entire life. Anyone can say prayers, but all the prayers you recite may not bring the connection you need. Peter once warned; *the end of the world is coming soon. Therefore, be earnest and disciplined in your prayers. Most important of all, continue to show deep love for each other, for love covers a multitude of sins.* (1 Peter 4:7-8, NLT) (63).

Why are most of us so reluctant to pray? Are we intimidated by God? I suppose we should be, but why would He want us to be intimidated in His presence while working so hard to get us there? Why would the very God that wants to hear from us do anything that would make us too uncomfortable to approach Him? Again, our ability to approach and have access to God was accomplished on the Cross. Do we think we are so bad at praying that we will embarrass ourselves before God? Our Father God is certainly not interested in shaming us out of an opportunity to talk to Him. I have always enjoyed hearing my children speak to me. Whether it is baby talk or adult conversations, I love to hear from them. How much more is God interested in hearing from his children? I think, a lot more.

And it came to pass, that, as he was praying in a certain place, when he ceased, one of his disciples said unto him, "Lord, teach us to pray, as John also taught his disciples." (Luke 11:1 KJV) (64).

This verse doesn't tell us which disciple asked Jesus to teach them how to pray. But he referred to John the Baptist having taught his disciples how to pray. Oddly enough this is the only place where it is mentioned that John taught people to pray. I suspect it was Andrew, Peter's brother, that brought up the subject. Because, John 1:40, reveals that Andrew was a follower of John before he began following Jesus. Apparently, simply witnessing Jesus as He was praying (talking to His Father), inspired the disciples to want to learn the language of prayer.

And he said unto them, "When ye pray, say, 'Our Father which art in heaven, Hallowed be thy name. Thy kingdom come. Thy will be done, as in heaven, so in earth. Give us day by day our daily bread. And forgive us our sins; for we also forgive every one that is indebted to us. And lead us not into temptation; but deliver us from evil.'" (Luke 11:2–4 KJV) (65).

That's it? That's all we need to know to be able to communicate with God. If this disciple would have asked one of the great religious leaders from the temple how to pray, I'm pretty sure he would have gotten more than a three-verse answer. But that's what we do. We think we have to have a seminary course on prayer before we can pray. My children learned to speak my language by listening to me speak. We learn to speak God's language by listening to Him speak. If we're not listening to God, then we're not learning to speak to Him. Jesus knew He was actually saying a lot when He taught them the Lord's prayer, but He also knew He was keeping it simple for these young new disciples, when He gave them their first lesson.

Jesus started the lesson by saying, *"When you pray, say."* When do we pray? When we are desperate and in trouble? When we need something we don't have or desire to have? Do we pray at bedtime or before eating our meal? Do we pray while others are watching, or do we wait for a closet where no one will see us? Do we pray when we feel like praying? Do we wait for the perfect moment to pray? Are we waiting for the right motivation to pray? Remember, it is GOD we are praying to, so it has to be good, right?

Real prayer can happen anywhere and anytime. Because of Christ and the work of Calvary, we have access to God, anywhere, anytime, and for any reason. Therefore, we should be bold, not timid, when it comes to talking to God.

Not with arrogance or pride, but with humility. He is our Father and thanks to his dear Son, Jesus, we can approach Him as a son also.

That was the whole idea of reconciliation. God wanted access to us; access that was lost when Adam and Eve disobeyed God in the garden. Their disobedience was not just the action of doing something they weren't supposed to be doing. Their choice to disobey was a breaking of the covenant God had with them which allowed mutual access. By disobeying, their sin separated them from continuing to have access to their creator. Rebellion violated the avenue between God and man and closed the door of communication for generations. God is not a man. He is not some egotistical narcissist craving to have a bunch of followers. He is the Father. A loving Father, and as our Father, we come to Him according to His provision and on His terms. He desires far more than being the Almighty God to us. He wants to restore access between us as a family. He wants us to know and communicate with Him as our Father.

Where is heaven? That's a big question. Millions have wanted to know the answer to that for a long time. So, here's one answer, "It's not Here!" But that's the beauty of this verse. Wherever heaven is, it does not keep God from hearing our prayers. And it certainly does not prevent us from hearing from Him.

I remember once when I was going through a very dark time in my life, one of many. I was driving down the highway, desperately longing for relief. In my misery I cried out to God and said, "Oh God, way up there in heaven somewhere, millions of miles away, please come down here and help me!"

Suddenly I heard a voice thunder in my heart and say, "*I am a very present help in times of trouble!*" Instantly, I realized God is not millions of miles away, nor would He have to make a very long trip in order to save me. At that moment I knew God was near, even in the car, and His presence was real and ready to help me. I was a very young man, and a new believer in Christ when I experienced that special moment. Thanks to that experience and answer to prayer, I never again doubted that God was always close to me, regardless of what I was going through or having to endure.

Jesus taught us to pray to the Father in heaven because it is from His throne that He helps us. And neither time nor distance can prevent the Father from reaching down to pick up His children when they cry out to Him. There have been many times in my life that I have had to look up to my Heavenly Father and say, "Daddy, pick me up!"

God is our refuge and strength, a very present help in trouble. Therefore, we will not fear, though the earth be removed, and though the mountains be carried into the midst of the sea; though the waters thereof roar and be troubled, though the mountains shake with the swelling thereof. Selah.

There is a river, the streams whereof shall make glad the city of God, the holy place of the tabernacles of the Most High. God is in the midst of her; she shall not be moved: God shall help her, and that right early.

The heathen raged, the kingdoms were moved: he uttered his voice, the earth melted. The Lord of hosts is with us; the God of Jacob is our refuge. Selah.

Come, behold the works of the Lord, what desolations he hath made in the earth. He maketh wars to cease unto the

*end of the earth; he breaketh the bow, and cutteth the spear
in sunder; he burneth the chariot in the fire.*

*Be still and know that I am God: I will be exalted among
the heathen, I will be exalted in the earth. The Lord of hosts
is with us; the God of Jacob is our refuge.* (Psalms 46 KJV) (66).

Praying to God is far more than offering petitions to a
mortal man. His name is Holy. His name is above every
other name. His name is to be praised. He is to be feared and
reverenced. He is the Holy God, the Lord of Lords, and the
King of Kings. At His name every knee will bow, and every
tongue confess, that He is the Lord of all!

Anything, or anyone less, than the Almighty God, is not
worth the time we spend in prayer. Some have prayed to
small idols made of wood or stone. Some have prayed to the
earth or the planets. Some pray to the unknown god. But we
pray to the Holy God, the Father of all, and the creator of all
things. We do not worship creation; we worship the One by
whom all creation was made.

*We also pray that you will be strengthened with all his
glorious power so you will have all the endurance and
patience you need. May you be filled with joy, always
thanking the Father. He has enabled you to share in the
inheritance that belongs to his people, who live in the light.
For he has rescued us from the kingdom of darkness and
transferred us into the Kingdom of his dear Son, who
purchased our freedom and forgave our sins.*

*Christ is the visible image of the invisible God. He
existed before anything was created and is supreme over all
creation, for through him God created everything in the
heavenly realms and on earth. He made the things we can
see and the things we can't see—such as thrones, kingdoms,
rulers, and authorities in the unseen world. Everything was*

created through him and for him. He existed before anything else, and he holds all creation together.

Christ is also the head of the church, which is his body. He is the beginning, supreme over all who rise from the dead. So he is first in everything. For God in all his fullness was pleased to live in Christ, and through him God reconciled everything to himself. He made peace with everything in heaven and on earth by means of Christ's blood on the cross.

This includes you who were once far away from God. You were his enemies, separated from him by your evil thoughts and actions. Yet now he has reconciled you to himself through the death of Christ in his physical body. As a result, he has brought you into his own presence, and you are holy and blameless as you stand before him without a single fault. (Colossians 1:11-22 NLT) (67).

Now this is the confidence that we have in Him, that if we ask anything according to His will, He hears us. And if we know that He hears us, whatever we ask, we know that we have the petitions that we have asked of Him. (1 John 5:14-15 NKJV) (68).

If we truly want to have confidence in our prayers it is imperative that we learn to pray according to God's will. But, how can we pray in line with God's will if we know nothing about God or His will? With little knowledge of God there is even less awareness of His will. This lack of understanding reduces our prayer life to desperate petitions when we have needs. True prayer, in the language of God, is experienced with growth and understanding of who the Father is and is not. This is revealed to us through the word of God. The more we read and learn His word, the better our prayers become.

Remember, prayer is communication with God. He does not struggle to understand what we are saying or trying to say. He is fully aware of our needs and wants, our true needs and deepest desires. And you can believe He knows His will for each of us. Praying for His will to be done simply increases our confidence that God will answer our prayers. Praying for the will of God releases Him to move and act on our behalf and in our best interest. Praying for His will sets the framework of our lives. It portrays our willingness to trust the very God of creation and the God that created us, to finish the work He began in us. This is not to say we can't petition God for what we desire or need. But it does reinforce the fact that we have a relationship with a God that is more than capable of supplying our needs, the ones we are aware of, and the ones we are not.

Yet you don't have what you want because you don't ask God for it. And even when you ask, you don't get it because your motives are all wrong—you want only what will give you pleasure. (James 4:2-3 NLT) (69).

In the beginning God created the Heaven and the earth. And the earth was without form, and void; and darkness was upon the face of the deep.

And the Spirit of God moved upon the face of the waters. And God said, "Let there be light: and there was light."

And God saw the light, that it was good: and God divided the light from the darkness. And God called the light Day, and the darkness he called Night. And the evening and the morning were the first day. (Genesis 1:1-5 KJV) (70).

Jesus told the disciples they needed to pray according to God's will. Now he adds that they should pray for God's will to be done on earth as it is in heaven. Most of the time we have no clue what God's will is on earth, so how in the world can we begin to know what God's will is in heaven? That's a big question. One for which I don't pretend to have all the answers. However, I can shed some light on it from the word of God.

Genesis starts with, *In the beginning God created the Heaven and the earth.* Then proceeds to tell us nothing about heaven while revealing that *the earth was without form, and void; and darkness was upon the face of the deep.*

So, let's presume that God created heaven first and then got started on the earth. And let's consider that what He did in heaven He now wants to mirror on this dark void of formless earth. Therefore, we can assume for the moment that heaven must be a place of light, noting the first thing God does for this blank canvas called earth, is to turn on the lights.

What is the first thing we do when entering a dark room? We turn on the lights. What do we normally do when we move into a new house? We get the power turned on so we can turn on the lights. It's pretty clear we don't enjoy living in darkness since turning on lights is one of our first priorities at anything we do in our lives. So, what is Jesus suggesting when he instructs them to pray *as in heaven so on earth?* Maybe we start by simply turning on some lights. So, let's start with what or who is light.

Then spake Jesus again unto them, saying, "I am the light of the world: he that followeth me shall not walk in darkness, but shall have the light of life." (John 8:12 KJV) (71).

Jesus did not come to this earth just to die on a cross. His death on the cross was paramount and of the highest priority because without His sacrifice we could never experience the full purpose of Calvary. He came to reveal Himself as the light of the world. Our lives were dark, formless and void because of sin. Through Calvary, Christ, the Son of God, once again, as at the beginning of creation, came to separate the darkness from the light in our hearts so we could have eyes to see His manifest glory, the Light of Almighty God. Without this light we continue to grope around in the darkness, stumbling over ourselves and our sin with no hope of seeing Him or ourselves in Him. His will in heaven is to light the way for man and all creation to find Him and see Him as He is, a God that can be found. He takes no pleasure in hiding from us. His words are recorded in Isaiah and Romans, *"I was found of them that sought me not."*

His will in heaven and especially on earth is that we find Him. And that is made possible by the Light revealed from the man that endured the cross at Calvary.

I must work the works of him that sent me, while it is day: the night cometh, when no man can work. As long as I am in the world, I am the light of the world. (John 9:4-5 KJV) (72).

In the beginning the Word already existed. The Word was with God, and the Word was God. He existed in the beginning with God. God created everything through him, and nothing was created except through him. The Word gave life to everything that was created, and his life brought light to everyone. The light shines in the darkness, and the darkness can never extinguish it. (John 1:1-5 NLT) (73).

God sent a man, John the Baptist, to tell about the light so that everyone might believe because of his testimony. John himself was not the light; he was simply a witness to tell about the light. The one who is the true light, who gives light to everyone, was coming into the world. He came into the very world he created, but the world didn't recognize him. He came to his own people, and even they rejected him. But to all who believed him and accepted him, he gave the right to become children of God. They are reborn—not with a physical birth resulting from human passion or plan, but a birth that comes from God. (John 1:6-13 NLT) (74).

So the Word became human and made his home among us. He was full of unfailing love and faithfulness. And we have seen his glory, the glory of the Father's one and only Son.

John testified about him when he shouted to the crowds, "This is the one I was talking about when I said, 'Someone is coming after me who is far greater than I am, for he existed long before me.'"

From his abundance we have all received one gracious blessing after another. For the law was given through Moses, but God's unfailing love and faithfulness came through Jesus Christ. No one has ever seen God. But the one and only Son is himself God and is near to the Father's heart. He has revealed God to us. (John 1:14-18 NLT) (75).

Typically, we don't worry about bread until we discover we have none. Not having what we need for our daily lives can often become a major distraction. Distractions draw our attention away from prayer and communion with God. Asking God to take care of our daily needs reduces worry and eliminates stress, thereby freeing us to commune with God.

God understands our daily needs. He should. He created us. We should remember that we are not bothering God when we ask Him to supply the things we have need of on a daily basis. That is what He instructed us to do. All too often we tend to leave God alone with the little stuff and only bother Him with the big desperate stuff. But what we fail to understand is communion with God is an exercise we must practice in order to develop more confidence when we pray to God. We become better at growing our faith in God when we practice communion with Him. Learning to ask and rely on God for our daily concerns teaches us to depend on Him as a father, for all of our needs. Simply stated we need Him every day, not just on bad days.

I remember one of those bad days. I was still a young man and I had taken a job with a very unpleasant man. It was a time when the economy was in the tank and many of my friends had been laid off from their jobs and couldn't find work. I tried to remind myself every day that I should be thankful that I even had a job.

The project we were doing was sixty-five miles away in another town and I had to meet this man very early at the shop to make the ride to the job. I would sit quietly in the passenger seat each day trying to meditate on the Lord and be thankful for the work. It didn't pay much but it was better than nothing. One morning I decided to quit because I couldn't take it anymore, but someone stole my toolbox. I had left it by the main entrance door while I was working on the opposite side of the building. You couldn't walk up on a jobsite in those days without tools, so I felt forced to stay. Thank God I did because I had a job with that man for the entire time the economy was down, while my friends remained unemployed for a year.

Every morning about half-way to our destination we would round a large curve in the road and suddenly there would be a large farm with acres of crops as far as you could see. I was always amazed at the size of that farm. Over the course of the year I had watched the plowing, the planting and the growing. It was interesting to witness the process as men sowed seed and trusted that a crop would grow, and a harvest would come.

Then one morning as we rounded the curve and passed the tree line to view the vast open farm, there were tractors everywhere harvesting the crops. It was something to watch as we sped past on the way to our jobsite. Several days later the tractors were gone, and the fields appeared barren and desolate, and I began once again to feel the barrenness and desolation in myself. After months of watching this scene through the window of the truck while trying to distract myself from the miserable driver I shared my morning meditation with, enduring his cigarette smoke, the loud radio and the coffee spills, I looked at the empty fields and wondered why I felt so empty and alone. Had God forgotten me? Didn't He know how miserable it was to spend every day of my year with this guy? Didn't He know I needed more money and a better job to provide for my new family, my wife and newborn son? How was I going to survive another day of this season of my life?

The following morning at the shop, waiting for my ride, I was more miserable than ever. The feelings of the day before were still fresh and I was sure I had reached my limit, but there was nowhere to go. I didn't even look forward to seeing the farm this morning because it would still be empty and barren. Or so I thought. As we rounded the curve one more time and passed the end of the tree line which had been blocking my view, I witnessed something I have only seen one time in my entire life. There were millions and millions of birds on and over all the fields for as far as I could see. The sky was black with them circling above the land below. The ground looked alive and moving with the birds on the ground gleaning what was left behind by the harvesters. I couldn't believe my eyes. I had never seen so many birds in one place before; a place that was miles long and wide. How did they know to come here? Who had called them to this massive feast?

Then I heard a still small voice in my head. A voice clearer than the blaring radio and the constant coughing of my driver. A voice that said, *"You see all these birds? I care about you and your needs more than every one of these birds!"* The tears shot out of my eyes. I slumped down in my seat as though I were sleeping trying to hide my face from my companion, trying to hide my tears so I wouldn't have to explain to him what was going on with me. But these were not tears of sorrow, these were tears of intense joy and I was trying desperately to keep this feeling locked inside, so I didn't embarrass myself in front of this other man. I had never felt such love and care from anyone, and here was God displaying His great care for me and my needs in the most awkward situation. I carried this feeling daily for the remainder of my time at that company. And I still carry the memory of God's love, care and concern for my needs, to this day.

Then He said to His disciples, "Therefore I say to you, do not worry about your life, what you will eat; nor about the body, what you will put on. Life is more than food, and the body is more than clothing. Consider the ravens, for they neither sow nor reap, which have neither storehouse nor barn; and God feeds them. Of how much more value are you than the birds? And which of you by worrying can add one cubit to his stature? If you then are not able to do the least, why are you anxious for the rest? Consider the lilies, how they grow: they neither toil nor spin; and yet I say to you, even Solomon in all his glory was not arrayed like one of these. If then God so clothes the grass, which today is in the field and tomorrow is thrown into the oven, how much more will He clothe you, O you of little faith?

"And do not seek what you should eat or what you should drink, nor have an anxious mind. For all these things the nations of the world seek after, and your Father knows that you need these things. But seek the kingdom of God, and all these things shall be added to you.

"Do not fear, little flock, for it is your Father's good pleasure to give you the kingdom." (Luke 12:22-32 NKJV) (76).

Now we come to one of the most important parts of learning the language of God. If we are to truly find access to God, we have to come to grips with the fact that we are all sinners and need to come to God for forgiveness. Jesus was keenly aware that He came to become the door for this access when He included this portion in his lesson on prayer. In order to properly begin our journey into a new life in Christ, it is imperative that we come to grips with our own sinfulness and turn to God asking for His forgiveness.

If we claim we have no sin, we are only fooling ourselves and not living in the truth. But if we confess our sins to him, he is faithful and just to forgive us our sins and to cleanse us from all wickedness. If we claim we have not sinned, we are calling God a liar and showing that his word has no place in our hearts.

My dear children, I am writing this to you so that you will not sin. But if anyone does sin, we have an advocate who pleads our case before the Father. He is Jesus Christ, the one who is truly righteous. He himself is the sacrifice that atones for our sins—and not only our sins but the sins of all the world. (1 John 1:8-2:2 NLT) (77).

Is there a difference between healing and forgiveness of sin? In either case there is need for a remedy beyond our ability to provide. And when the one that is doing the suffering is asking for healing or forgiveness, either request becomes a simple matter of word choices. The desire to be whole from sin or sickness is foremost in the mind of the one in pain.

There is nothing new about confusion over the sin-disease question. For some, what was once a bad choice which led to addiction is now called a disease. For others, calling sin a disease provides the illusion of a scapegoat for out of control behavior. Regardless of our understanding or position on the subject of *is it sin or a disease*, there is one thing for sure, we need to be healed.

Jesus provided the path for our healing by instructing us to simply ask Him for forgiveness of our sins. Whether we ask for forgiveness or ask to be healed, we are still coming to the one with the power to do either, when we bring our request to Him.

When Jesus returned to Capernaum several days later, the news spread quickly that he was back home. Soon the house where he was staying was so packed with visitors that there was no more room, even outside the door. While he was preaching God's word to them, four men arrived carrying a paralyzed man on a mat. They couldn't bring him to Jesus because of the crowd, so they dug a hole through the roof above his head. Then they lowered the man on his mat, right down in front of Jesus.

Seeing their faith, Jesus said to the paralyzed man, "My child, your sins are forgiven."

But some of the teachers of religious law who were sitting there thought to themselves, "What is he saying? This is blasphemy! Only God can forgive sins!"

Jesus knew immediately what they were thinking, so he asked them, "Why do you question this in your hearts? Is it easier to say to the paralyzed man 'Your sins are forgiven,' or 'Stand up, pick up your mat, and walk?' So I will prove to you that the Son of Man has the authority on earth to forgive sins."

Then Jesus turned to the paralyzed man and said, "Stand up, pick up your mat, and go home!"

And the man jumped up, grabbed his mat, and walked out through the stunned onlookers. They were all amazed and praised God, exclaiming, "We've never seen anything like this before!" (Mark 2:1-12 NLT) (78).

Seeing our need for healing and forgiveness is quite remarkable. But Jesus also taught us that a major component of learning the language of prayer involved our willingness and ability to forgive others who owed us.

You know that our ancestors were told, "Do not murder" and "A murderer must be brought to trial." But I promise you that if you are angry with someone, you will have to stand trial. If you call someone a fool, you will be taken to court. And if you say that someone is worthless, you will be in danger of the fires of hell.

So if you are about to place your gift on the altar and remember that someone is angry with you, leave your gift there in front of the altar. Make peace with that person, then come back and offer your gift to God. (Matthew 5:21-24 CEV) (79).

I am never more distracted than when I attempt to pray. I remember everything I need to get done. I constantly check my watch so I'm not late for work, or whatever. I'm bombarded with thoughts of people who have done me wrong or simply hurt my feelings. Which is precisely why

Jesus pointed out to the disciples in His lesson on prayer, they must forgive those indebted to them when they pray.

Who is indebted to us? Do we have to let them off the hook if they owe us money? What is the debt? See, a distraction! To experience access to God through prayer, it is best to remove distractions. And things that distract us the most can usually be found in our relationships with other people. I have often joked that if it weren't for people I would be just fine.

I fully understand the first portion of this passage. I clearly have a problem if I am filled with thoughts of condescension, anger, and even murder towards others when I come to prayer. But if someone has a problem with me, why should I have to go to them first in order to present my gift at the altar? Why didn't Jesus tell them to come make it right with me? They're angry with me – I'm not angry with them. We may conclude that if we truly want to make peace with God (who we don't see) then it will help to make peace with (who we do see), our fellow man. The object is *peace*. Peace with God and man; and access to our fellow man through peace and access to God. We must learn to communicate using the language of God without the distractions. This is best accomplished when our hearts are filled with forgiveness rather than overloaded with hurt.

Take heed to yourselves: If thy brother trespass against thee, rebuke him; and if he repent, forgive him. And if he trespass against thee seven times in a day, and seven times in a day turn again to thee, saying, I repent; thou shalt forgive him. (Luke 17:3-4 KJV) (80).

I am not overstating it when I say that the man who caused all the trouble hurt all of you more than he hurt me. Most of you opposed him, and that was punishment enough.

Now, however, it is time to forgive and comfort him. Otherwise he may be overcome by discouragement. So, I urge you now to reaffirm your love for him.

I wrote to you as I did to test you and see if you would fully comply with my instructions. When you forgive this man, I forgive him, too. And when I forgive whatever needs to be forgiven, I do so with Christ's authority for your benefit, so that Satan will not outsmart us. For we are familiar with his evil schemes. (2 Corinthians 2:5-11 NLT) (81).

Jesus also pointed out in the Lord's Prayer that we should pray that God lead us not into temptation. Seriously? Do we really believe God would lead us into temptation?

All of us at one time or another have either said, or heard someone say, "God must be testing me." This statement could never be further from the truth. If Jesus is teaching us how to pray to the Father, why would part of that prayer ask that God *not* lead us into temptation?

Consider this, as a parent we often allow young children some freedom of mobility as they wonder around the room. The room may be filled with many obstacles such as the very things we purchased for the child to play with. Then there's furniture in the room, especially tables. We've all seen or heard of a toddler tripping over his own stuff only to bump his head against the edge of a table. However, with all the potential for some possible hurt to the child, we still leave the furniture in place and allow the child to scatter his toys all over the room, thus creating much of his own risk. We all understand we can only "child-proof" the house to a certain level. The ultimate child-proof room is the one you don't bring the child into. Simply stated, it's a challenge to grow up.

Therefore, are we leading the child into temptation by allowing him into the room? Are we setting him up for failure by leaving potential hazards in the room? Or, are we standing by him, watching and waiting to catch him before he falls, while allowing him to grow and learn to navigate around the obstacles in the room?

Remember, this prayer started with *Our Father,* and we have to view God as a father when we pray to Him. When we look to our Father in heaven, we have to believe that His only intentions towards us are good. If they are anything else, we will be afraid to approach Him. Prayer through Christ Jesus is our most available access to God, and while there may be obstacles of learning in the path and process, we should remain committed to understanding the language of God in order to fully comprehend his love and passion for us as our Father.

Jesus specifically included the words *and lead us not into temptation* for a reason. Even though the Spirit led Him into the wilderness to face temptation, He understood it was His choice and His freewill to face what was ahead in that place where His most ardent enemy awaited. While God is not the one doing the tempting, it can often be seen that He has allowed things to remain in the room for our growth and education. It helps if we learn to understand where temptation comes from and what God's role is in temptation. Then it will help to recognize the role temptation plays in our spiritual growth and development. According to the verses below, much of our temptation starts with us.

Let no man say when he is tempted, I am tempted of God: for God cannot be tempted with evil, neither tempteth he any man: (James 1:13 KJV) (82).

God blesses those who patiently endure testing and temptation. Afterward they will receive the crown of life that God has promised to those who love him. And remember, when you are being tempted, do not say, "God is tempting me." God is never tempted to do wrong, and he never tempts anyone else.

Temptation comes from our own desires, which entice us and drag us away. These desires give birth to sinful actions. And when sin is allowed to grow, it gives birth to death. (James 1:12-15 NLT) (83).

Okay. Hang in there, we're almost done with our language lesson. Why would Jesus instruct us to ask to be delivered from evil when we pray? Are the wicked forces of evil going to attack us when we pray? They might! We just read about being distracted in prayer. Is *evil* a problem for me when I'm not praying? Yes! We may be surrounded by evil or be the ones filled with evil. In either case, whether within or without, we need to be delivered from evil, especially if we are to have access to approach God. Don't misunderstand this statement. We can never come to God because of our own worthiness. But we have access to the Father through the righteousness of His dear Son, Jesus Christ. Evil keeps us from the door. Christ became the door in order to give us access to God. Deliverance from evil clears the way for communion with Christ and communication with the Father in another facet of His own language, the language of love.

But evil people and impostors will flourish. They will deceive others and will themselves be deceived. But you must remain faithful to the things you have been taught. (2 Timothy 3:13-14 NLT) (84)

And this is the condemnation, that light is come into the world, and men loved darkness rather than light, because their deeds were evil. For everyone that doeth evil hateth the light, neither cometh to the light, lest his deeds should be reproved. But he that doeth truth cometh to the light, that his deeds may be made manifest, that they are wrought in God. (John 3:19-21 KJV) (85).

Beloved, follow not that which is evil, but that which is good. He that doeth good is of God: but he that doeth evil hath not seen God. (3 John 11 KJV) (86).

Let's pray. Dear Lord Jesus, we ask You today to teach us to pray. Motivate us to pray more often. And give us the confidence to pray bold prayers as we humble ourselves before You. Teach us to pray according to Your will and Your word. Help us to apply all the skills provided by Your Spirit and teach us to become fervent people of prayer in Jesus name. Amen.

Chapter Nine

Blood Sweat & Tears

There's been a lot of debate regarding the legitimacy of the historical account of Jesus sweating blood in the garden while He prayed. This is not one of those debates. This is an opportunity to remember what one man did for the benefit of others. Everything Jesus did during His short visit to this planet was a well laid plan devised by a Father willing to provide the ultimate sacrifice, His Son, in order to recover something as equally precious, you!

When Jesus entered the Garden of Gethsemane that night, He knew this was the point of no return. This was not a moment like the others where He hid Himself in the crowd and left the scene because it was not yet His time. But this was His time, a time in which He still possessed the *freewill* to refuse to stick to the plan. But Jesus was no ordinary man, and this was no ordinary plan. This was a plan to take back that which had been stolen. This was the moment in time when a fallen angel would be reminded of his coming defeat. This man was about to cross the abyss that none were allowed to return from, and this passage would empower Him to take captivity captive and set men's souls free.

Then Jesus went with them to the olive grove called Gethsemane, and he said, "Sit here while I go over there to pray."

He took Peter and Zebedee's two sons, James and John, and he became anguished and distressed. He told them, "My soul is crushed with grief to the point of death. Stay here and keep watch with me."

He went on a little farther and bowed with his face to the ground, praying, "My Father! If it is possible, let this cup of suffering be taken away from me. Yet I want your will to be done, not mine."

Then he returned to the disciples and found them asleep. He said to Peter, "Couldn't you watch with me even one hour? Keep watch and pray, so that you will not give in to temptation. For the spirit is willing, but the body is weak!"

Then Jesus left them a second time and prayed, "My Father! If this cup cannot be taken away unless I drink it, your will be done." When he returned to them again, he found them sleeping, for they couldn't keep their eyes open. So he went to pray a third time, saying the same things again.

Then he came to the disciples and said, "Go ahead and sleep. Have your rest. But look—the time has come. The Son of Man is betrayed into the hands of sinners. Up, let's be going. Look, my betrayer is here!" (Matthew 26:36-46 NLT) (87).

What did Jesus expect from these three men? They were tired. They had given up several years of their lives to follow this man all over the countryside because they saw something in Him that promised, what they believed, to offer a better opportunity for a better life. They had endured His mood swings, listened to his stories and teachings, and even witnessed a few miracles. This was just another night under the stars waiting for whatever was to happen as a result of following this man around to finally come. And besides, they were tired, and this was probably not the first night they dosed off while Jesus prayed.

And even as Jesus said this, Judas, one of the twelve disciples, arrived with a crowd of men armed with swords and clubs. They had been sent by the leading priests and elders of the people.

The traitor, Judas, had given them a prearranged signal: "You will know which one to arrest when I greet him with a kiss."

So Judas came straight to Jesus. "Greetings, Rabbi!" he exclaimed and gave him the kiss.

Jesus said, "My friend, go ahead and do what you have come for."

Then the others grabbed Jesus and arrested him. But one of the men with Jesus pulled out his sword and struck the high priest's slave, slashing off his ear.

"Put away your sword," Jesus told him. "Those who use the sword will die by the sword. Don't you realize that I could ask my Father for thousands of angels to protect us, and he would send them instantly? But if I did, how would the Scriptures be fulfilled that describe what must happen now?"

Then Jesus said to the crowd, "Am I some dangerous revolutionary, that you come with swords and clubs to arrest me? Why didn't you arrest me in the Temple? I was there teaching every day. But this is all happening to fulfill the words of the prophets as recorded in the Scriptures." At that point, all the disciples deserted him and fled. (Matthew 26:47-56 NLT) (88).

This was not the first time Jesus had come to pray at this garden, but it would be the last. It was not the first time His disciples slept while He prayed. Remember, Judas knew exactly where to find Jesus, once he committed to betraying Him.

Jesus knew this was the night, His last night. He could have gone somewhere else. He could have avoided the garden altogether. But earlier, He had told Judas to go do what he was going to do. Judas was going to betray Jesus, and he knew just where to bring the soldiers so they could make the arrest.

Rather than run or avoid His appointed time on this particular evening, Jesus embraced the will of God, as painful as it was, and laid his will down that night in the garden. Before Jesus ever took all our sins to the cross, He took our will to hold on to those sins to the garden. None of his previous visits to this favorite prayer spot produced blood. What made this night so much more excruciating? Was it the waiting Cross? Was it His anxiety over the coming trial, the forty lashes, or the crown of thorns?

For us to fully appreciate the sacrifice Christ made for us, we have to look deeper than the single event of his death on the Cross and recognize the work of Calvary that took place in every one of His actions. He had warned His own mother at the age of twelve that He had to be about His Father's business. Years before the Cross, He was mindful even as a child, of the purpose of His arrival. He would allow the soldiers to nail our sins on the cross in His body. He would submit to their lashes to secure our healing. And tonight, he would resist till he sweated blood as He took our freewill, the same freewill we use to disobey and rebel against the will of God and surrender it all with His will in the garden.

We wouldn't have asked for the cup to be removed. We would have avoided it at any cost. He, being fully human, asked for it to be taken away, but being fully God, remembered why He had to drink. He was here to lose His life so we could find ours.

Every step Jesus took, was at one level or another for the express purpose of fulfilling prophecy and securing what had been stolen from God by a rebellious defector from His own creation. The cost to redeem the lost would require all the equity God held dear in the earthly body of His only beloved Son. Are we really worth such a high price? Obviously, we are! God paid the ultimate price to buy back his ultimate loss – us.

So Jesus told them this story: "If a man has a hundred sheep and one of them gets lost, what will he do? Won't he leave the ninety-nine others in the wilderness and go to search for the one that is lost until he finds it? And when he has found it, he will joyfully carry it home on his shoulders. When he arrives, he will call together his friends and neighbors, saying, 'Rejoice with me because I have found my lost sheep.' In the same way, there is more joy in heaven over one lost sinner who repents and returns to God than over ninety-nine others who are righteous and haven't strayed away!

"Or suppose a woman has ten silver coins and loses one. Won't she light a lamp and sweep the entire house and search carefully until she finds it? And when she finds it, she

will call in her friends and neighbors and say, 'Rejoice with me because I have found my lost coin.' In the same way, there is joy in the presence of God's angels when even one sinner repents." (Luke 15:3-10 NLT) (89).

Was His anguish over the fear of His coming torture and death? Were the drops of blood in the garden the result of His inner battle to obey or not to obey? What had He spent His life doing? Being about the will of His Father. What was the will of His Father? To seek and save that which was lost. In the garden His search would reach a new level. God was tearing His house apart to find the missing coin. The shepherd was scouring the countryside to locate the one that was missing. In order for the coin and the sheep to be found and secured once and forever, a Lamb was about to be slain. And not just any lamb. The time for the Lamb of God had arrived and the ultimate test of free will, had also arrived. It was the time for more than talk and parables; it was the time for sacrifice and death. His death.

He asked for it to be removed, anyone of us would have done the same. He agreed to drink it if that was the only way it would pass from Him, as an empty cup. We would have run away, but He stayed, and the start of His shedding blood had come. He shed blood in the garden, He shed blood at the trial when the thorns were pushed into His head. He shed more blood at the whipping post as the soldiers ripped the flesh from His back. He hung there on the cross dripping with blood as it ran down the tree to the ground below. And even after He gave up His spirit and took our sins, sickness, and self-will to hell below, He shed more blood, and the water of His very life when a soldier pierced His side with a spear to verify that His death was complete.

The deed was about to be carried out. More prophecies

were coming to pass. The will of God in heaven was about to be done in the earth. The heavens, the earth, and hell below, were about to witness the Lamb which was slain from the foundation of the world. And this evening of prayer in the Garden of Gethsemane would place the Son of God and the Son of Man at the threshold of heaven to redeem and reunite the Creator with that which was lost.

Dear Lord Jesus. Your first disciples asked You to teach them how to pray. We now ask You to teach us to prayer. Teach us to endure in prayer. Help us to pray with purpose and passion. Empower us to pray with power in order to stand against principalities and wickedness in high places. Teach us to pray for our enemies and our friends. Strengthen us to pray according to Your Word and Your will. Help us to stay awake and pray with You at every opportunity. Teach us to pray without ceasing. We ask this in Your name. Amen.

Chapter Ten

Arrested in the Night

There are few things more disturbing than an illicit and unjustified arrest. History is filled with stories of people having been falsely accused, tried, convicted and condemned of crimes they did not commit. And often, without any concern for getting the facts right or wrong from witnesses, bystanders and spectators participating in the process. There may also be little concern for the legitimacy or accuracy of the process. But there has never been a more unjust breach of due process than that committed against Jesus of Nazareth.

Although His death was part of a divine and grand design, it was still an evil and despicable act of behavior on the part of those who carried out this supreme injustice upon a truly innocent man. As we take a deeper look at this trial, we should constantly bear in mind that it was each one of us that deserved to be the ones under scrutiny for our actions.

Mob rule is a very frightening experience. Especially if you find yourself in the crosshairs of their condemnation. People worked up into a frenzy by events, incidents and occurrences of various kinds can draw conclusions and demand actions on those conclusions, with very little appetite for truth or reality. And most of the time it only takes one instigator to stir a crowd into doing something that as individuals, would have never ventured into such a realm of behavior. In fact, their activism requires them to take on the role of a victim or act as the defender of a victim, in order to keep things adequately stirred up. Sadly, many in the mob manipulated to carry out the desires of the instigators, can tell you very little of what is actually taking place. Much of the same crowd crying, "Hosanna," when Jesus entered the city, took up the cry for crucifixion at his trial. Simply stated, people can support you then turn on you with very little provocation. And all it took to turn the crowd from praise to persecution in the case of Jesus, was a miracle.

But, not just any miracle. He had amazed the crowd by healing the sick. Many questioned what sort of man He was by opening blind eyes and restoring withered limbs. He healed lepers with His touch rather than avoiding contact with them like others. But when He crossed over the barrier of death itself and raised a man from the dead, He had to be stopped. No one could overcome death, no one till now. And if death couldn't stop Him, who could?

Then Jesus shouted, "Lazarus, come out!" And the dead man came out, his hands and feet bound in graveclothes, his face wrapped in a headcloth. Jesus told them, "Unwrap him and let him go!"

Many of the people who were with Mary believed in Jesus when they saw this happen. But some went to the Pharisees and told them what Jesus had done. Then the leading priests and Pharisees called the high council together.

"What are we going to do?" they asked each other. "This man certainly performs many miraculous signs. If we allow him to go on like this, soon everyone will believe in him. Then the Roman army will come and destroy both our Temple and our nation."

Caiaphas, who was high priest at that time, said, "You don't know what you're talking about! You don't realize that it's better for you that one man should die for the people than for the whole nation to be destroyed."

He did not say this on his own; as high priest at that time he was led to prophesy that Jesus would die for the entire nation. And not only for that nation, but to bring together and unite all the children of God scattered around the world.

So from that time on, the Jewish leaders began to plot Jesus' death. As a result, Jesus stopped his public ministry among the people and left Jerusalem. He went to a place near the wilderness, to the village of Ephraim, and stayed there with his disciples. (John 11:44-54 NLT) (90).

Did you catch that last paragraph? As a result of their plot to kill Him, Jesus stopped His public ministry and went into the wilderness and stayed there with His disciples. Why? Was He afraid of the people? Did He fear for His life, a life He came to sacrifice? Was He trying to regroup and plan His next move?

Jesus had travelled openly; taught openly; healed openly; and performed miracles openly. He had nothing to hide and He certainly wasn't hiding now. He had just demonstrated that even the grave could not defy Him. The dead could not resist His power. Only the living had the ability to resist His love by using a gift from God above called freewill, which is often used to resist His only Son. And the time had arrived for prophecy to have its way with Him. The ultimate rejection was about to be revealed and regardless of all God was willing to do to redeem man back to Himself, man was still willing to resist, reject and murder the love of His life – His only begotten Son.

Jesus crossed the Kidron Valley with his disciples and entered a grove of olive trees. Judas, the betrayer, knew this place, because Jesus had often gone there with his disciples.

The leading priests and Pharisees had given Judas a contingent of Roman soldiers and Temple guards to accompany him. Now with blazing torches, lanterns, and weapons, they arrived at the olive grove. (John 18:1-3 NLT) (91).

While no exact number is given as to how many men it took to arrest Jesus, it is clear that the authorities sent a very large team to capture the man. Some sources report historically that a *contingent* could have been as many as six-hundred soldiers. Six-hundred Roman soldiers carrying torches, lanterns and weapons during the middle of the night, a frightening sight for anyone in their way as they marched towards the olive grove where Jesus was praying with His disciples.

The soldiers were armed and ready. They had been mustered in the night to embark on a mission. One they may have been privy to or not. Their training prepared them for the worst of encounters. Other than the officers among them, they probably knew little about the battle ahead. The fact that so many of them had been deployed for tonight's mission, more than likely put them on edge, noting this was a lot of force for a simple arrest within the city boundaries.

Who was this enemy? What were they about to encounter? Prepared, earnest, and on edge, soldiers trained to kill without emotion or regard for the life of the enemy they faced, now marched in the night for an encounter with God. The rank and file didn't know what level of resistance to expect. They could, however, look around them and consider they were taking a lot of men with them to get the job done. And they were ready for battle, because they were Roman soldiers.

In addition to the Roman soldiers, the priests and Pharisees included a group of their own Temple Guards to participate in the arrest. We are provided little detail about their numbers either, but we can tell that this was no small matter to the priests, and they weren't willing to take any chances with the execution of their warrant to capture a man claiming to be the Son of God. They had heard of His miracles, His authoritative teaching, and His power over demons. They did not know what He was fully capable of doing, but the stories of raising the dead had them on full alert. For all they knew, this Jesus, had the power to take life from the living as well as returning life to the dead; and they wanted to assuage their fear of the unknown by sending plenty of force.

How was it that the Jewish priests and Pharisees even had the authority to send hundreds of Roman soldiers along with their own Temple guards to make the arrest? It was apparent the Jewish leaders were already working with the Roman government in some manner to carry out their desire to destroy Jesus. This was no small effort to stop a man that had taught people in parables and healed a few sick folks.

Knowing now that He could raise the dead, changed the game and there was no telling what He could do if He chose to resist arrest. An arrest they apparently feared to carry out because of the sheer fire power they decided to deploy. Besides, the Jews had historical data for things like this. When a king sent soldiers to arrest the prophet Elijah in the book of 2nd Kings, he called fire down from heaven to destroy them, twice. What could Jesus do?

One day Israel's new king, Ahaziah, fell through the latticework of an upper room at his palace in Samaria and was seriously injured. So he sent messengers to the temple of Baal-zebub, the god of Ekron, to ask whether he would recover.

But the angel of the Lord told Elijah, who was from Tishbe, "Go and confront the messengers of the king of Samaria and ask them, 'Is there no God in Israel? Why are you going to Baal-zebub, the god of Ekron, to ask whether the king will recover? Now, therefore, this is what the Lord says: You will never leave the bed you are lying on; you will surely die.'" So Elijah went to deliver the message.

When the messengers returned to the king, he asked them, "Why have you returned so soon?"

They replied, "A man came up to us and told us to go back to the king and give him this message. 'This is what the Lord says: Is there no God in Israel? Why are you sending men to Baal-zebub, the god of Ekron, to ask whether you will recover? Therefore, because you have done this, you will never leave the bed you are lying on; you will surely die.'"

"What sort of man was he?" the king demanded. "What did he look like?"

They replied, "He was a hairy man, and he wore a leather belt around his waist."

"Elijah from Tishbe!" the king exclaimed.

Then he sent an army captain with fifty soldiers to arrest him. They found him sitting on top of a hill. The captain said to him, "Man of God, the king has commanded you to come down with us."

But Elijah replied to the captain, "If I am a man of God, let fire come down from heaven and destroy you and your fifty men!" Then fire fell from heaven and killed them all.

So the king sent another captain with fifty men. The captain said to him, "Man of God, the king demands that you come down at once."

Elijah replied, "If I am a man of God, let fire come down from heaven and destroy you and your fifty men!" And again the fire of God fell from heaven and killed them all.

Once more the king sent a third captain with fifty men. But this time the captain went up the hill and fell to his knees before Elijah. He pleaded with him, "O man of God, please spare my life and the lives of these, your fifty servants. See how the fire from heaven came down and destroyed the first two groups. But now please spare my life!"

Then the angel of the Lord said to Elijah, "Go down with him, and don't be afraid of him." So Elijah got up and went with him to the king. (2 Kings 1:2-15 NLT) (92).

What could Jesus do? Anything He wanted. What would Jesus do? Fortunately for the small army deployed to capture Him, He would submit to the will of His Father God, without regard for the intimidating presence of the soldiers before Him. Whether they realized it or not they were simply tools in the hands of an Almighty God being used to carry out His will in order to fulfill His prophetic word as revealed by generations of prophets before them.

Jesus fully realized all that was going to happen to him, so he stepped forward to meet them. "Who are you looking for?" he asked.

"Jesus the Nazarene," they replied.

"I AM he," Jesus said. (Judas, who betrayed him, was standing with them.) As Jesus said, "I AM he," they all drew back and fell to the ground!

Once more he asked them, "Who are you looking for?"

And again they replied, "Jesus the Nazarene."

"I told you that I AM he," Jesus said. "And since I am the one you want, let these others go."

He did this to fulfill his own statement: "I did not lose a single one of those you have given me." (John 18:4-9 NLT) (93).

What an amazing moment. He was confronted by a small army that under normal circumstances would not have been concerned with the request of their prisoner. However, this was not a normal circumstance or a normal man. Nor was He their prisoner as they may have supposed.

He was the Son of God, the Messiah, God come in the flesh, the Word by whom all things were made, from the beginning, and *to fulfill his own statement*, He narrowed the focus of this army, which were there to confront Him and His army, to allow His followers to go free while arresting only Himself.

From the moment of their first contact and the betrayer's kiss, He demonstrated his available power then humbly submitted Himself to their arrest. He submitted because He fully realized all that was about to happen to Him. Upon their first approach He asked who they were looking for and when they said, "Jesus the Nazarene," he said, "I AM he!" At that moment this powerful contingent stood face to face with the great *I AM*. And this Nazarene, armed only with the power of his Word, caused them *all* to step back and fall down to the ground in the way worshippers of the *Almighty* might lay prostrate before God in contrite obeisance.

In His presence and at His word they could not stand and be able to carry out their orders on their own power. They could only fall because they were now face to face with the *I AM,* who stood before them as the simple Son of a carpenter.

When they were finally able to get up and resume their stance for battle, He asked them again who they were looking for and once again they replied, Jesus. He now had their attention. He had now demonstrated how powerless they actually were against Him. They had no problem honoring His request to allow the others to go. Besides, the soldiers may have wondered, had He imparted this power to His disciples as well? They understood this lone man was coming with them willingly and they weren't willing to push their luck. The spectators assumed the soldiers were in charge as they returned their prisoner to the Temple, but the soldiers still remembered what they saw in the face of the *I AM,* and what they felt as they stared at the ground.

So the soldiers, their commanding officer, and the Temple guards arrested Jesus and tied him up. First they took him to Annas, the father-in-law of Caiaphas, the high priest at that time. Caiaphas was the one who had told the other Jewish leaders, "It's better that one man should die for the people." (John 18:12-14 NLT) (94).

The soldiers were following orders to arrest Jesus. They did not concern themselves with politeness as they executed orders. And after what they just experienced, they were taking no chances. How soon they forgot that His words alone contained the power to subdue them and no other weapon was necessary. Nonetheless, they tied Him up and made great spectacle of dragging their prisoner off to the former official high priest, Annas.

The time had come, and aged-old prophecies were being fulfilled. The disciples were spared and scattered as Jesus was marched through the streets in the night with an entourage that carried swords and torches. The fishermen and tax collectors had gone into hiding thinking their dreams were dashed by the arrest of the man they had hoped was the Messiah. Now they were unsure on many levels and could only hope that the outcome for the man they followed for several years would turn out okay. Despite Jesus' attempts to teach and prepare them for what was going to happen to Him, they still escaped into the night confused and dejected. Only a few dared to follow at a distance as Jesus was taken to appear before a one-man grand jury.

Annas actually had no right or authority to question Jesus, and if this had been a *real* trial, he would have been concerned about getting to the truth about this man's guilt or innocence. But this trial was rigged, and true justice was not the goal. Annas still looked over the family business by insuring that his ability to insert himself into temple matters remained intact by keeping sons and son-in-law's, in positions of the highest authority. Annas was a curious meddling old man and asked Jesus about His followers and His teaching. There was no interest in innocence. The fact that Jesus had the hearts of the common people more than the leaders of the temple was reason enough to establish guilt. They were jealous and their relevance among the faithful was waning. Jesus simply had to go.

Inside, the high priest began asking Jesus about his followers and what he had been teaching them. Jesus replied, "Everyone knows what I teach. I have preached regularly in the synagogues and the Temple, where the people gather. I have not spoken in secret. Why are you asking me this question? Ask those who heard me. They know what I said."

Then one of the Temple guards standing nearby slapped Jesus across the face. "Is that the way to answer the high priest?" he demanded.

Jesus replied, "If I said anything wrong, you must prove it. But if I'm speaking the truth, why are you beating me?"

Then Annas bound Jesus and sent him to Caiaphas, the high priest. (John 18:19-24 NLT) (95).

The man that stood before Annas didn't look like the Son of God. Now that he had the chance to meet this Jesus, he saw an ordinary looking man. Could this have really been the same man that the people claimed performed miracles and raised people from the dead? Annas wanted to know more about His teaching and what sort of people would follow a man like this just to hear what He taught. The people that Annas taught from the Temple didn't follow him around in such manner.

Even the guard standing near Jesus sensed no threat from this so-called miracle worker as he struck Him in the face for the way Jesus responded to Annas' questioning. This guard must not have been one of the guards in the garden when they apprehended Jesus, because he would have remembered staring at the ground after Jesus answered the soldiers' question. Annas didn't even ask about the miracles. There was no way the man standing before him was a miracle worker, let alone the Son of God. Besides, not all of Jesus' followers had fled the scene. Peter was nearby but he wasn't in any shape to answer questions. Peter was also about to deny all the questions he would be asked. So Annas had the guards take Jesus to Caiaphas.

Simon Peter followed Jesus, as did another of the disciples. That other disciple was acquainted with the high priest, so he was allowed to enter the high priest's courtyard with Jesus. Peter had to stay outside the gate. Then the disciple who knew the high priest spoke to the woman watching at the gate, and she let Peter in.

The woman asked Peter, "You're not one of that man's disciples, are you?"

"No," he said, "I am not."

Because it was cold, the household servants and the guards had made a charcoal fire. They stood around it, warming themselves, and Peter stood with them, warming himself. (John 18:15-18 NLT) (96).

Meanwhile, as Simon Peter was standing by the fire, they asked him again, "You're not one of his disciples, are you?"

He denied it, saying, "No, I am not."

But one of the household slaves of the high priest, a relative of the man whose ear Peter had cut off, asked, "Didn't I see you out there in the olive grove with Jesus?"

Again Peter denied it. And immediately a rooster crowed. (John 18:25-27 NLT) (97).

Jesus told Peter he would deny that he knew Him. And here was Peter minding his own business trying to get warm by a fire and the person standing next to him was none other than a relative of the man that Peter took a sword and cut off his ear. Of all the stinking luck to be standing next to someone who actually saw him in the garden. The same someone that God would use to catch Peter in his lie, just as Jesus had predicted.

Peter's real problem was not that he was ashamed of knowing Jesus, it was that he was fearful and afraid to let other people *know* that he followed Jesus. At that moment, his fear had probably escalated because he was afraid of getting arrested for being with Jesus. But just like many other things that Peter had a habit of forgetting, he may have forgotten that Jesus convinced the guards and the soldiers in the garden to let His followers go free. And despite being given a chance to get away like the others, Peter still ventured onto the courtyard grounds to keep an eye on Jesus' fate. Peter simply feared what other people thought about what he did with his life and he usually tried to fend off that fear by making bold promises he had difficulty keeping.

Why should any of us care what others think about our decision to follow Jesus? Like Peter, we know what the Lord has done for us, but still act timid when required to give an answer for our faith. Knowing that the people around us need Jesus to intervene in their lives just as He has done for us, we should be more thoughtful of their response to Him rather than their reaction to us.

Most people I encounter are interested in knowing more about Jesus when given the opportunity. The one standing at the fire next to Peter simply asked, *"Didn't I see you out there in the olive grove with Jesus?"* It was Peter's fear that began to torment him with that question. Why are they asking me this? Are they going to report me and have me arrested? What if they simply wanted to know more about Jesus and this was their first chance to actually talk to one of his followers?

Don't be afraid. Peter would later overcome his fears with the help of the Holy Spirit and would effectively preach Jesus to thousands of willing listeners. Don't be afraid when

God gives you opportunities to share your faith when others are curious about your decision to be a follower of Jesus.

Lord Jesus. Help me to recognize my weakness and Your innocence. Help me to appreciate the price You paid. I should have been arrested for my sins, but You stepped in at the right moment and took my place. Thank you! Have mercy on me a sinner. In Jesus name. Amen.

Chapter Eleven

The Trial of Trials

Jesus' preliminary hearing in the presence of the Grand Jury, if you please, would be held in the court of the religious. Why are those who are so quick to judge others also the ones willing to condemn others for their perceived sins? And who appointed this crowd to be the judge of the Son of God?

And those who had laid hold of Jesus led Him away to Caiaphas the high priest, where the scribes and the elders were assembled. Now the chief priests, the elders, and all the council sought false testimony against Jesus to put Him to death, but found none. (Matthew 26:57, 59-60 NKJV) (98).

They weren't looking for the truth. They had no interest in His innocence or His origin. They tried to find *false testimony* and found none. The purpose of this trial was nothing more than an attempt to condemn the man they determined was a threat to their position and power.

Even though many false witnesses came forward, they found none. But at last two false witnesses came forward and said, "This fellow said, 'I am able to destroy the temple of God and to build it in three days.'" (Matthew 26:60-61 NKJV) (99).

First of all, Jesus didn't say He would destroy the temple or rebuild it. He had previously been asked to show them a sign. He replied by referring to His body, death and resurrection, *"Destroy this temple, and in three days I will raise it up."* He knew the Jews didn't want a sign, they wanted Him dead. But, not only did He have the power to raise Lazarus from the dead, He had the power to raise Himself from the dead. By fulfilling prophecy and completing His calling, He was to take *our* place in hell for *our* sins, not His. He did not come to explain it or search for an escape. He came to finish the work He was sent to do. The false witnesses were a necessary evil to finish the job.

And the high priest arose and said to Him, "Do You answer nothing? What is it these men testify against You?"

But Jesus kept silent.

And the high priest answered and said to Him, "I put You under oath by the living God: Tell us if You are the Christ, the Son of God!" (Matthew 26:62-63 NKJV) (100).

Isn't that the question every religious Jew wanted answered? Didn't these priests devote their entire lives to searching the scriptures in order to recognize the arrival of the Messiah? Why were they so blind and ignorant to the answer of their prayers as He stood before them? Why did the descendants of Abraham, Isaac and Jacob, fail to understand the prophecies were being fulfilled before their very eyes? Yet as Jesus finally broke His silence and agreed with the high priest's assessment, Jesus' acknowledgement of who the high priest asserted He was, secured a cry for the death sentence, a sentence in which they lacked the authority to carry out. They would need the help of their oppressors, the Romans.

Jesus said to him, "It is as you said. Nevertheless, I say to you, hereafter you will see the Son of Man sitting at the right hand of the Power, and coming on the clouds of heaven."

Then the high priest tore his clothes, saying, "He has spoken blasphemy! What further need do we have of witnesses? Look, now you have heard His blasphemy! What do you think?"

They answered and said, "He is deserving of death."

Then they spat in His face and beat Him; and others struck Him with the palms of their hands, saying, "Prophesy to us, Christ! Who is the one who struck You?" (Matthew 26:64-68 NKJV) (101).

Have you ever been accused of doing something in which you had nothing to do? Did your pleas of, "I am innocent," go unheeded and ignored? The problem with a fake court and false witnesses is that none of the participants in the assembled court are interested in the truth. They have another agenda. They have already made up their mind that the accused is guilty of all charges. The trial is a sham because the verdict has been decided before the evidence has been presented.

History is filled with stories of hangings, firing squads, and crucifixions, of the wrongly accused, innocent, and falsely convicted individuals, whose crime was that of being in the wrong place at the wrong time. Or simply of being a convenient scapegoat for a blood thirsty gang. They were treated as *guilty* by a mob that was more interested in carrying out a sentence of death than learning the real truth of the matter.

Jesus had defended a woman literally caught in the act of adultery and instead of allowing a mob to stone her to death, challenged them with their own guilt to have mercy. Her accusers caught her in the act but failed to condemn the man caught in the act with her. He was probably one of the men in the mob, holding a stone in his hand, and ready to kill her with the rest of the accusers. How did they catch her in the act, unless it was a setup for no other purpose than to accuse Jesus of blasphemy? It is often easier for us to attempt to destroy the evidence of our sin, rather than repent of the sin altogether.

Jesus had no sin of His own. He knew this time would come. He spent His earthly life getting prepared to be the scapegoat, the sacrificial lamb. The soldiers may have thought they brought Him to face this trial, but He actually came on His own terms and in His own time. He had the power and the resources to resist but chose to submit to this travesty of justice. Because, the trial that could have happened in the Garden of Eden centuries earlier was being held now. Justice was finally being served. But, instead of being served on those that fell, it was falling on an innocent replacement. The Lamb, slain from the foundation of the world, would now bear the sin of the whole world on Himself, and we the guilty, were throwing the first stones!

Jesus' trial before Caiaphas ended in the early hours of the morning. Then he was taken to the headquarters of the Roman governor. His accusers didn't go inside because it would defile them. (John 18:28 NLT) (102).

That's odd; they didn't see themselves as being defiled when insisting on the death of an innocent man that they simply wanted to get rid of and destroy.

And they wouldn't be allowed to celebrate the Passover. So Pilate, the governor, went out to them and asked, "What is your charge against this man?"

"We wouldn't have handed him over to you if he weren't a criminal!" they retorted.

"Then take him away and judge him by your own law," Pilate told them.

"Only the Romans are permitted to execute someone," the Jewish leaders replied. (This fulfilled Jesus' prediction about the way he would die.)

Then Pilate went back into his headquarters and called for Jesus to be brought to him. "Are you the king of the Jews?" he asked him. (John 18:28-33 NLT) (103).

Now that's the question! His accusers had handed Him over to Pilate without answering Pilate's question of what He was being charged with. They presented Him as a criminal worthy of death and expected the Roman Governor to act on their accusation without proof. Pilate discerned their jealousy for this man and no doubt had heard stories about Him. He didn't ask if He was a king, he specifically asked if He was the King of the Jews. In essence he was mocking his accusers.

Jesus replied, "Is this your own question, or did others tell you about me?"

"Am I a Jew?" Pilate retorted. "Your own people and their leading priests brought you to me for trial. Why? What have you done?"

Jesus answered, "My Kingdom is not an earthly kingdom. If it were, my followers would fight to keep me from being handed over to the Jewish leaders. But my Kingdom is not of this world."

Pilate said, "So you are a king?"

Jesus responded, "You say I am a king. Actually, I was born and came into the world to testify to the truth. All who love the truth recognize that what I say is true." (John 18:34-37 NLT) (104).

Pay attention to what Jesus just said to Pilate. Jesus is standing before a Governor of the Roman empire as an accused liar by the religious Jews. They want to know if He claims to be the Son of God or a king. He makes two simple statements that clears the way to understanding who He really is, and it goes right over their heads. Pilate is always remembered for asking, *"What is truth?"* But little attention is ever paid to what prompted his famous question.

Actually, He *was born and came into the world to testify to the truth.* The world was in darkness and had been since the fall in the garden. Jesus was the Light and the Word of Truth that had come to effectively dispel the darkness and to vanquish the lies of the serpent. The problem? There were many then and still are today, that have no desire for light or truth. Therefore, this *smart* crowd of so-called experts effortlessly missed the point. Those who love the truth will recognize that what Jesus says is true. Do you love truth?

"What is truth?" Pilate asked.

Then he went out again to the people and told them, "He is not guilty of any crime. But you have a custom of asking me to release one prisoner each year at Passover. Would you like me to release this 'King of the Jews'?"

But they shouted back, "No! Not this man. We want Barabbas!" (Barabbas was a revolutionary). (John 18:38-40 NLT) (105).

No! They didn't want the innocent man. Instead, they wanted a man that was indeed a criminal. After centuries of studying the scrolls and searching the prophecies for their deliverer, the Messiah, they ignored the stories as rumors and rejected the very one they had hoped would come. Jesus didn't meet their expectations of what a real messiah would be like, so this imposter would have to die. Little did they know that His death was exactly what the story called for, and their guilt would be with them for generations to follow.

Then Pilate had Jesus flogged with a lead-tipped whip. The soldiers wove a crown of thorns and put it on his head, and they put a purple robe on him. "Hail! King of the Jews!" they mocked, as they slapped him across the face.

Pilate went outside again and said to the people, "I am going to bring him out to you now, but understand clearly that I find him not guilty." (John 19:1-4 NLT) (106).

The Roman authority did not find Him guilty, but still carried out the Jews desire to put Him to death. He used this opportunity to mock them for their jealousy and contempt for an innocent man. A man whose only crime was to come to seek and find those which were lost. He did not come *this time* to be their king, He came to be their savior.

Then Jesus came out wearing the crown of thorns and the purple robe. And Pilate said, "Look, here is the man!"

When they saw him, the leading priests and Temple guards began shouting, "Crucify him! Crucify him!" (John 19:5-6 NLT) (107).

So here stood the Son of the Living God; the Messiah; the Word; the Light; the Truth; the Chief Cornerstone; the Lamb; the Hope of the world; the God of their fathers, Abraham, Isaac and Jacob; their Deliverer; and now their sacrifice. But they had delivered Him to a Roman Governor in the early hours of the morning to condemn and kill Him, because He didn't fit their narrative. They sent Roman soldiers and temple guards in the night to His place of prayer and dragged Him without resistance to a curious ex-high priest for interrogation. Then He was taken to the current high priest, the son-in-law to the former priest, to face accusation and condemnation from men looking for any excuse available to carry out their thirst for blood, His blood. And when they thought they had sufficient reason to taste His blood, they presented Him to Pilate, to execute their evil desire upon an innocent man.

In their self-righteous need to remain clean in order to celebrate Passover, they stayed outside while Jesus was taken in alone to stand before Pilate and his soldiers. Hollywood has always gotten it wrong. There was no crowd of witnesses as He was punished without cause by the Roman soldiers. They didn't need an audience while they beat Him to His knees with lashes designed to tear flesh away from His body. They weren't entertaining anyone but themselves when they made a crown of thorns and shoved it down on His head. Their disdain for the Jews and this man they brought to them, was all too evident as they slapped His face and hailed Him as a king, a king for whom they certainly had no respect. The soldiers loved their job and hated the Jews. This was not the great assignment for which they had enlisted. This was a tour of duty that Pilate and his men no doubt longed to finish so they could return to their beloved homeland.

When they finished playing with Jesus, they put the purple robe back on Him that Herod had sent Him back to Pilate wearing. A robe that the soldiers would later gamble to keep in one piece. It was used to add further insult to the

Jews who had brought their *king* to the Romans to exact their revenge. The soldiers had their morning workout, unaware that the Creator had just permitted them to treat the Son in such a way without vengeance and retribution. The Romans and Jews alike were simply pawns, pieces of a puzzle used to carry out a prophecy, and a plan capable of saving their souls.

Then they brought this beaten, mocked and blood-soaked man back out to the priests and the temple guards that had brought Him there, out to the place where they thought they could remain clean for the Passover, and declared, "Look, here is the man!"

To which *the leading priest and Temple guards* began to chant, *"Crucify him! Crucify him! Crucify him! Crucify him!"* (John 19:6 NLT) (108).

Those demands were not initiated by a random crowd. The cry for the death of the Savior of the world was started by the pastors and the temple security guards of that day. The so-called leaders of the people were calling for the execution of the man which had simply come to save the people. Politicians, if you please, looking out for themselves rather than looking out for the people they represented. There is truly nothing new under the sun. It's always the same story at a different place and time. But this was the time that mattered the most. This time it was the Son of God, and they had all played into the hand that used them to fulfill the will of the Most High God!

"Take him yourselves and crucify him," Pilate said. *"I find him not guilty."* (John 19:6 NLT) (109).

Despite their cries to have an innocent man murdered, Pilate insisted this man was not guilty of any crimes. Were it not for the Jews bringing Jesus to the governor's house this morning, Pilate could have enjoyed the morning as he had many others. Instead, he became a key player in the crime of eternity and all the water in Jerusalem would not be enough to cleanse him of his involvement.

The Jewish leaders replied, "By our law he ought to die because he called himself the Son of God."

When Pilate heard this, he was more frightened than ever. He took Jesus back into the headquarters again and asked him, "Where are you from?" (John 19:7-9 NLT) (110).

What had started out as a morning to humor a crowd of jealous Jewish leaders, now turned to fear and darkness. Pilate become unsure of himself and had to know who this man was. Why didn't this prisoner of the religious beg for mercy? Why didn't this Jesus, defend Himself and insist on being innocent? Pilate had never encountered a man like this.

But Jesus gave no answer.

"Why don't you talk to me?" Pilate demanded. "Don't you realize that I have the power to release you or crucify you?"

Then Jesus said, "You would have no power over me at all unless it were given to you from above. So the one who handed me over to you has the greater sin."

Then Pilate tried to release him, but the Jewish leaders shouted, "If you release this man, you are no friend of Caesar. Anyone who declares himself a king is a rebel against Caesar." (John 19:9-12 NLT) (111).

Those religious despots were now challenging his loyalty to Caesar. They were willing to stoop to any depth of intimidation to have their death wish carried out on their unwanted Messiah. Their determination to reject the Chief Cornerstone had no limit. One had to die, and they were convinced it had to be Jesus.

When they said this, Pilate brought Jesus out to them again. Then Pilate sat down on the judgment seat on the platform that is called the Stone Pavement (in Hebrew, Gabbatha). It was now about noon on the day of preparation for the Passover. And Pilate said to the people, "Look, here is your king!"

"Away with him," they yelled. "Away with him! Crucify him!"

"What? Crucify your king?" Pilate asked.

"We have no king but Caesar," the leading priests shouted back. (John 19:13-15 NLT) (112).

And there it was. They despised Caesar. They wanted nothing more than to be free from Roman rule. They hated every day that the Romans ruled over them and their beloved homeland. They studied their whole lives to understand what the scriptures revealed about their coming king. And now their king had come, humble and meek, a lamb for sacrifice instead of the lion they hoped for. So, they played right into the place prepared for them. The place of shame and disgrace as they insisted that their real king be crucified while they pledged their allegiance to an earthly king they hated. The religious experts, blind with pride and rage, chose a reprobate Barabbas over Jesus, and a Roman Caesar over the King of Kings.

Then Pilate turned Jesus over to them to be crucified. (John 19:16 NLT) (113).

Father in heaven. It is hard to fathom the cruelty Your Son endured on our behalf. He could have walked away. He could have returned to His rightful place at Your side, but He chose to stand in our place instead. His trial should have been our trial. We were the ones that deserved judgement. But You provided the perfect Lamb as the sacrifice for us.

Chapter Twelve

The Crucifixion

How do you tell the story of the crucifixion of Jesus Christ? How do you describe His consummate sacrifice? His death should not have been a surprise to anyone. The religious leaders knew the prophecies of His birth, resurrection and ultimate return. How did they miss the fulfillment of those prophecies standing before them in the form of Jesus?

His own disciples and followers had heard Him openly predict His own death. A great cloud of witnesses watched from heaven and earth as all creation stopped for a front row seat to the sacrifice of a Lamb which was slain from the foundation of the world.

Wherefore seeing we also are compassed about with so great a cloud of witnesses, let us lay aside every weight, and the sin which doth so easily beset us, and let us run with patience the race that is set before us, looking unto Jesus the author and finisher of our faith; who for the joy that was set before him endured the cross, despising the shame, and is set down at the right hand of the throne of God. For consider him that endured such contradiction of sinners against himself, lest ye be wearied and faint in your minds. (Hebrews 12:1-3 KJV) (114).

All of history since the fall in the garden had looked forward to this incredible event. Now we, and all from that moment to now, continue to look back at the ultimate price God was willing to pay for our redemption. The cross became the center piece for all time; past, present, and future.

Jesus repeatedly told His followers what He came to do. The outcome would not come as a surprise to Jesus, and if they had listened, it would not have been a surprise to them as well. But they had not listened, and they only heard what they wanted to hear.

From then on, Jesus began telling his disciples what would happen to him. He said, "I must go to Jerusalem. There the nation's leaders, the chief priests, and the teachers of the Law of Moses will make me suffer terribly. I will be killed, but three days later I will rise to life." (Matthew 16:21 CEV) (115).

While Jesus and his disciples were going from place to place in Galilee, he told them, "The Son of Man will be handed over to people who will kill him. But three days later he will rise to life." All of this made the disciples very sad. (Matthew 17:22-23 CEV) (116).

As Jesus was on his way to Jerusalem, he took his twelve disciples aside and told them in private, "We are now on our way to Jerusalem, where the Son of Man will be handed over

to the chief priests and the teachers of the Law of Moses.
They will sentence him to death, and then they will hand him
over to foreigners who will make fun of him. They will beat
him and nail him to a cross. But on the third day he will rise
from death." (Matthew 20:17-19 CEV) (117).

Now the time of His death was near. The course was
sure. The prophecies were true and about to be fulfilled. In
the garden that night where He prayed, an angel had
appeared to provide Him strength for the hours ahead. But
His own disciples slept when He was about to be delivered
to the men that would come to carry out a death sentence He
did not earn.

He would be too exhausted to carry His own cross
without the help of a stranger. There is no mention of the two
men hanging on either side of Him being forced to carry their
crosses. He had been betrayed by one of His own in the
garden. He had first been taken to Annas, before being
delivered to Caiaphas. The sacrifice did not resist or fight
back. He barely answered them. It wouldn't have made any
difference if He did. They did not want to hear anything He
had to say, they only wanted Him dead.

He had been up all night, being accused, abused and
humiliated. Caiaphas brought Him to Pilate. Pilate wanted
nothing to do with this travesty. His own wife had warned
him. He saw an opportunity to send Him to Herod, only to
have Him returned with Herod's fancy robe after Jesus
refused to answer Herod's questions or provide him with a
much-wanted sign or miracle.

Pilate had Him flogged and beaten, hoping it would be
enough for this blood-thirsty and jealous crowd, but it was
not enough. He repeatedly tried to pass off the responsibility
of this innocent man's judgement, but when his loyalty to

Caesar was challenged, he gave the mob what they wanted and delivered Him back to them to carry out the desire of their wicked hearts. The desire to crucify the Son of God, their Messiah, and to reject once again, what the God of their fathers had provided them.

Finally, Pilate handed him over to them to be crucified. So the soldiers took charge of Jesus. Carrying his own cross, he went out to the place of the Skull (which in Aramaic is called Golgotha). Here they crucified him, and with him two others— one on each side and Jesus in the middle.

Pilate had a notice prepared and fastened to the cross. It read: JESUS OF NAZARETH, THE KING OF THE JEWS. Many of the Jews read this sign, for the place where Jesus was crucified was near the city, and the sign was written in Aramaic, Latin and Greek. The chief priests of the Jews protested to Pilate, "Do not write 'The King of the Jews,' but that this man claimed to be king of the Jews."

Pilate answered, "What I have written, I have written."

When the soldiers crucified Jesus, they took his clothes, dividing them into four shares, one for each of them, with the undergarment remaining. This garment was seamless, woven in one piece from top to bottom. "Let's not tear it," they said to one another. "Let's decide by lot who will get it."

This happened that the scripture might be fulfilled which said, "They divided my garments among them and cast lots for my clothing." So this is what the soldiers did.

Near the cross of Jesus stood his mother, his mother's sister, Mary the wife of Clopas, and Mary Magdalene. When Jesus saw his mother there, and the disciple whom he loved standing nearby, he said to his mother, "Dear woman, here is your son," and to the disciple, *"Here is your mother."* *From that time on, this disciple took her into his home.*

Later, knowing that all was now completed, and so that the Scripture would be fulfilled, Jesus said, "I am thirsty."

A jar of wine vinegar was there, so they soaked a sponge in it, put the sponge on a stalk of the hyssop plant, and lifted it to Jesus' lips. When he had received the drink, Jesus said, "It is finished." With that, he bowed his head and gave up his spirit.

Now it was the day of Preparation, and the next day was to be a special Sabbath. Because the Jews did not want the bodies left on the crosses during the Sabbath, they asked Pilate to have the legs broken and the bodies taken down. The soldiers therefore came and broke the legs of the first man who had been crucified with Jesus, and then those of the other. But when they came to Jesus and found that he was already dead, they did not break his legs. Instead, one of the soldiers pierced Jesus' side with a spear, bringing a sudden flow of blood and water.

The man who saw it has given testimony, and his testimony is true. He knows that he tells the truth, and he testifies so that you also may believe. These things happened so that the scripture would be fulfilled: "Not one of his bones will be broken," and, as another scripture says, "They will look on the one they have pierced." (John 19:16-37 NIV) (118).

THEY WILL LOOK ON THE ONE THEY HAVE PIERCED!

"And I will pour on the house of David and on the inhabitants of Jerusalem the Spirit of grace and supplication; then they will look on Me whom they pierced.

Yes, they will mourn for Him as one mourns for his only son, and grieve for Him as one grieves for a firstborn. (Zechariah 12:10 NKJV) (119).

AND THEY WILL LOOK ON ME WHOM THEY HAVE PIERCED!

I have heard it said my whole life that Jesus died for me. That He was nailed to a cross for my sins. And He was pierced in his side and that the blood and water which flowed out was so I could have His forgiveness and His life.

Please try to understand what I have written here. I do agree that Jesus died for us; that He willingly gave his life for our sins and that through His blood we have grace and forgiveness. But I also believe that we have forgotten, or failed to recognize, or missed altogether, the depth of what happened at Calvary.

We share the guilt of the soldier that pierced Him. We are accomplices with the crowd that shouted down Pilate and demanded that Christ be crucified. The water that was not sufficient to wash Pilate's hands of his participation in the death of God's Son proves inadequate to cleanse us also. We may as well have been one of the soldiers that dragged Him from His prayer garden and delivered Him to men wanting Him dead. Our sins were the nails driven through His hands and feet which held Him on a cross He had not earned. And we also will look on the one WE pierced.

Because, Jesus not only died on the cross for us, He died because of us! He died for our sin, not His own. By taking our sins on Himself, He took the blame for everything we have ever thought, said, or have done. It was not His failure to obey God that placed Him there, it was OUR disobedience, OUR failures, and OUR sins that hammered the nails through His hands and feet to the wooden cross.

By assuming OUR guilt on that tree, He left us with nothing but a completely clean slate. He cleansed us from what we've done, what we are doing, and what we will do. He paid the total debt, the complete price, for our fallen state and condition. With the currency of blood, He met the demand for payment and covered all of our losses up to that anticipated moment, where in the twinkle of an eye, we will be forever changed.

We are covered till we arrive through the glory of death and redemption, and shed this corruptible, fallen and sinful nature, manifested through this temporary body, and take on one that is incorruptible, totally awesome, forever new, immortal, and sinless. A heavenly body complete with the nature of the Almighty God Himself, where and when, we will wear that new mansion He promised to prepare for us. Not a building of brick and mortar, but a body He has prepared for us.

Because, when we see Him in His resurrected glorious state, we will be like Him because we will then see Him as He really is. Once we behold Him in his spotless risen glory, we will manifest His spotless glory as well, being adorned in white robes of righteousness – never to possess or share or see our fallen state and condition, ever again. The full and unimaginable depth of suffering on His part, or ours, is nothing to compare to the glory that shall be revealed in us.

The cross, for Christ, was about the price for OUR failure, not His. We rightfully belonged there, not Him. OUR sins required payment. He was without sin. The cross relieved OUR debt. He owed nothing and no one. We must come face to face with the reality that He not only died on the cross for us, He died upon that cross instead of us. Remembering Calvary is more than remembering what Jesus did, why He did it, or for whom He did it.

We should also consider what Calvary would have looked like if we had been assaulted and placed there for OUR crimes. His death was even more horrible, because He was innocent. OUR death would be considered justified and would have been celebrated because justice was served.

Would we have stood before our accusers as dumb without saying a word in OUR defense? We would not. We would have screamed and pleaded non-stop for OUR lives to be spared. We would have begged to OUR dying breath for mercy, but there would have been no grace for a death we deserved. Imagine billions of crosses covering the landscape as each of us received OUR just reward. But Jesus didn't ask us to die on a cross, He simply asked that we carry OUR cross. He had someone else help carry His cross; and I am certain He will help us carry OURS.

Again, the cross was what Jesus did to satisfy the debt we cannot pay. It's what He did for others and it's what He did for us. He did it for His Father. Remember, it was not His will to suffer this way. Who would want to suffer as He suffered, especially if you were innocent? He had asked that the cup pass from Him, but He drank it in obedience to satisfy the will of His Father. He drank from a cup filled with the bitterness of OUR sins. A cup that also should have been OURS to drink.

Many of us are familiar with the twenty-third Psalm and find great comfort in the words. But hundreds of years before Christ came and died a horrible death at the hands of sinners, David saw the future in his twenty-second Psalm. The men that cried out for the death of their Messiah were aware of this Psalm, but it did not stop them from playing right into the hands of this prophetic vision of the price that had to be paid for them and all the rest of us as well.

My God, my God, why have you abandoned me? Why are you so far away when I groan for help? Every day I call to you, my God, but you do not answer. Every night you hear my voice, but I find no relief.

Yet you are holy, enthroned on the praises of Israel. Our ancestors trusted in you, and you rescued them. They cried out to you and were saved. They trusted in you and were never disgraced.

But I am a worm and not a man. I am scorned and despised by all! Everyone who sees me mocks me. They sneer and shake their heads, saying, "Is this the one who relies on the Lord? Then let the Lord save him! If the Lord loves him so much, let the Lord rescue him!"

Yet you brought me safely from my mother's womb and led me to trust you at my mother's breast. I was thrust into your arms at my birth. You have been my God from the moment I was born.

Do not stay so far from me, for trouble is near, and no one else can help me. My enemies surround me like a herd of bulls; fierce bulls of Bashan have hemmed me in! Like lions they open their jaws against me, roaring and tearing into their prey. My life is poured out like water, and all my bones are out of joint. My heart is like wax, melting within me. My strength has dried up like sunbaked clay. My tongue sticks to the roof of my mouth. You have laid me in the dust and left me for dead. My enemies surround me like a pack of dogs; an evil gang closes in on me. They have pierced my hands and feet. I can count all my bones. My enemies stare at me and gloat. They divide my garments among themselves and throw dice for my clothing.

O Lord, do not stay far away! You are my strength; come quickly to my aid! Save me from the sword; spare my precious life from these dogs. Snatch me from the lion's jaws and from the horns of these wild oxen.

I will proclaim your name to my brothers and sisters. I will praise you among your assembled people. Praise the Lord, all you who fear him! Honor him, all you descendants of Jacob! Show him reverence, all you descendants of Israel! For he has not ignored or belittled the suffering of the needy. He has not turned his back on them, but has listened to their cries for help.

I will praise you in the great assembly. I will fulfill my vows in the presence of those who worship you. The poor will eat and be satisfied. All who seek the Lord will praise him. Their hearts will rejoice with everlasting joy. The whole earth will acknowledge the Lord and return to him. All the families of the nations will bow down before him. For royal power belongs to the Lord. He rules all the nations.

Let the rich of the earth feast and worship. Bow before him, all who are mortal, all whose lives will end as dust. Our children will also serve him. Future generations will hear about the wonders of the Lord. His righteous acts will be told to those not yet born. They will hear about everything he has done. A psalm of David. (Psalms 22:1-31 NLT) (120).

How could it be possible they did not know who this man was? Every one of those Jews, from the least to the greatest, had listened to the reading of the prophecies their entire lives, which foretold of the very things they were now witnessing with their own eyes. Their promised Messiah had finally arrived after generations had waited for this day and had not lived to be its witnesses. The very ones orchestrating His crucifixion knew the scriptures more than all that were there on that day of prophetic fulfillment. But their disdain for this man claiming to be the Son of the God of their fathers was more than they could tolerate. Despite what they knew and had long heard from the reading of the scriptures, they chose to be deaf, dumb, blind and determined, to deny the Christ their forefathers had longed to see. Their unwillingness to recognize Jesus as the Christ, demonstrated they had spent their entire lives looking for a different redeemer than the one standing before them. They hated the Romans as much as their fathers hated the Egyptians. They were looking for a lion, and who was this lamb anyway?

What makes things any different today than then? What kind of a savior are we waiting for? Will He give us a mansion? Will He make us wealthy? Will we be immortal? Which one of us will get to sit on His right or His left? Wasn't His crucifixion all about us and what we could get out of it? If it was only about what we could get, doesn't it seem like an excessive price to pay? Couldn't the charge have been less? Why the need for all this blood? Just how bad was the fall of man anyway? Sounds like a high price to pay for a little disobedience. It was only one tree and a small piece of fruit. What grand plan did that mess up? And where did that serpent come from anyway?

I realize that sounds like a lot of foolish questions, but what have we learned from the crowd that thought they were doing God a favor by killing Jesus? Apart from the redemption that was individually granted as a result of His death, we have learned nothing. If He returned again in another time, and in the same way as before, another religious crowd would attempt to kill Him again. However,

He's not returning for that kind of treatment again, because there is a grand plan and a great lion and king is coming one day to initiate that plan.

His first appearance was to redeem that which was lost. His next appearance will be to conquer and establish an eternal kingdom that will not fail. Your acceptance of His terms now, will determine your position then, when that day comes. The price was high. The plan is grand. Your time to decide is now.

The crowd at Calvary on that prophesied day made their decision. They chose to reject the very thing they needed the most with their cries for crucifixion. They chose to close their eyes and their ears to the scriptures they heard all their lives only to become savage and guilty participants in a death intended for their own redemption. Read what they knew.

See, my servant will prosper; he will be highly exalted. But many were amazed when they saw him. His face was so disfigured he seemed hardly human, and from his appearance, one would scarcely know he was a man. And he will startle many nations. Kings will stand speechless in his presence. For they will see what they had not been told; they will understand what they had not heard about.

Who has believed our message? To whom has the Lord revealed his powerful arm? My servant grew up in the Lord's presence like a tender green shoot, like a root in dry ground.

There was nothing beautiful or majestic about his appearance, nothing to attract us to him. He was despised and rejected— a man of sorrows, acquainted with deepest grief. We turned our backs on him and looked the other way. He was despised, and we did not care.

Yet it was our weaknesses he carried; it was our sorrows that weighed him down. And we thought his troubles were a punishment from God, a punishment for his own sins! But he was pierced for our rebellion, crushed for our sins. He was beaten so we could be whole. He was whipped so we could be healed.

All of us, like sheep, have strayed away. We have left God's paths to follow our own. Yet the Lord laid on him the sins of us all. He was oppressed and treated harshly, yet he never said a word. He was led like a lamb to the slaughter. And as a sheep is silent before the shearers, he did not open his mouth. Unjustly condemned, he was led away. No one cared that he died without descendants, that his life was cut short in midstream. But he was struck down for the rebellion of my people. He had done no wrong and had never deceived anyone.

But he was buried like a criminal; he was put in a rich man's grave. But it was the Lord's good plan to crush him and cause him grief. Yet when his life is made an offering for sin, he will have many descendants. He will enjoy a long life, and the Lord's good plan will prosper in his hands.

When he sees all that is accomplished by his anguish, he will be satisfied. And because of his experience, my righteous servant will make it possible for many to be counted righteous, for he will bear all their sins. I will give him the honors of a victorious soldier, because he exposed himself to death. He was counted among the rebels. He bore the sins of many and interceded for rebels. (Isaiah 52:13-53:12 NLT) (121).

Oh Lord our God. Open our eyes that we may see. We wonder around in darkness even though You have given us access to Your glorious Light of the World, Jesus. We thank You for providing the necessary sacrifice for our debts and ask You to forgive our many sins against You. Turn our hearts and our attention to You. Draw us by Your Spirit and we will run after You. We have nowhere else to go. Only You can pave the way for eternal life. You alone have made the way for us to break free of the outcome that insures our destruction. Let us be found safe in Your forgiveness and Your redemption. We ask You in the precious name of Jesus. Amen.

Chapter Thirteen

The Body of Christ

It is finished. At least that's what they hoped. Jesus was just a man like every other man. He could be killed, and the Romans and the Priests just proved it was possible. He hung there for all to see; the blood-soaked body of a man purported to be the Son of God. A body battered beyond recognition and a face barely resembling human form. Many in the crowd had not noticed when He took His last breath during this spontaneous social event of the day. Today only three men met their fate on the crosses. The Romans were so prolific at this deadly task that it was difficult for the community not to be calloused to the entire event. The one in the center seemed to be a little more famous than the men on either side of Him. They didn't know the names of the other men, but the one in the middle was known as a

Nazarite. Jesus was His name. So why did the sign say, "King of the Jews?" And now that He was dead the party was over. Besides a storm was coming.

Later, Joseph of Arimathea asked Pilate for the body of Jesus. Now Joseph was a disciple of Jesus, but secretly because he feared the Jews. With Pilate's permission, he came and took the body away. He was accompanied by Nicodemus, the man who earlier had visited Jesus at night. Nicodemus brought a mixture of myrrh and aloes, about seventy-five pounds.

Taking Jesus' body, the two of them wrapped it, with the spices, in strips of linen. This was in accordance with Jewish burial customs. At the place where Jesus was crucified, there was a garden, and in the garden a new tomb, in which no one had ever been laid. Because it was the Jewish day of Preparation and since the tomb was nearby, they laid Jesus there. (John 19:38-42 NIV) (122).

Joseph of Arimathea and Nicodemus were well known men among the Jewish leaders. Joseph was a prominent council member and a man longing for the coming kingdom of God. He knew there was something particularly important about Jesus and may have had his own thoughts about His death. This series of events carried many similarities to scriptures he had read and studied his entire life.

Nicodemus had a rather curious exchange with Jesus early in His ministry. Later, he took some push-back from fellow Pharisees while trying to defend Jesus' actions. The first time Nicodemus met Jesus; the Lord told this leader of Israel what was really required of him. It is also a requirement of each one of us, without exception.

After dark one evening, he came to speak with Jesus. "Rabbi," he said, "we all know that God has sent you to teach us. Your miraculous signs are evidence that God is with you."

Jesus replied, "I tell you the truth, unless you are born again, you cannot see the Kingdom of God."

"What do you mean?" exclaimed Nicodemus. "How can an old man go back into his mother's womb and be born again?"

Jesus replied, "I assure you, no one can enter the Kingdom of God without being born of water and the Spirit. Humans can reproduce only human life, but the Holy Spirit gives birth to spiritual life. So don't be surprised when I say, 'You must be born again.' The wind blows wherever it wants. Just as you can hear the wind but can't tell where it comes from or where it is going, so you can't explain how people are born of the Spirit."

"How are these things possible?" Nicodemus asked.

Jesus replied, "You are a respected Jewish teacher, and yet you don't understand these things? I assure you, we tell you what we know and have seen, and yet you won't believe our testimony. But if you don't believe me when I tell you about earthly things, how can you possibly believe if I tell you about heavenly things? No one has ever gone to heaven and returned. But the Son of Man has come down from heaven. And as Moses lifted up the bronze snake on a pole in the wilderness, so the Son of Man must be lifted up, so that everyone who believes in him will have eternal life.

"For God loved the world so much that he gave his one and only Son, so that everyone who believes in him will not perish but have eternal life. God sent his Son into the world not to judge the world, but to save the world through him.

"There is no judgment against anyone who believes in him. But anyone who does not believe in him has already been judged for not believing in God's one and only Son.

"And the judgment is based on this fact: God's light came into the world, but people loved the darkness more than the light, for their actions were evil. All who do evil hate the light and refuse to go near it for fear their sins will be exposed. But those who do what is right come to the light so others can see that they are doing what God wants." (John 3:2-21 NLT) (123).

Nicodemus had gone to church his entire life. He had been taught by the best in the business of religion. He was a pretty good teacher himself. Today, as he saw Jesus lifted up on the cross, he remembered that early encounter when Jesus told him about Moses lifting a bronze snake up on a poll. When he saw the soldier pierce His side with a spear, he remembered the words Jesus said about having to be born of water and Spirit to enter the kingdom of God. It made sense now. Jesus was lifted up so we could look on Him and find healing for our body and salvation for our soul. He remembered the part about being born again and the words of Jesus about earthly things and heavenly things. It wasn't about having to be reborn from his mother's womb as an adult. It was about being made as new as a newborn child in his spirit. It was more than a re-start; it was a rebirth. And it was only possible with God because of what just happened to Jesus Christ on this wooden cross.

We have the same problem as Nicodemus. We get so blinded by our religion or lack thereof; that we fail to grasp the heavenly change that God wants to bring about in us. A change that can only be done by God. Simply deciding to be better and do better is not what Jesus died to help us with.

He gave His life and finished the requirement for redemption – a requirement that we would never earn or accomplish on our own. By all right, we should have been on that cross. But we didn't have to because Jesus endured it on our behalf. How is that even possible?

For when we were still without strength, in due time Christ died for the ungodly. For scarcely for a righteous man will one die; yet perhaps for a good man someone would even dare to die. But God demonstrates His own love toward us, in that while we were still sinners, Christ died for us. Much more then, having now been justified by His blood, we shall be saved from wrath through Him. For if when we were enemies we were reconciled to God through the death of His Son, much more, having been reconciled, we shall be saved by His life. And not only that, but we also rejoice in God through our Lord Jesus Christ, through whom we have now received the reconciliation. (Romans 5:6-11 NKJV) (124).

Reconciliation is a work we receive, not a work that we do. And as Nicodemus helped Joseph prepare the body of Jesus for burial, the Spirit of the Living God was helping him remember the words Jesus told him when they first met. Even before Jesus would raise from the dead, Nicodemus was being raised to a new level of understanding about who this man actually was. Jesus had said that He was the light that lights the way of every man that comes into the world and the lights were on during this dark and tragic afternoon. And the light of understanding was filling Nicodemus with a new sense of hope and purpose for his life. He had been taught all his life about the need to make yearly sacrifices to atone for his sins. Now, as he looked up at Jesus on the pole, he witnessed his last sacrifice. It is definitely finished. So, what about us? What benefit do we derive from Jesus laying His body down?

But to each one of us grace was given according to the measure of Christ's gift.

Therefore He says: "When He ascended on high, He led captivity captive, and gave gifts to men."

(Now this, "He ascended" — what does it mean but that He also first descended into the lower parts of the earth? He who descended is also the One who ascended far above all the heavens, that He might fill all things.)

And He Himself gave some to be apostles, some prophets, some evangelists, and some pastors and teachers, for the equipping of the saints for the work of ministry, for the edifying of the body of Christ, till we all come to the unity of the faith and of the knowledge of the Son of God, to a perfect man, to the measure of the stature of the fullness of Christ; that we should no longer be children, tossed to and fro and carried about with every wind of doctrine, by the trickery of men, in the cunning craftiness of deceitful plotting, but, speaking the truth in love, may grow up in all things into Him who is the head — Christ — from whom the whole body, joined and knit together by what every joint supplies, according to the effective working by which every part does its share, causes growth of the body for the edifying of itself in love. (Ephesians 4:7-16 NKJV) (125).

Christ not only made a place for us in the coming Kingdom of God, He made a place for us in His body in the here and now. The work He accomplished for us could now be done through us. Not a building, but a body. Buildings will come and go, or as we experienced in 2020, can even become off limits. But if we are His body, and we are, there are no limits to fulfilling His will and purpose, as His body.

Therefore, always remember, the Church is the Church, and the building is just a building. The building is as simple as our flesh. If the life leaves the flesh, the flesh is dead. If the Church leaves the building, the building is empty. Unfortunately, there are many buildings said to look like churches, with people inside, that don't know they are the body. If we are to truly experience the depth of our calling, we will have to stop being distracted by our buildings. I happen to believe God gave us an opportunity in 2020, to do just that.

For as the body is one and has many members, but all the members of that one body, being many, are one body, so also is Christ. For by one Spirit we were all baptized into one body — whether Jews or Greeks, whether slaves or free — and have all been made to drink into one Spirit. For in fact the body is not one member but many.

If the foot should say, "Because I am not a hand, I am not of the body," is it therefore not of the body? And if the ear should say, "Because I am not an eye, I am not of the body," is it therefore not of the body? If the whole body were an eye, where would be the hearing? If the whole were hearing, where would be the smelling? But now God has set the members, each one of them, in the body just as He pleased. And if they were all one member, where would the body be?

But now indeed there are many members, yet one body. And the eye cannot say to the hand, "I have no need of you;" nor again the head to the feet, "I have no need of you." No, much rather, those members of the body which seem to be weaker are necessary. And those members of the body which we think to be less honorable, on these we bestow greater honor; and our unpresentable parts have greater modesty, but our presentable parts have no need. But God composed the body, having given greater honor to that part which lacks it, that there should be no schism in the body, but that the members should have the same care for one another. And if one member suffers, all the members suffer with it; or if one member is honored, all the members rejoice with it. Now you are the body of Christ, and members individually. (1 Corinthians 12:12-27 NKJV) (126).

Christ equipped all of us with many different gifts. Abilities that can be used to benefit all of us as a whole Church, or Body, if you please. The real Church of God, the Body of Christ, was not designed for one individual to do all the spiritual work of the ministry while everyone else keeps the pews warm. Christ spent very little time in the temple waiting for the people to come to Him. He went to the people and ministered to their needs wherever they were. Our churches were never intended to serve as retail ministry outlets for the lost to come shop for salvation. They are useful for gathering, teaching and discipling. But equipping the saints provides the most benefit to others when we take what we have learned and received out of our doors to those in need.

Maybe this is different than you expected to come after the story of the crucifixion. Two old men with a mission to recover the body of Jesus were not aware that He would only be needing the grave for a few days. As I look upon the landscape of the Church in America, I see the need to recover the Body of Christ. Have our buildings become tombs? Have we forgotten the price of our redemption? Is our resurrection possible?

Let's pray. Father, just as You raised Jesus from the dead, we ask that You raise the Body of Christ from the dead.

Lift us up to once again fulfill Your calling and purpose in the earth. Fill us fresh with Your life and Spirit. Make these dry bones live once again and activate Your Church to do Your work in this land. The dead do not praise You. Raise us to praise and serve You again. In Jesus name. Amen.

Chapter Fourteen

The Resurrection

How long must the Church lie in state in her own buildings? Did anyone notice she was dead? Do we remember the last time someone came forward to give their life to Christ in our buildings? How long has it been since a young man or woman came to a pastor and expressed a calling from God to enter into the ministry or go to the mission field? Where is the next generation of blood-bought, God-called, Spirit-filled servants of God? Something smells of death and we either need a burial or a resurrection.

Nicodemus and Joseph buried the body of Jesus in time for the Passover. The Romans, at the request of the Jewish leaders that had Him killed, placed guards at the tomb. They seriously doubted the stories about His resurrection but still didn't want to take any chances with His disciples stealing

His body and claiming He raised from the dead. By the way, where were His disciples? They had followed Him around for several years and were now nowhere to be found. Well, there was one of them at the crucifixion.

Now there stood by the cross of Jesus His mother, and His mother's sister, Mary the wife of Clopas, and Mary Magdalene. When Jesus therefore saw His mother, and the disciple whom He loved standing by, He said to His mother, "Woman, behold your son!"

Then He said to the disciple, "Behold your mother!" And from that hour that disciple took her to his own home. (John 19:25-27 NKJV) (127).

John had always stayed as close as possible to Jesus. And here at the end of His earthly ministry He instructed John to take care of His mother. The same John that would go on to face persecution and attempted murder, the one that would write the Revelation of Jesus Christ during exile on an island, and the only apostle that would die a natural death. John witnessed the murder of Jesus on the cross and lived a long life to tell about it. The other apostles, that were absent at the crucifixion, faced their own martyrdoms one by one. Even the two brothers that insisted they could drink the same cup and baptism. However, all but Judas would see Jesus again after the resurrection.

Suddenly there was a great earthquake! For an angel of the Lord came down from heaven, rolled aside the stone, and sat on it. His face shone like lightning, and his clothing was as white as snow. The guards shook with fear when they saw him, and they fell into a dead faint.

Then the angel spoke to the women. "Don't be afraid!" he said. "I know you are looking for Jesus, who was crucified. He isn't here! He is risen from the dead, just as he

said would happen. Come, see where his body was lying.
And now, go quickly and tell his disciples that he has risen
from the dead, and he is going ahead of you to Galilee. You
will see him there. Remember what I have told you."

The women ran quickly from the tomb. They were very
frightened but also filled with great joy, and they rushed to
give the disciples the angel's message. And as they went,
Jesus met them and greeted them. And they ran to him,
grasped his feet, and worshiped him.

Then Jesus said to them, "Don't be afraid! Go tell my
brothers to leave for Galilee, and they will see me there."
(Matthew 28:2-10 NLT) (128).

Jesus didn't need an angel to roll a stone away so He could get out. They needed the stone rolled away so they could see in. How often do we find heavy stones rolled in our way that keep us from seeing the risen Lord at work in our lives? The cross is a very important thing to remember, because without it we would not understand the price that was paid for our salvation. But the resurrection is where we gain understanding about the power we need to walk in victory over the things of the world. Jesus died so we could be saved from our sinful condition through His sacrifice on the cross. He rose so our real life could begin and continue through eternity. Nevertheless, we are the ones with whom the decisions rest. We can choose to obey or disobey. We can use our gift of freewill to live or die. Many question what a loving God would do when they see trouble befall the people around them. A loving God gives us the choice.

Being a Christian does not exempt us from choices, good or bad ones. We still have freewill. Jesus' death and resurrection provided us with the opportunity for a different outcome from our choices. Through history God's people have been presented with choices. But those choices also come with consequences. Any nation, including those whose claim is of being a nation under God, will face the consequences of their choices. The children of Israel provide our greatest evidence of what happens to a nation that chooses to obey and disobey.

You know God's laws, and it isn't impossible to obey them. His commands aren't in heaven, so you can't excuse yourselves by saying, "How can we obey the Lord's commands? They are in heaven, and no one can go up to get them, then bring them down and explain them to us."

And you can't say, "How can we obey the Lord's commands? They are across the sea, and someone must go across, then bring them back and explain them to us."

No, these commands are nearby, and you know them by heart. All you have to do is obey! Today I am giving you a choice. You can choose life and success or death and disaster. I am commanding you to be loyal to the Lord, to live the way he has told you, and to obey his laws and teachings. You are about to cross the Jordan River and take the land that he is giving you. If you obey him, you will live and become successful and powerful.

On the other hand, you might choose to disobey the Lord and reject him. So, I'm warning you that if you bow down and worship other gods, you won't have long to live.

Right now, I call the sky and the earth to be witnesses that I am offering you this choice. Will you choose for the Lord to make you prosperous and give you a long life? Or will he put you under a curse and kill you? Choose life!

Be completely faithful to the Lord your God, love him, and do whatever he tells you. The Lord is the only one who can give life, and he will let you live a long time in the land that he promised to your ancestors Abraham, Isaac, and Jacob. (Deuteronomy 30:11-20 CEV) (129).

The choice is still, and always has been, America's choice to make. She has made many good choices and She has made many bad choices. And She has had to live with the consequences of Her choices year after year. Those choices were shaped and decided by Her people, and the leaders Her people have elected to represent Her. Currently She appears to have lost Her sense of direction and purpose. Many voices, whether whispering or yelling, are calling for Her to change. And not all the changes they are calling for are good. God told the Church in Laodicea she had lost her first love. Many in America are wondering the same thing. Is America a Christian nation? Was God instrumental in the founding of America? Is God judging America for Her sin and rebellion? Can America be saved or is it too late?

Let me say this. America was discovered and developed over several hundred years by imperfect humans, longing for a better life for themselves and their families. Some came here willingly and some against their will. Some came as free and some came as slaves. But the intent of the American dream has always remained the same.

"We hold these truths to be self-evident, that all men are created equal, that they are endowed by their Creator with certain unalienable Rights, that among these are Life, Liberty and the pursuit of Happiness." (Thomas Jefferson - The Declaration of Independence - Second Continental Congress - Philadelphia, Pennsylvania).

American's have tried for generations to get it right. They didn't get it 100% right two-hundred years ago and they don't have it 100% right today. But they're not finished yet. Despite Her imperfections and failures, it doesn't take an expert or a genius to recognize She still maintains Her quest to be a good and great nation for all. However, Her land has been filled with many voices. Voices that do not share Her dream of equality for all. The voices of hate and division that She opened Her arms to, are calling for Her destruction. Many are using their "right to," and their "freedom to," to do as they see fit, which is to tear this country down. Their desire is to transform this country into something many of us won't recognize. And now the battle has evolved from the ballot box and moved into the streets. What is next? Some are calling for revolution while others only wish to get back to normal. But the truth of the matter is, we have never had a normal. There have always been issues and problems to fix and overcome. Remember, we are not perfect, and we do not have a perfect union.

But one thing we do have and must reinforce as fast as possible, is the place we have reserved for God! God still desires that we be one nation under Him. If we continue to disobey and reject the principles that have made us great, we will collapse, and the dust of our fall will be smelled over the entire planet.

Where is the Church? Is She cowering in fear or is She prepared to intervene? Have Her prayers turned inward or is She ready to stand for God and take a fresh stand for this nation? She has lost ground in the courts; She has lost ground with the people; and She has lost ground with God. How is She planning to take back what She has lost? Jesus once told John to write a letter to some churches. Here is just one of those letters.

Write this letter to the angel of the church in Laodicea. This is the message from the one who is the Amen—the faithful and true witness, the beginning of God's new creation:

"I know all the things you do, that you are neither hot nor cold. I wish that you were one or the other! But since you are like lukewarm water, neither hot nor cold, I will spit you out of my mouth! You say, 'I am rich. I have everything I want. I don't need a thing!' And you don't realize that you are wretched and miserable and poor and blind and naked. So I advise you to buy gold from me—gold that has been purified by fire. Then you will be rich. Also buy white garments from me so you will not be shamed by your nakedness, and ointment for your eyes so you will be able to see. I correct and discipline everyone I love. So be diligent and turn from your indifference.

"Look! I stand at the door and knock. If you hear my voice and open the door, I will come in, and we will share a meal together as friends. Those who are victorious will sit with me on my throne, just as I was victorious and sat with my Father on his throne.

"Anyone with ears to hear must listen to the Spirit and understand what he is saying to the churches." (Revelation 3:14-22 NLT) (130).

I can't think of a better description of the Church in America than what we just read. All my life I have seen the painting depicting Jesus knocking on the door. And for all those years I've heard my grandmother and a multitude of preachers claim that depiction was Jesus knocking on the door of our hearts. But in reality, He is knocking on the door of the Church. How many churches are so busy with their methods and meetings that they have literally left Jesus locked out of their buildings? It's easy for the Church to look at the crazy world we live in only to think that it's high time for God to judge this world. But be careful what you wish for. Look what Peter wrote about judgement.

For the time has come for judgment to begin at the house of God; and if it begins with us first, what will be the end of those who do not obey the gospel of God?

Now "If the righteous one is scarcely saved, where will the ungodly and the sinner appear?"

Therefore, let those who suffer according to the will of God commit their souls to Him in doing good, as to a faithful Creator. (1 Peter 4:17-19 NKJV) (131).

Where does judgement begin? If you are a member of the Church, the Body of Christ, it begins with us. If we want the nation to be saved, we better know that we are saved. We better listen to what Jesus told Nicodemus, and make sure we understand that we must be born again of water and Spirit. We better leave the past behind and set our sight on Christ and His coming kingdom. We need to know His grace and His forgiveness. We need to stand against fear and make our calling and election sure. Unlike other Christians in other nations, we have the right to choose our leaders and we better choose well. But more than that we better pray and intercede for the leaders we have, because they will either make us or break us.

Jesus rose from the dead and ascended to His Father. It is time for the Church to experience Her own resurrection. It is time for the Church to take off Her grave clothes and put on Her armor. It is time for these dead bones to live again. What must we do to be saved? We return to the Word of God. We repent of our sinful ways. We ask God to give us another chance. And we become the army of God we were intended to be. But our warfare is not with flesh and blood. Our warfare is in the heavenlies and we better learn to fight in our spirit against all the enemies of the cross. We have seen it before in other lands and we may even see it happen in this country. When they finish removing statues and monuments, they'll be coming after our crosses next. And they won't be asking for our permission. Are you ready?

And war broke out in heaven: Michael and his angels fought with the dragon; and the dragon and his angels fought, but they did not prevail, nor was a place found for them in heaven any longer. So the great dragon was cast out, that serpent of old, called the Devil and Satan, who deceives the whole world; he was cast to the earth, and his angels were cast out with him.

Then I heard a loud voice saying in heaven, "Now salvation, and strength, and the kingdom of our God, and the power of His Christ have come, for the accuser of our brethren, who accused them before our God day and night, has been cast down.

And they overcame him by the blood of the Lamb and by the word of their testimony, and they did not love their lives to the death. Therefore rejoice, O heavens, and you who dwell in them! Woe to the inhabitants of the earth and the sea! For the devil has come down to you, having great wrath, because he knows that he has a short time." (Revelation 12:7-12 NKJV) (132).

How do we win the battle for the heart and soul of our nation? We overcome by the blood of the Lamb, Jesus Christ. We win by the word of our testimony. And we overcome by not being afraid, not even of our own death. Why? Because we also will experience the same resurrection Jesus did at the last day.

Dear Lord Jesus. Make us ready! Help us turn our attention away from the world around us and help us turn our attention to You and Your kingdom. Help us to see all You have planned for us, and all that You have provided for us.

Give us the courage and the strength to walk in Your power. Help us to overcome as You intended us to do. We ask in Your name, the name above all names. Amen.

Chapter Fifteen

The Ascension

Jesus spent forty days with the disciples after His resurrection. Just as He had tried to prepare them for His death, He was now preparing them for His ascension. They might have thought, now that He is risen, the kingdom He spoke of and promised them, was now about to come to pass. But they failed to understand that although His earthly work was finished, theirs was not.

Some had given up on their dreams after the crucifixion. But now, He was spending the time between His resurrection and ascension to show them there was still hope, and there was much work to do. Those that wait for the instantaneous arrival of the kingdom of God know little and understand even less of the immense size of the kingdom that is coming. If God took six days to create the heavens and the earth, how long should it take to make a kingdom for us? I guess that depends on how big that kingdom will be.

Jesus did perform instant healings on people. But for the person getting healed, that miracle may have felt like a lifetime in coming. Many of the stories of His healing miracles involved people that had carried diseases and infirmities for years. So, you tell me what "instant" feels like.

When Jesus was first revealed to John the Baptist, and baptized, He went into the wilderness for forty days of testing. However, the real purpose of the testing was to prepare Him for the few short years of work He had to accomplish before finding Himself nailed to a cross because of our sins. The scriptures are filled with examples of God preparing men and women for their calling and purpose of life.

Moses spent forty years in Egypt and forty years in his own wilderness experience, in order to be prepared for going back to Egypt and spending forty years leading God's people to the promised land. David was prepared as a child while being a shepherd, so he could become a king, and continue the lineage of Jesus Christ. Joseph was prepared in slavery and in prison to later become the right-hand man to Pharaoh. In that place of leadership, God used him to spare the people of God, and his own family, from famine and extinction. Hebrews 11 and 12 tells story after story of heroes of faith, responsible for changing lives and nations because they trusted God when He chose them and used them for His glory and purpose. (Hebrews 11:1-12:29 NKJV) (133).

Very often, our entire lives are part of an eternal preparation that begins as a few chapters while on this earth. Jesus was with the Father at the beginning of creation. Then

He was born among men to fulfill the next chapter of His purpose and calling. Fortunately, this chapter for Him, resulted in redemption and eternal hope for us. And as He spent His last forty days on the earth, He used that time to prepare the disciples for their next chapter before He departed to begin His next assignment. I guess we didn't realize the amount of work that goes into the kingdom of God. What was the next assignment for Jesus?

Jesus said to his disciples, "Don't be worried! Have faith in God and have faith in me. There are many rooms in my Father's house. I wouldn't tell you this, unless it was true. I am going there to prepare a place for each of you. After I have done this, I will come back and take you with me. Then we will be together. You know the way to where I am going."

Thomas said, "Lord, we don't even know where you are going! How can we know the way?"

"I am the way, the truth, and the life!" Jesus answered. "Without me, no one can go to the Father. If you had known me, you would have known the Father. But from now on, you do know him, and you have seen him." (John 14:1-7 CEV) (134).

How great is that? Jesus is going to the Father's house, in which there are many rooms, and He is going to prepare all of those rooms in the Father's house, for each one of us. Think of the number of rooms and the preparations that are going on just for us because we are in Christ. And when He is done, He will come back and take us to be with Him, and we will have our own room in the house of the Father! What small minds we often have only to live meaningless lives on this earth thinking what we have for now is the best God has to offer. Even Thomas, who is witnessing the Word of God, standing and speaking before him in visible resurrected form, has the audacity to say he doesn't know the way. I suppose it only proves we see what we want to see. And for some that's not much.

Just think! God has let all of us in on a great secret. He has revealed His mystery to us, if we will only have the faith to see it. Paul shared it with us in one of his writings.

Friends, when I came and told you the mystery that God had shared with us, I didn't use big words or try to sound wise. In fact, while I was with you, I made up my mind to speak only about Jesus Christ, who had been nailed to a cross.

At first, I was weak and trembling with fear. When I talked with you or preached, I didn't try to prove anything by sounding wise. I simply let God's Spirit show his power. That way you would have faith because of God's power and not because of human wisdom.

We do use wisdom when speaking to people who are mature in their faith. But it isn't the wisdom of this world or of its rulers, who will soon disappear. We speak of God's hidden and mysterious wisdom that God decided to use for our glory long before the world began. The rulers of this world didn't know anything about this wisdom. If they had known about it, they would not have nailed the glorious Lord to a cross.

But it is just as the Scriptures say, "What God has planned for people who love him is more than eyes have seen or ears have heard. It has never even entered our minds!"

God's Spirit has shown you everything. His Spirit finds out everything, even what is deep in the mind of God. You are the only one who knows what is in your own mind, and God's Spirit is the only one who knows what is in God's mind. But God has given us his Spirit. That's why we don't think the same way that the people of this world think. That's also why we can recognize the blessings that God has given us.

Every word we speak was taught to us by God's Spirit, not by human wisdom. And this same Spirit helps us teach spiritual things to spiritual people. That's why only someone who has God's Spirit can understand spiritual blessings. Anyone who doesn't have God's Spirit thinks these blessings are foolish. People who are guided by the Spirit can make all kinds of judgments, but they cannot be judged by others.

The Scriptures ask, "Has anyone ever known the thoughts of the Lord or given him advice?"

But we understand what Christ is thinking. (1 Corinthians 2:1-16 CEV) (135).

How do we understand what Christ is thinking? By being filled with the Spirit of God. How can we know what is in God's mind? By being filled with God's Spirit.

God's plans for us are so wonderful and so great that words fail us to describe them. His plans haven't even entered our imagination at any level. I love mysteries and I love surprises. I can't wait to see and experience what Christ is preparing for me in the Father's house. But the only way I will get to see or experience any of this is by going through Christ and Him alone. There is no other way. There are NOT many ways to God and His promised blessings for us. There is only one way and it is through His Son, Christ Jesus. There is no compromise available in this path to eternal life. It makes no difference what other men or religions have claimed. Jesus, the Son of God, the Word of God, stated clearly to Thomas, and anyone after him, *"I am the way, the truth, and the life!" Jesus answered. "Without me, no one can go to the Father."* No one!

Jesus appeared to many after His resurrection. He left no doubt of His footprint upon the earth after His death. To deny it not only proves a lack of faith, it demonstrates a lack of historical integrity. Many across the centuries have tried to change or eliminate His story, but to no avail. Some have tried to wipe out His followers. And when that failed, they simply tried to get those followers to doubt themselves and fail to walk in what they should have known as believers. We need to go back to the Word of God and pay close attention to His instructions to those present, before He was lifted up into heaven.

The former account I made, O Theophilus, of all that Jesus began both to do and teach, until the day in which He was taken up, after He through the Holy Spirit had given commandments to the apostles whom He had chosen, to whom He also presented Himself alive after His suffering by many infallible proofs, being seen by them during forty days and speaking of the things pertaining to the kingdom of God.

And being assembled together with them, He commanded them not to depart from Jerusalem, but to wait for the Promise of the Father, "which," He said, "you have heard from Me; for John truly baptized with water, but you shall be baptized with the Holy Spirit not many days from now."

Therefore, when they had come together, they asked Him, saying, "Lord, will You at this time restore the kingdom to Israel?"

And He said to them, "It is not for you to know times or seasons which the Father has put in His own authority. But you shall receive power when the Holy Spirit has come upon you; and you shall be witnesses to Me in Jerusalem, and in all Judea and Samaria, and to the end of the earth."

Now when He had spoken these things, while they watched, He was taken up, and a cloud received Him out of their sight. And while they looked steadfastly toward heaven as He went up, behold, two men stood by them in white apparel, who also said, "Men of Galilee, why do you stand gazing up into heaven? This same Jesus, who was taken up from you into heaven, will so come in like manner as you saw Him go into heaven."

Then they returned to Jerusalem from the mount called Olivet, which is near Jerusalem, a Sabbath day's journey. And when they had entered, they went up into the upper room where they were staying: Peter, James, John, and Andrew; Philip and Thomas; Bartholomew and Matthew; James the son of Alphaeus and Simon the Zealot; and Judas the son of James. These all continued with one accord in prayer and supplication, with the women and Mary the mother of Jesus, and with His brothers. (Acts 1:1-14 NKJV) (136).

Jesus said, "It is finished!" However, He was speaking of His work upon the earth to redeem us to the Father. Then He went to the Father's house, because there is much work to do there before the time to come and get us to go be with Him forever. His followers were instructed to go and wait for the power they would need to do what they had been taught and continue His work on the earth through Him. The students were now ready for graduation, but they would need the Holy Spirit to empower and lead them for the work ahead.

We also need that power because there is still much work to do. For too many years the Church has functioned from memory instead of power. When Jesus left this earth, He promised the Holy Spirit would come. And He did come, and is still here, for the work that continues. Instead of tapping into that power, the Church has continued for centuries to debate the authenticity and availability of the power Christ promised. As a result, much of the Church stands powerless against the onslaught of the devil.

If we would have had the power of the Holy Spirit in our midst, would the government have succeeded at running us out of our buildings through what they called a pandemic? If we were filled with the power of the Holy Spirit would we have gone to hide in our houses until the government said it was okay to come out? Many of the believers hid after the crucifixion. But now at His ascension, Jesus was telling the Church, you will not have to hide or be afraid if you will follow my instructions and go wait for the Power of God to come in the form of the Holy Spirit. If the modern day Church would also follow the instructions of Jesus and get filled with the power of the Holy Spirit, our buildings would become irrelevant to us, because the call to proclaim the good news of the gospel would once again become our primary focus.

We praise God for the birth of Jesus. We rejoice that Jesus took our place and our sins on the cross. We can't wait to see the place He has prepared for us. And we long for the day He returns as the risen King of Kings and establishes the Kingdom of God on the earth. However, we continue to skip over the part about being filled with the power of the Holy Spirit and fulfilling our calling as obedient servants doing the work of the kingdom until He returns. There is still much work to be done and it is the Church's responsibility to do the work. But She needs the tools and the power God has provided to do that work successfully. However, instead of equipping Her and teaching Her to work, Her shepherds have deprived Her of Her tools and steered Her away from the power. Why would they do that? Don't they know they will have to answer to God? That's the problem! Shepherds, leaders, prophets, priests and politicians all, have failed the people they are intended to serve and have instead rigged the system to serve themselves. This is not a new thing. People entrusted with leadership have often disappointed – and yes, they will be held accountable. If not by the people who put them there, then certainly at the appointed time by God.

"My people have been lost sheep. Their shepherds have led them astray; they have turned them away on the mountains. They have gone from mountain to hill; they have forgotten their resting place. All who found them have devoured them; and their adversaries said, 'We have not offended, because they have sinned against the Lord, the habitation of justice, the Lord, the hope of their fathers.'" (Jeremiah 50:6-7 NKJV) (137).

This is what the Lord Almighty says: "Look! Disaster is spreading from nation to nation; a mighty storm is rising from the ends of the earth."

At that time those slain by the Lord will be everywhere, from one end of the earth to the other. They will not be mourned or gathered up or buried but will be like refuse lying on the ground.

Weep and wail, you shepherds; roll in the dust, you leaders of the flock. For your time to be slaughtered has come; you will fall and be shattered like fine pottery. The shepherds will have nowhere to flee, the leaders of the flock no place to escape.

Hear the cry of the shepherds, the wailing of the leaders of the flock, for the Lord is destroying their pasture. The peaceful meadows will be laid waste because of the fierce anger of the Lord. Like a lion he will leave his lair, and their land will become desolate because of the sword of the oppressor and because of the Lord's fierce anger. (Jeremiah 25:32-38 NIV) (138).

We really are witnessing disaster spreading from "*nation to nation.*" What is the role of the Church in the midst of this chaos? Is She to cower in fear and run away? What if Her leaders and shepherds don't lead? Then She better start with finding or developing new leaders, because there is still much work to do. The power of God imparted to us at Pentecost after the ascension of Jesus, leaves us with no excuses when it comes to leadership. Instead of waiting on these leaders to repent or grow up, we need to call on the Holy Ghost to do His job and empower us, the Church, for the work that still needs to be done.

There are no more excuses. There is no more time to waste. We are witnessing daily the evidence that the devil knows that his time is limited and he's working to destroy all he can with the time he has left. And Church, if his time is limited, then so is ours, and there is still much work to be done. Rise up! God has given us the power and the tools, and it's about time for us to jump in.

You leaders of my people are like shepherds that kill and scatter the sheep. You were supposed to take care of my people, but instead you chased them away. So now I'll really take care of you, and believe me, you will pay for your crimes!

I will bring the rest of my people home from the lands where I have scattered them, and they will grow into a mighty nation. I promise to choose leaders who will care for them like real shepherds. All of my people will be there, and they will never again be frightened.

Someday I will appoint an honest king from the family of David, a king who will be wise and rule with justice. As long as he is king, Israel will have peace, and Judah will be safe. The name of this king will be "The Lord Gives Justice." A time will come when you will again worship me. But you will no longer call me the Living God who rescued Israel from Egypt. Instead, you will call me the Living God who rescued you from the land in the north and from all the other countries where I had forced you to go. And you will once again live in your own land.

When I think of the prophets, I am shocked, and I tremble like someone drunk, because of the Lord and his sacred words. Those unfaithful prophets misuse their power all over the country. So God turned the pasturelands into scorching deserts.

The Lord told me to say: You prophets and priests think so little of me, the Lord, that you even sin in my own temple! Now I will punish you with disaster, and you will slip and fall in the darkness. I, the Lord, have spoken. (Jeremiah 23:1-12 CEV) (139).

We have a shepherd! We have a high priest! We have a savior! We have what we need to do the work of Christ. What we don't have, is another excuse.

Now these are the gifts Christ gave to the church: the apostles, the prophets, the evangelists, and the pastors and teachers. Their responsibility is to equip God's people to do his work and build up the church, the body of Christ. This will continue until we all come to such unity in our faith and knowledge of God's Son that we will be mature in the Lord, measuring up to the full and complete standard of Christ.

Then we will no longer be immature like children. We won't be tossed and blown about by every wind of new

teaching. We will not be influenced when people try to trick us with lies so clever, they sound like the truth. Instead, we will speak the truth in love, growing in every way more and more like Christ, who is the head of his body, the church. He makes the whole body fit together perfectly. As each part does its own special work, it helps the other parts grow, so that the whole body is healthy and growing and full of love.
(Ephesians 4:11-16 NLT) (140).

This world is the same world it was at the time of the crucifixion and the ascension. It is a world that needs Jesus. It's a world that needs to turn from sin and rebellion and turn to God. The commission of the Church in this world has not changed. The message of the Church is the same. The names have changed, the world is more modern. The tools and toys are more advanced. But the heart without Christ is still the same one that needs to find salvation in the only one that can provide it, Christ Jesus. What are we lacking? Power from God to do the work that is before us! And that power has been and is available since the day it was first imparted to the early church on the day of Pentecost.

Churches in America had hoped to reopen in 2020 on the day of Pentecost, in order to celebrate some symbolic return to their buildings. But the world needs more than a symbolic return from the Church. The world needs to witness the power of God in the Church, and find its heart pierced beyond the ability to resist the convicting and drawing power of God to come humbly and repentant to salvation. Revolutions come and go, but salvation lasts for eternity!

On the day of Pentecost all the believers were meeting together in one place. Suddenly, there was a sound from heaven like the roaring of a mighty windstorm, and it filled the house where they were sitting. Then, what looked like flames or tongues of fire appeared and settled on each of them. And everyone present was filled with the Holy Spirit and began speaking in other languages, as the Holy Spirit gave them this ability.

At that time there were devout Jews from every nation living in Jerusalem. When they heard the loud noise, everyone came running, and they were bewildered to hear their own languages being spoken by the believers.

They were completely amazed. "How can this be?" they exclaimed. "These people are all from Galilee, and yet we hear them speaking in our own native languages! Here we are—Parthians, Medes, Elamites, people from Mesopotamia, Judea, Cappadocia, Pontus, the province of Asia, Phrygia, Pamphylia, Egypt, and the areas of Libya around Cyrene, visitors from Rome (both Jews and converts to Judaism), Cretans, and Arabs. And we all hear these people speaking in our own languages about the wonderful things God has done!"

They stood there amazed and perplexed. "What can this mean?" they asked each other.

But others in the crowd ridiculed them, saying, "They're just drunk, that's all!

Then Peter stepped forward with the eleven other apostles and shouted to the crowd, "Listen carefully, all of you, fellow Jews and residents of Jerusalem! Make no mistake about this. These people are not drunk, as some of you are assuming. Nine o'clock in the morning is much too early for that. No, what you see was predicted long ago by the prophet Joel: 'In the last days,' God says, 'I will pour out my Spirit upon all people. Your sons and daughters will prophesy. Your young men will see visions, and your old men will dream dreams. In those days I will pour out my Spirit

*even on my servants—men and women alike—and they will
prophesy.*

*And I will cause wonders in the heavens above and signs
on the earth below—blood and fire and clouds of smoke. The
sun will become dark, and the moon will turn blood red
before that great and glorious day of the Lord arrives. But
everyone who calls on the name of the Lord will be saved.'*
(Acts 2:1-21 NLT) (141).

Lord Jesus. We need all You have given us to do the
work of the kingdom of God. We are not too old or too
young. We have been given authority by Your word, now we
ask for courage to do the work. Raise up the warrior spirit in
Your Church and give us the resolve to do Your mighty and
powerful work in the earth. We will not fear what people will
try to do to oppose us. Rather we will fear to fail at walking
in Your word and finishing the course set before us. Thank
You for Your power supply for our cause, the Holy Ghost!

Chapter Sixteen

The Return

Every eye shall see Him! Whether you believe in Him or not, you will see Him! Whether you faithfully served Him or not, you will see Him. Everyone on the face of the earth, you are going to behold Him in His mighty power, and there will be no place to hide or escape. Even those who pierced Him will see Him.

Grace to you and peace from Him who is and who was and who is to come, and from the seven Spirits who are before His throne, and from Jesus Christ, the faithful witness, the firstborn from the dead, and the ruler over the kings of the earth.

To Him who loved us and washed us from our sins in His own blood and has made us kings and priests to His God and

Father, to Him be glory and dominion forever and ever. Amen.

Behold, He is coming with clouds, and every eye will see Him, even they who pierced Him. And all the tribes of the earth will mourn because of Him. Even so, Amen.

"I am the Alpha and the Omega, the Beginning and the End," says the Lord, "who is and who was and who is to come, the Almighty." (Revelation 1:4-8 NKJV) (142).

The same Jesus that came meek and lowly as a lamb will come again as a powerful and reigning King. His story did not end in the garden. His story did not end at the cross. And His story did not end at the ascension where a small crowd of people were told by angels He would return again.

For centuries men have tried to hide the truth of His life, His death, and His resurrection. But there is coming a day when no one will be able to hide from His return. Modern America and the world alike have repeatedly tried to ignore His word and His promise to return again. But His day is coming, and no one will fail to recognize who He is; King of Kings, and Lord of Lords.

Some will accuse this writer of being just another crazy fanatic, and claim the words are meaningless or simply taken out of context. But this writer knows and understands which words in this book belong to him and which words are His words. His words are quick and powerful, and have endured time, and prevailed over the death of every leader the world has known. The heavens know Him, the dead know Him, and soon the earth will know Him.

For the word of God is living and powerful, and sharper than any two-edged sword, piercing even to the division of soul and spirit, and of joints and marrow, and is a discerner of the thoughts and intents of the heart. And there is no creature hidden from His sight, but all things are naked and open to the eyes of Him to whom we must give account. (Hebrews 4:12-13 NKJV) (143).

And who must give account? All of us! We have all given our lives and energy to the things we felt were most valuable. God also demonstrated what was valuable to Him when He permitted His own creation to dishonor and destroy His only begotten Son, Jesus. How can it be possible that we have failed to recognize our own value and worth to God? But we did. And for some, it wasn't enough just to reject Him. Some gave their lives to trying to destroy all that He stood for and accomplished. We are without excuse, and the day of His return is at hand, and nothing is going to stop Him from coming. When He comes, the mocking will cease because every eye will see Him.

The kings of the earth, its famous people, and its military leaders hid in caves or behind rocks on the mountains. They hid there together with the rich and the powerful and with all the slaves and free people. Then they shouted to the mountains and the rocks, "Fall on us! Hide us from the one who sits on the throne and from the anger of the Lamb. That terrible day has come! God and the Lamb will show their anger, and who can face it?" (Revelation 6:15-17 CEV) (144).

So, in the meantime, what is the Church to do? I would say we need to take up the cause and preach the gospel which is able to save our souls. I would suggest we remember our calling and if we have fallen away from the simplicity of the gospel of Christ, we immediately get busy bringing our hearts back to the Lord as fast as we can. This is not a joke; this is life and death. Our nation and our world is sick unto death, and only God's healing touch can bring us back from the brink of our own demise. Our people destroy their own cities and their country while listening to and believing lies. Only the gospel of Christ and the power of the Holy Spirit can save us from certain annihilation. These destroyers, walking in the evil anointing of their father, also work like their end is near. But God, who is rich in mercy stands ready to forgive and restore their tormented hearts and souls.

Therefore, lay aside all filthiness and overflow of wickedness, and receive with meekness the implanted word, which is able to save your souls.

But be doers of the word, and not hearers only, deceiving yourselves. For if anyone is a hearer of the word and not a doer, he is like a man observing his natural face in a mirror; for he observes himself, goes away, and immediately forgets what kind of man he was. But he who looks into the perfect law of liberty and continues in it and is not a forgetful hearer but a doer of the work, this one will be blessed in what he does. (James 1:21-25 NKJV) (145).

Just so I'm clear; this is not a book about the end times. This a book about the times we are living in right now. This is a call to the hurting heart to turn and return to the God that saves. America is not perfect. No individual is and certainly no nation is. However, even with all Her imperfection there has never been another nation in the world that has worked as hard or paid as high of a price, to make itself and every other nation a better place to live for those that live on the earth. And the only reason for this effort, is because America is a land in which many with the freedom She has provided, have used that freedom to worship God and help Her fellow man.

Regardless of Her faults She has been faithful to help others. Despite Her sins, She has forgiven those who have trespassed against Her. And true to the heart of Her people,

She has loved others the same way She has loved Herself. This nation has been generous to Her friends and Her enemies. She has repented of wrong-doing and found ways to make amends and do better. Yes, She has fallen often. But rather than lay in shame and disgrace indefinitely, She pulled Herself up above the fool's choice, and said I can do better, and I can be better.

For those that long to rejoice at Her destruction, remember that the ship you are trying to sink, is the same ship that you and your family needs to get back to shore. America has been blessed by God with a great hull, and just like Noah's ark, God has used America to keep the rest of the world safe from a multitude of floods.

And the Lord shall utter his voice before his army: for his camp is very great: for he is strong that executes his word: for the day of the Lord is great and very terrible; and who can abide it?

Therefore, also now, saith the Lord, turn ye even to me with all your heart, and with fasting, and with weeping, and with mourning: And rend your heart, and not your garments, and turn unto the Lord your God: for he is gracious and merciful, slow to anger, and of great kindness, and repents him of the evil. (Joel 2:11-13 KJV) (146).

"Then, after doing all those things, I will pour out my Spirit upon all people. Your sons and daughters will prophesy. Your old men will dream dreams, and your young men will see visions. In those days I will pour out my Spirit even on servants—men and women alike. And I will cause wonders in the heavens and on the earth—blood and fire and columns of smoke. The sun will become dark, and the moon will turn blood red before that great and terrible day of the

Lord arrives. But everyone who calls on the name of the Lord will be saved." (Joel 2:28-32 NLT) (147).

It is time again for America to be saved. What do I mean by that? America has been saved from many things. She has been saved in war. She has been saved in economic collapse. She has been saved from many of the calamities that have befallen other nations. But every new generation in America seems to miss that She is great because God has made Her great. And She has enjoyed the blessings of Her greatness because of Her consistent dedication to sending aid and missionaries, with the gospel message, to every nation of the world. She is also blessed because She sends Her young men and women of the military to deliver, protect, and keep safe, multiple other nations around the world.

But America has never been more at risk than She is right now. While having Her share of foreign enemies to deal with, She seems to have never been as overrun by domestic enemies within as She is at this time. She has never appeared to be more divided than She is at this moment in time. And recently She is finding less and less opportunity to catch Her breath from onslaught after onslaught. Peace has been taken from Her. Prosperity has been stolen from Her. And common sense seems headed out the door. Her only hope is for God to intervene. Her necessary courage and peace will have to come from God. Her strength and resolve to rise above the latest ashes will have to be provided by God. America can never survive if She tries to go it alone without God. Because, be sure of this one thing, it has only been because Her people have prayed harder than any other nation on the earth, that She has maintained the greatest stature of all the nations of the world. For America to be great again and for America to be saved again, Americans are going to have to pray again.

Behold what manner of love the Father has bestowed on us, that we should be called children of God! Therefore, the world does not know us, because it did not know Him. Beloved, now we are children of God; and it has not yet been revealed what we shall be, but we know that when He is revealed, we shall be like Him, for we shall see Him as He is. And everyone who has this hope in Him purifies himself, just as He is pure. (1 John 3:1-3 NKJV) (148).

Every eye will see Him. But every eye will not be glad to see Him. And if we know Him, when we do see Him, we will become like Him, because we will see Him as He is.

Dear Jesus. Open our hearts and our eyes to see You clearly. We repent of our sins and turn our hearts to You and ask that You finish the great work You began in us. We admit we can't do this work without You. Lord help us to accomplish Your will and fulfill Your purpose. Oh God, have mercy on us and save us from becoming nothing more than someone's memory in time. Lord, our times are in Your hands and we ask that You make America saved again. Amen.

SCRIPTURES IN ORDER OF USE

CHAPTER 1
(1) Jeremiah 29:11-14 NIV
11 For I know the plans I have for you," declares the Lord, "plans to prosper you and not to harm you, plans to give you hope and a future. 12 Then you will call upon me and come and pray to me, and I will listen to you. 13 You will seek me and find me when you seek me with all your heart. 14 I will be found by you," declares the Lord, "and will bring you back from captivity. b I will gather you from all the nations and places where I have banished you," declares the Lord, "and will bring you back to the place from which I carried you into exile." NIV

(2) Proverbs 19:21 NIV
21 Many are the plans in a man's heart, but it is the Lord's purpose that prevails. NIV

(3) Proverbs 19:3 NLT
3 People ruin their lives by their own foolishness and then are angry at the Lord. Holy Bible, New Living Translation ®, copyright © 1996, 2004 by Tyndale Charitable Trust. Used by permission of Tyndale House Publishers. All rights reserved.

(4) Proverbs 21:2 NKJV
2 Every way of a man *is* right in his own eyes, But the Lord weighs the hearts. NKJV

(5) Numbers 22-24 NKJV
22 Then the children of Israel moved, and camped in the plains of Moab on the side of the Jordan *across from* Jericho. 2 Now Balak the son of Zippor saw all that Israel had done to the Amorites. 3 And Moab was exceedingly afraid of the people because they *were* many, and Moab was sick with dread because of the children of Israel. 4 So Moab said to the elders of Midian, "Now this company will lick up everything around us, as an ox licks up the grass of the field." And Balak the son of Zippor *was* king of the Moabites at that time. 5 Then he sent messengers to Balaam the son of Beor at Pethor, which *is* near the River* in the land of the sons of his people,* to call him, saying: "Look, a people has come from Egypt. See, they cover the face of the earth, and are settling next to me! 6 Therefore please come at once, curse this people for me, for they *are* too mighty for me. Perhaps I shall be able to defeat them and drive them out of the land, for I know that he whom you bless *is* blessed, and he whom you curse is cursed." 7 So the elders of Moab and the elders of Midian departed with the diviner's fee in their hand, and they came to Balaam and spoke to him the words of Balak. 8 And he said to them, "Lodge here tonight, and I will bring back word to you, as the Lord speaks to me." So the princes of Moab stayed with Balaam. 9 Then God came to Balaam and said, "Who *are* these men with you?" 10 So Balaam said to God, "Balak the son of Zippor, king of Moab, has sent to me, *saying,* 11 'Look, a people has come out of Egypt, and they cover the face of the earth. Come now, curse them for me; perhaps I shall be able to overpower them and drive them out.'" 12 And God said to Balaam, "You shall not go with them; you shall not curse the people, for they *are* blessed." 13 So Balaam rose in the morning and said to the princes of Balak, "Go back to your land, for the Lord has refused to give me permission to go with you." 14 And the princes of Moab rose and went to Balak, and said, "Balaam refuses to come with us." 15 Then Balak again sent princes, more numerous and more honorable than they. 16 And they came to Balaam and said to him, "Thus says Balak the son of Zippor: 'Please let nothing hinder you from coming to me; 17 for I will certainly honor you greatly, and I will do whatever you say to me.

Therefore please come, curse this people for me.'" 18 Then Balaam answered and said to the servants of Balak, "Though Balak were to give me his house full of silver and gold, I could not go beyond the word of the Lord my God, to do less or more. 19 Now therefore, please, you also stay here tonight, that I may know what more the Lord will say to me." 20 And God came to Balaam at night and said to him, "If the men come to call you, rise *and* go with them; but only the word which I speak to you — that you shall do." 21 So Balaam rose in the morning, saddled his donkey, and went with the princes of Moab.

Balaam, the Donkey, and the Angel

22 Then God's anger was aroused because he went, and the Angel of the Lord took His stand in the way as an adversary against him. And he was riding on his donkey, and his two servants *were* with him. 23 Now the donkey saw the Angel of the Lord standing in the way with His drawn sword in His hand, and the donkey turned aside out of the way and went into the field. So Balaam struck the donkey to turn her back onto the road. 24 Then the Angel of the Lord stood in a narrow path between the vineyards, *with* a wall on this side and a wall on that side. 25 And when the donkey saw the Angel of the Lord, she pushed herself against the wall and crushed Balaam's foot against the wall; so he struck her again. 26 Then the Angel of the Lord went further, and stood in a narrow place where there *was* no way to turn either to the right hand or to the left. 27 And when the donkey saw the Angel of the Lord, she lay down under Balaam; so Balaam's anger was aroused, and he struck the donkey with his staff. 28 Then the Lord opened the mouth of the donkey, and she said to Balaam, "What have I done to you, that you have struck me these three times?" 29 And Balaam said to the donkey, "Because you have abused me. I wish there were a sword in my hand, for now I would kill you!" 30 So the donkey said to Balaam, "*Am* I not your donkey on which you have ridden, ever since *I became* yours, to this day? Was I ever disposed to do this to you?" And he said, "No." 31 Then the Lord opened Balaam's eyes, and he saw the Angel of the Lord standing in the way with His drawn sword in His hand; and he bowed his head and fell flat on his face. 32 And the Angel of the Lord said to him, "Why have you struck your donkey these three times? Behold, I have come out to stand against you, because *your* way is perverse before Me. 33 The donkey saw Me and turned aside from Me these three times. If she had not turned aside from Me, surely I would also have killed you by now, and let her live." 34 And Balaam said to the Angel of the Lord, "I have sinned, for I did not know You stood in the way against me. Now therefore, if it displeases You, I will turn back." 35 Then the Angel of the Lord said to Balaam, "Go with the men, but only the word that I speak to you, that you shall speak." So Balaam went with the princes of Balak. 36 Now when Balak heard that Balaam was coming, he went out to meet him at the city of Moab, which *is* on the border at the Arnon, the boundary of the territory. 37 Then Balak said to Balaam, "Did I not earnestly send to you, calling for you? Why did you not come to me? Am I not able to honor you?" 38 And Balaam said to Balak, "Look, I have come to you! Now, have I any power at all to say anything? The word that God puts in my mouth, that I must speak." 39 So Balaam went with Balak, and they came to Kirjath Huzoth. 40 Then Balak offered oxen and sheep, and he sent *some* to Balaam and to the princes who *were* with him.

Balaam's First Prophecy

41 So it was, the next day, that Balak took Balaam and brought him up to the high places of Baal, that from there he might observe the extent of the people.

The Prophecies of Balaam

23 Then Balaam said to Balak, "Build seven altars for me here, and prepare for me here seven bulls and seven rams." 2 And Balak did just as Balaam had spoken, and Balak and Balaam offered a bull and a ram on *each* altar. 3 Then Balaam said to Balak, "Stand by your burnt offering, and I will go; perhaps the Lord will come to meet me, and whatever He shows me I will tell you." So he went to a desolate height. 4 And God met Balaam, and he said to Him, "I have prepared the seven altars, and I have offered on *each* altar a bull and a ram." 5 Then the Lord put a word in Balaam's mouth, and said, "Return to Balak, and thus you shall speak." 6 So he returned to him, and there he was, standing by his burnt offering, he and all the princes of Moab. 7 And he took up his oracle and said: "Balak the

king of Moab has brought me from Aram, From the mountains of the east. 'Come, curse Jacob for me, And come, denounce Israel!' 8 "How shall I curse whom God has not cursed? And how shall I denounce *whom* the Lord has not denounced? 9 For from the top of the rocks I see him, And from the hills I behold him; There! A people dwelling alone, Not reckoning itself among the nations. 10 "Who can count the dust* of Jacob, Or number one-fourth of Israel? Let me die the death of the righteous, And let my end be like his!" 11 Then Balak said to Balaam, "What have you done to me? I took you to curse my enemies, and look, you have blessed *them* bountifully!" 12 So he answered and said, "Must I not take heed to speak what the Lord has put in my mouth?"

Balaam's Second Prophecy
13 Then Balak said to him, "Please come with me to another place from which you may see them; you shall see only the outer part of them, and shall not see them all; curse them for me from there." 14 So he brought him to the field of Zophim, to the top of Pisgah, and built seven altars, and offered a bull and a ram on *each* altar. 15 And he said to Balak, "Stand here by your burnt offering while I meet* *the* Lord over there." 16 Then the Lord met Balaam, and put a word in his mouth, and said, "Go back to Balak, and thus you shall speak." 17 So he came to him, and there he was, standing by his burnt offering, and the princes of Moab were with him. And Balak said to him, "What has the Lord spoken?" 18 Then he took up his oracle and said: "Rise up, Balak, and hear! Listen to me, son of Zippor! 19 "God *is* not a man, that He should lie, Nor a son of man, that He should repent. Has He said, and will He not do? Or has He spoken, and will He not make it good? 20 Behold, I have received *a command* to bless; He has blessed, and I cannot reverse it. 21 "He has not observed iniquity in Jacob, Nor has He seen wickedness in Israel. The Lord his God *is* with him, And the shout of a King *is* among them. 22 God brings them out of Egypt; He has strength like a wild ox. 23 "For *there is* no sorcery against Jacob, Nor any divination against Israel. It now must be said of Jacob And of Israel, 'Oh, what God has done!' 24 Look, a people rises like a lioness, And lifts itself up like a lion; It shall not lie down until it devours the prey, And drinks the blood of the slain." 25 Then Balak said to Balaam, "Neither curse them at all, nor bless them at all!" 26 So Balaam answered and said to Balak, "Did I not tell you, saying, 'All that the Lord speaks, that I must do'?"

Balaam's Third Prophecy
27 Then Balak said to Balaam, "Please come, I will take you to another place; perhaps it will please God that you may curse them for me from there." 28 So Balak took Balaam to the top of Peor, that overlooks the wasteland.* 29 Then Balaam said to Balak, "Build for me here seven altars, and prepare for me here seven bulls and seven rams." 30 And Balak did as Balaam had said, and offered a bull and a ram on *every* altar.

Balaam Foretells the Happiness of Israel
24 Now when Balaam saw that it pleased the Lord to bless Israel, he did not go as at other times, to seek to use sorcery, but he set his face toward the wilderness. 2 And Balaam raised his eyes, and saw Israel encamped according to their tribes; and the Spirit of God came upon him. 3 Then he took up his oracle and said: "The utterance of Balaam the son of Beor, The utterance of the man whose eyes are opened, 4 The utterance of him who hears the words of God, Who sees the vision of the Almighty, Who falls down, with eyes wide open: 5 "How lovely are your tents, O Jacob! Your dwellings, O Israel! 6 Like valleys that stretch out, Like gardens by the riverside, Like aloes planted by the Lord, Like cedars beside the waters. 7 He shall pour water from his buckets, And his seed *shall be* in many waters. "His king shall be higher than Agag, And his kingdom shall be exalted. 8 "God brings him out of Egypt; He has strength like a wild ox; He shall consume the nations, his enemies; He shall break their bones And pierce *them* with his arrows. 9 'He bows down, he lies down as a lion; And as a lion, who shall rouse him?'* "Blessed *is* he who blesses you, And cursed *is* he who curses you." 10 Then Balak's anger was aroused against Balaam, and he struck his hands together; and Balak said to Balaam,"I called you to curse my enemies, and look, you have bountifully blessed *them* these three times! 11 Now therefore, flee to your place. I said I would greatly honor you, but in fact, the Lord has kept you back from honor." 12 So Balaam said to Balak, "Did I not also speak to your messengers whom you sent to me,

saying, 13 'If Balak were to give me his house full of silver and gold, I could not go beyond the word of the Lord, to do good or bad of my own will. What the Lord says, that I must speak'? 14 And now, indeed, I am going to my people. Come, I will advise you what this people will do to your people in the latter days."

Balaam's Fourth Prophecy

15 So he took up his oracle and said: "The utterance of Balaam the son of Beor, And the utterance of the man whose eyes are opened; 16 The utterance of him who hears the words of God, And has the knowledge of the Most High, *Who* sees the vision of the Almighty, *Who* falls down, with eyes wide open: 17 "I see Him, but not now; I behold Him, but not near; A Star shall come out of Jacob; A Scepter shall rise out of Israel, And batter the brow of Moab, And destroy all the sons of tumult.* 18 "And Edom shall be a possession; Seir also, his enemies, shall be a possession, While Israel does valiantly. 19 Out of Jacob One shall have dominion, And destroy the remains of the city." 20 Then he looked on Amalek, and he took up his oracle and said: "Amalek *was* first among the nations, But *shall be* last until he perishes." 21 Then he looked on the Kenites, and he took up his oracle and said: "Firm is your dwelling place, And your nest is set in the rock; 22 Nevertheless Kain shall be burned. How long until Asshur carries you away captive?" 23 Then he took up his oracle and said: "Alas! Who shall live when God does this? 24 But ships *shall come* from the coasts of Cyprus,* And they shall afflict Asshur and afflict Eber, And so shall *Amalek,** until he perishes." 25 So Balaam rose and departed and returned to his place; Balak also went his way. NKJV

(6) Ephesians 1:7-12 NKJV

7 In Him we have redemption through His blood, the forgiveness of sins, according to the riches of His grace 8 which He made to abound toward us in all wisdom and prudence, 9 having made known to us the mystery of His will, according to His good pleasure which He purposed in Himself, 10 that in the dispensation of the fullness of the times He might gather together in one all things in Christ, both* which are in heaven and which are on earth — in Him. 11 In Him also we have obtained an inheritance, being predestined according to the purpose of Him who works all things according to the counsel of His will, 12 that we who first trusted in Christ should be to the praise of His glory. NKJV

(7) Numbers 24:9 NKJV

9 'He bows down, he lies down as a lion; And as a lion, who shall rouse him?'* "Blessed *is* he who blesses you, And cursed *is* he who curses you." NKJV

(8) Ephesians 2:4-10 NKJV

4 But God, who is rich in mercy, because of His great love with which He loved us, 5 even when we were dead in trespasses, made us alive together with Christ (by grace you have been saved), 6 and raised *us* up together, and made *us* sit together in the heavenly *places* in Christ Jesus, 7 that in the ages to come He might show the exceeding riches of His grace in *His* kindness toward us in Christ Jesus. 8 For by grace you have been saved through faith, and that not of yourselves; *it is* the gift of God, 9 not of works, lest anyone should boast. 10 For we are His workmanship, created in Christ Jesus for good works, which God prepared beforehand that we should walk in them. NKJV

CHAPTER 2

(9) Matthew 24:1-2 NKJV

1 Then Jesus went out and departed from the temple, and His disciples came up to show Him the buildings of the temple. 2 And Jesus said to them, "Do you not see all these things? Assuredly, I say to you, not one stone shall be left here upon another, that shall not be thrown down." NKJV

(10) John 3:16 NKJV

For God so loved the world that He gave His only begotten Son, that whoever believes in Him should not perish but have everlasting life. NKJV

(11) 2 Chronicles 7:12-22 NKJV
12 Then the Lord appeared to Solomon by night, and said to him: "I have heard your prayer, and have chosen this place for Myself as a house of sacrifice. 13 When I shut up heaven and there is no rain, or command the locusts to devour the land, or send pestilence among My people, 14 if My people who are called by My name will humble themselves, and pray and seek My face, and turn from their wicked ways, then I will hear from heaven, and will forgive their sin and heal their land. 15 Now My eyes will be open and My ears attentive to prayer *made* in this place. 16 For now I have chosen and sanctified this house, that My name may be there forever; and My eyes and My heart will be there perpetually. 18 As for you, if you walk before Me as your father David walked, and do according to all that I have commanded you, and if you keep My statutes and My judgments, 18 then I will establish the throne of your kingdom, as I covenanted with David your father, saying, 'You shall not fail *to have* a man as ruler in Israel.' 19 "But if you turn away and forsake My statutes and My commandments which I have set before you, and go and serve other gods, and worship them, 20 then I will uproot them from My land which I have given them; and this house which I have sanctified for My name I will cast out of My sight, and will make it a proverb and a byword among all peoples. 21 "And *as for* this house, which is exalted, everyone who passes by it will be astonished and say, 'Why has the Lord done thus to this land and this house?' 22 Then they will answer, 'Because they forsook the Lord God of their fathers, who brought them out of the land of Egypt, and embraced other gods, and worshiped them and served them; therefore He has brought all this calamity on them.'" NKJV

(12) Revelation 19:6-8 NKJV
6 And I heard, as it were, the voice of a great multitude, as the sound of many waters and as the sound of mighty thunderings, saying, "Alleluia! For the Lord God Omnipotent reigns! 7 Let us be glad and rejoice and give Him glory, for the marriage of the Lamb has come, and His wife has made herself ready" 8 And to her it was granted to be arrayed in fine linen, clean and bright, for the fine linen is the righteous acts of the saints. NKJV

(13) 1 John 4:18 NKJV
There is no fear in love; but perfect love casts out fear, because fear involves torment. But he who fears has not been made perfect in love. NKJV

(14) 2 Timothy 1:7 NKJV
For God has not given us a spirit of fear, but of power and of love and of a sound mind. NKJV

(15) Matthew 28:5-8 NKJV
5 But the angel answered and said to the women, "Do not be afraid, for I know that you seek Jesus who was crucified. 6 He is not here; for He is risen, as He said. Come, see the place where the Lord lay. 7 And go quickly and tell His disciples that He is risen from the dead, and indeed He is going before you into Galilee; there you will see Him. Behold, I have told you." 8 So they went out quickly from the tomb with fear and great joy and ran to bring His disciples word. NKJV

(16) 1 Corinthians 10:13 NKJV
No temptation has overtaken you except such as is common to man; but God *is* faithful, who will not allow you to be tempted beyond what you are able, but with the temptation will also make the way of escape, that you may be able to bear *it*. NKJV

CHAPTER 3
(17) Jeremiah 1:5 NKJV

"Before I formed you in the womb I knew you; Before you were born I sanctified you; I ordained you a prophet to the nations." NKJV

(18) Philippians 3:13-14 KJV
13 Brethren, I count not myself to have apprehended: but this one thing I do, forgetting those things which are behind, and reaching forth unto those things which are before, 14 I press toward the mark for the prize of the high calling of God in Christ Jesus. KJV

(19) Romans 11:29 NKJV
For the gifts and the calling of God *are* irrevocable. NKJV

(20) 1 Samuel 1:1-4:1 NKJV
1:1 Now there was a certain man of Ramathaim Zophim, of the mountains of Ephraim, and his name *was* Elkanah the son of Jeroham, the son of Elihu, the son of Tohu, the son of Zuph, an Ephraimite. 2 And he had two wives: the name of one *was* Hannah, and the name of the other Peninnah. Peninnah had children, but Hannah had no children. 3 This man went up from his city yearly to worship and sacrifice to the Lord of hosts in Shiloh. Also, the two sons of Eli, Hophni and Phinehas, the priests of the Lord, *were* there. 4 And whenever the time came for Elkanah to make an offering, he would give portions to Peninnah his wife and to all her sons and daughters. 5 But to Hannah he would give a double portion, for he loved Hannah, although the Lord had closed her womb. 6 And her rival also provoked her severely, to make her miserable, because the Lord had closed her womb. 7 So it was, year by year, when she went up to the house of the Lord, that she provoked her; therefore, she wept and did not eat. 8 Then Elkanah her husband said to her, "Hannah, why do you weep? Why do you not eat? And why is your heart grieved? *Am* I not better to you than ten sons?" 9 So Hannah arose after they had finished eating and drinking in Shiloh. Now Eli the priest was sitting on the seat by the doorpost of the tabernacle of the Lord. 10 And she *was* in bitterness of soul and prayed to the Lord and wept in anguish. 11 Then she made a vow and said, "O Lord of hosts, if You will indeed look on the affliction of Your maidservant and remember me, and not forget Your maidservant, but will give Your maidservant a male child, then I will give him to the Lord all the days of his life, and no razor shall come upon his head." 12 And it happened, as she continued praying before the Lord, that Eli watched her mouth. 13 Now Hannah spoke in her heart; only her lips moved, but her voice was not heard. Therefore, Eli thought she was drunk. 14 So Eli said to her, "How long will you be drunk? Put your wine away from you!" 15 But Hannah answered and said, "No, my lord, I *am* a woman of sorrowful spirit. I have drunk neither wine nor intoxicating drink but have poured out my soul before the Lord. 16 Do not consider your maidservant a wicked woman, for out of the abundance of my complaint and grief I have spoken until now." 17 Then Eli answered and said, "Go in peace, and the God of Israel grant your petition which you have asked of Him." 18 And she said, "Let your maidservant find favor in your sight." So, the woman went her way and ate, and her face was no longer sad. 19 Then they rose early in the morning and worshiped before the Lord and returned and came to their house at Ramah. And Elkanah knew Hannah his wife, and the Lord remembered her. 20 So it came to pass in the process of time that Hannah conceived and bore a son, and called his name Samuel, saying, "Because I have asked for him from the Lord." 21 Now the man Elkanah and all his house went up to offer to the Lord the yearly sacrifice and his vow. 22 But Hannah did not go up, for she said to her husband, "Not until the child is weaned; then I will take him, that he may appear before the Lord and remain there forever." 23 So Elkanah her husband said to her, "Do what seems best to you; wait until you have weaned him. Only let the Lord establish His word." Then the woman stayed and nursed her son until she had weaned him. 24 Now when she had weaned him, she took him up with her, with three bulls, one ephah of flour, and a skin of wine, and brought him to the house of the Lord in Shiloh. And the child *was* young. 25 Then they slaughtered a bull, and brought the child to Eli. 26 And she said, "O my lord! As your soul lives, my lord, I *am* the woman who stood by you here, praying to the Lord.

27 For this child I prayed, and the Lord has granted me my petition which I asked of Him. 28 Therefore I also have lent him to the Lord; as long as he lives he shall be lent to the Lord." So they worshiped the Lord there. 2:1 And Hannah prayed and said: "My heart rejoices in the Lord; My horn is exalted in the Lord. I smile at my enemies, because I rejoice in Your salvation. 2 No one is holy like the Lord, for *there is* none besides You, nor *is there* any rock like our God. 3 Talk no more so very proudly; let no arrogance come from your mouth, for the Lord *is* the God of knowledge; and by Him actions are weighed. 4 The bows of the mighty men *are* broken, and those who stumbled are girded with strength. 5 *Those who were* full have hired themselves out for bread, and the hungry have ceased *to hunger.* Even the barren has borne seven, and she who has many children has become feeble. 6 The Lord kills and makes alive; He brings down to the grave and brings up. 7 The Lord makes poor and makes rich; He brings low and lifts up. 8 He raises the poor from the dust a*nd* lifts the beggar from the ash heap, to set *them* among princes and make them inherit the throne of glory. For the pillars of the earth *are* the Lord's, and He has set the world upon them. 9 He will guard the feet of His saints, but the wicked shall be silent in darkness. For by strength no man shall prevail. 10 The adversaries of the Lord shall be broken in pieces; from heaven He will thunder against them. The Lord will judge the ends of the earth. He will give strength to His king, and exalt the horn of His anointed." 11 Then Elkanah went to his house at Ramah. But the child ministered to the Lord before Eli the priest. 12 Now the sons of Eli *were* corrupt; they did not know the Lord. 13 And the priests' custom with the people *was that* when any man offered a sacrifice, the priest's servant would come with a three-pronged fleshhook in his hand while the meat was boiling. 14 Then he would thrust *it* into the pan, or kettle, or caldron, or pot; and the priest would take for himself all that the fleshhook brought up. So they did in Shiloh to all the Israelites who came there. 15 Also, before they burned the fat, the priest's servant would come and say to the man who sacrificed, "Give meat for roasting to the priest, for he will not take boiled meat from you, but raw." 16 And *if* the man said to him, "They should really burn the fat first; *then* you may take *as much* as your heart desires," he would then answer him, *"No, but you must give it* now; and if not, I will take *it* by force." 17 Therefore the sin of the young men was very great before the Lord, for men abhorred the offering of the Lord. 18 But Samuel ministered before the Lord, *even as* a child, wearing a linen ephod. 19 Moreover his mother used to make him a little robe, and bring *it* to him year by year when she came up with her husband to offer the yearly sacrifice. 20 And Eli would bless Elkanah and his wife, and say, "The Lord give you descendants from this woman for the loan that was given to the Lord." Then they would go to their own home. 21 And the Lord visited Hannah, so that she conceived and bore three sons and two daughters. Meanwhile the child Samuel grew before the Lord. 22 Now Eli was very old; and he heard everything his sons did to all Israel, and how they lay with the women who assembled at the door of the tabernacle of meeting. 23 So he said to them, "Why do you do such things? For I hear of your evil dealings from all the people. 24 No, my sons! For *it is* not a good report that I hear. You make the Lord's people transgress. 25 If one man sins against another, God will judge him. But if a man sins against the Lord, who will intercede for him?" Nevertheless they did not heed the voice of their father, because the Lord desired to kill them. 26 And the child Samuel grew in stature, and in favor both with the Lord and men. 27 Then a man of God came to Eli and said to him, "Thus says the Lord: 'Did I not clearly reveal Myself to the house of your father when they were in Egypt in Pharaoh's house? 28 Did I not choose him out of all the tribes of Israel *to be* My priest, to offer upon My altar, to burn incense, and to wear an ephod before Me? And did I not give to the house of your father all the offerings of the children of Israel made by fire? 29 Why do you kick at My sacrifice and My offering which I have commanded *in My* dwelling place, and honor your sons more than Me, to make yourselves fat with the best of all the offerings of Israel My people?' 30 Therefore the Lord God of Israel says: 'I said indeed *that* your house and the house of your father would walk before Me forever.' But now the Lord says: 'Far be it from Me; for those who honor Me I will honor, and those who despise Me shall be lightly esteemed. 31 Behold, the days are coming that I will cut off your arm and the arm of your father's house, so that

there will not be an old man in your house. 32 And you will see an enemy *in My* dwelling place, *despite* all the good which God does for Israel. And there shall not be an old man in your house forever. 33 But any of your men *whom* I do not cut off from My altar shall consume your eyes and grieve your heart. And all the descendants of your house shall die in the flower of their age. 34 Now this *shall be* a sign to you that will come upon your two sons, on Hophni and Phinehas: in one day they shall die, both of them. 35 Then I will raise up for Myself a faithful priest *who* shall do according to what *is* in My heart and in My mind. I will build him a sure house, and he shall walk before My anointed forever. 36 And it shall come to pass that everyone who is left in your house will come *and* bow down to him for a piece of silver and a morsel of bread, and say, "Please, put me in one of the priestly positions, that I may eat a piece of bread."""3:1 Now the boy Samuel ministered to the Lord before Eli. And the word of the Lord was rare in those days; *there was* no widespread revelation. 2 And it came to pass at that time, while Eli *was* lying down in his place, and when his eyes had begun to grow so dim that he could not see, 3 and before the lamp of God went out in the tabernacle of the Lord where the ark of God *was,* and while Samuel was lying down, 4 that the Lord called Samuel. And he answered, "Here I am!" 5 So he ran to Eli and said, "Here I am, for you called me." And he said, "I did not call; lie down again." And he went and lay down. 6 Then the Lord called yet again, "Samuel!" So Samuel arose and went to Eli, and said, "Here I am, for you called me." He answered, "I did not call, my son; lie down again." 7 (Now Samuel did not yet know the Lord, nor was the word of the Lord yet revealed to him.) 8 And the Lord called Samuel again the third time. So he arose and went to Eli, and said, "Here I am, for you did call me." Then Eli perceived that the Lord had called the boy. 9 Therefore Eli said to Samuel, "Go, lie down; and it shall be, if He calls you, that you must say, 'Speak, Lord, for Your servant hears.'" So Samuel went and lay down in his place. 10 Now the Lord came and stood and called as at other times, "Samuel! Samuel!" And Samuel answered, "Speak, for Your servant hears." 11 Then the Lord said to Samuel: "Behold, I will do something in Israel at which both ears of everyone who hears it will tingle. 12 In that day I will perform against Eli all that I have spoken concerning his house, from beginning to end. 13 For I have told him that I will judge his house forever for the iniquity which he knows, because his sons made themselves vile, and he did not restrain them. 14 And therefore I have sworn to the house of Eli that the iniquity of Eli's house shall not be atoned for by sacrifice or offering forever." 15 So Samuel lay down until morning, and opened the doors of the house of the Lord. And Samuel was afraid to tell Eli the vision. 16 Then Eli called Samuel and said, "Samuel, my son!" He answered, "Here I am." 17 And he said, "What *is* the word that *the* Lord spoke to you? Please do not hide *it* from me. God do so to you, and more also, if you hide anything from me of all the things that He said to you." 18 Then Samuel told him everything, and hid nothing from him. And he said, "It *is* the Lord. Let Him do what seems good to Him." 19 So Samuel grew, and the Lord was with him and let none of his words fall to the ground. 20 And all Israel from Dan to Beersheba knew that Samuel *had been* established as a prophet of the Lord. 21 Then the Lord appeared again in Shiloh. For the Lord revealed Himself to Samuel in Shiloh by the word of the Lord. 4:1 And the word of Samuel came to all Israel. NKJV

(21) Psalms 139:14-16 NKJV
14 I will praise You, for I am fearfully *and* wonderfully made; marvelous are Your works, and *that* my soul knows very well. 15 My frame was not hidden from You, when I was made in secret, *and* skillfully wrought in the lowest parts of the earth. 16 Your eyes saw my substance, being yet unformed. And in Your book, they all were written, the days fashioned for me, when *as yet there were* none of them. NKJV

(22) 1 Corinthians 1:26-31 NKJV
26 For you see your calling, brethren, that not many wise according to the flesh, not many mighty, not many noble, *are called.* 27 But God has chosen the foolish things of the world to put to shame the wise, and God has chosen the weak things of the world to put to shame

the things which are mighty; 28 and the base things of the world and the things which are despised God has chosen, and the things which are not, to bring to nothing the things that are, 29 that no flesh should glory in His presence. 30 But of Him you are in Christ Jesus, who became for us wisdom from God — and righteousness and sanctification and redemption — 31 that, as it is written, *"He who glories, let him glory in the Lord."* * NKJV

CHAPTER 4
(23) Matthew 28:18-20 NKJV
18 And Jesus came and spoke to them, saying, "All authority has been given to Me in heaven and on earth. 19 Go therefore* and make disciples of all the nations, baptizing them in the name of the Father and of the Son and of the Holy Spirit, 20 teaching them to observe all things that I have commanded you; and lo, I am with you always, *even* to the end of the age." Amen.* NKJV

(24) 2 Timothy 1:7 KJV
7 For God hath not given us the spirit of fear; but of power, and of love, and of a sound mind. KJV

(25) Matthew 10:28 KJV
28 And fear not them which kill the body, but are not able to kill the soul: but rather fear him which is able to destroy both soul and body in hell. KJV

(26) Romans 12:1 – 16:27 NLT
12 And so, dear brothers and sisters,* I plead with you to give your bodies to God because of all he has done for you. Let them be a living and holy sacrifice—the kind he will find acceptable. This is truly the way to worship him.* 2 Don't copy the behavior and customs of this world, but let God transform you into a new person by changing the way you think. Then you will learn to know God's will for you, which is good and pleasing and perfect. 3 Because of the privilege and authority* God has given me, I give each of you this warning: Don't think you are better than you really are. Be honest in your evaluation of yourselves, measuring yourselves by the faith God has given us.* 4 Just as our bodies have many parts and each part has a special function, 5 so it is with Christ's body. We are many parts of one body, and we all belong to each other. 6 In his grace, God has given us different gifts for doing certain things well. So if God has given you the ability to prophesy, speak out with as much faith as God has given you. 7 If your gift is serving others, serve them well. If you are a teacher, teach well. 8 If your gift is to encourage others, be encouraging. If it is giving, give generously. If God has given you leadership ability, take the responsibility seriously. And if you have a gift for showing kindness to others, do it gladly. 9 Don't just pretend to love others. Really love them. Hate what is wrong. Hold tightly to what is good. 10 Love each other with genuine affection,* and take delight in honoring each other. 11 Never be lazy, but work hard and serve the Lord enthusiastically.* 12 Rejoice in our confident hope. Be patient in trouble, and keep on praying. 13 When God's people are in need, be ready to help them. Always be eager to practice hospitality. 14 Bless those who persecute you. Don't curse them; pray that God will bless them. 15 Be happy with those who are happy, and weep with those who weep. 16 Live in harmony with each other. Don't be too proud to enjoy the company of ordinary people. And don't think you know it all! 17 Never pay back evil with more evil. Do things in such a way that everyone can see you are honorable. 18 Do all that you can to live in peace with everyone. 19 Dear friends, never take revenge. Leave that to the righteous anger of God. For the Scriptures say, "I will take revenge; I will pay them back,"* says the Lord. 20 Instead, "If your enemies are hungry, feed them. If they

are thirsty, give them something to drink. In doing this, you will heap burning coals of shame on their heads."* 21 Don't let evil conquer you, but conquer evil by doing good.

Respect for Authority

13 Everyone must submit to governing authorities. For all authority comes from God, and those in positions of authority have been placed there by God. 2 So anyone who rebels against authority is rebelling against what God has instituted, and they will be punished. 3 For the authorities do not strike fear in people who are doing right, but in those who are doing wrong. Would you like to live without fear of the authorities? Do what is right, and they will honor you. 4 The authorities are God's servants, sent for your good. But if you are doing wrong, of course you should be afraid, for they have the power to punish you. They are God's servants, sent for the very purpose of punishing those who do what is wrong. 5 So you must submit to them, not only to avoid punishment, but also to keep a clear conscience. 6 Pay your taxes, too, for these same reasons. For government workers need to be paid. They are serving God in what they do. 7 Give to everyone what you owe them: Pay your taxes and government fees to those who collect them, and give respect and honor to those who are in authority.

Love Fulfills God's Requirements

8 Owe nothing to anyone—except for your obligation to love one another. If you love your neighbor, you will fulfill the requirements of God's law. 9 For the commandments say, "You must not commit adultery. You must not murder. You must not steal. You must not covet."* These—and other such commandments—are summed up in this one commandment: "Love your neighbor as yourself."* 10 Love does no wrong to others, so love fulfills the requirements of God's law. 11 This is all the more urgent, for you know how late it is; time is running out. Wake up, for our salvation is nearer now than when we first believed. 12 The night is almost gone; the day of salvation will soon be here. So remove your dark deeds like dirty clothes, and put on the shining armor of right living. 13 Because we belong to the day, we must live decent lives for all to see. Don't participate in the darkness of wild parties and drunkenness, or in sexual promiscuity and immoral living, or in quarreling and jealousy. 14 Instead, clothe yourself with the presence of the Lord Jesus Christ. And don't let yourself think about ways to indulge your evil desires.

The Danger of Criticism

14 Accept other believers who are weak in faith, and don't argue with them about what they think is right or wrong. 2 For instance, one person believes it's all right to eat anything. But another believer with a sensitive conscience will eat only vegetables. 3 Those who feel free to eat anything must not look down on those who don't. And those who don't eat certain foods must not condemn those who do, for God has accepted them. 4 Who are you to condemn someone else's servants? They are responsible to the Lord, so let him judge whether they are right or wrong. And with the Lord's help, they will do what is right and will receive his approval. 5 In the same way, some think one day is more holy than another day, while others think every day is alike. You should each be fully convinced that whichever day you choose is acceptable. 6 Those who worship the Lord on a special day do it to honor him. Those who eat any kind of food do so to honor the Lord, since they give thanks to God before eating. And those who refuse to eat certain foods also want to please the Lord and give thanks to God. 7 For we don't live for ourselves or die for ourselves. 8 If we live, it's to honor the Lord. And if we die, it's to honor the Lord. So whether we live or die, we belong to the Lord. 9 Christ died and rose again for this very purpose—to be Lord both of the living and of the dead. 10 So why do you condemn another believer*? Why do you look down on another believer? Remember, we will all stand before the judgment seat of God. 11 For the Scriptures say, "'As surely as I live,' says the Lord, 'every knee will bend to me, and every tongue will confess and give praise to God.*'" 12 Yes, each of us will give a personal account to God. 13 So let's stop condemning each other. Decide instead to

live in such a way that you will not cause another believer to stumble and fall. 14 I know and am convinced on the authority of the Lord Jesus that no food, in and of itself, is wrong to eat. But if someone believes it is wrong, then for that person it is wrong. 15 And if another believer is distressed by what you eat, you are not acting in love if you eat it. Don't let your eating ruin someone for whom Christ died. 16 Then you will not be criticized for doing something you believe is good. 17 For the Kingdom of God is not a matter of what we eat or drink, but of living a life of goodness and peace and joy in the Holy Spirit. 18 If you serve Christ with this attitude, you will please God, and others will approve of you, too. 19 So then, let us aim for harmony in the church and try to build each other up. 20 Don't tear apart the work of God over what you eat. Remember, all foods are acceptable, but it is wrong to eat something if it makes another person stumble. 21 It is better not to eat meat or drink wine or do anything else if it might cause another believer to stumble. 22 You may believe there's nothing wrong with what you are doing, but keep it between yourself and God. Blessed are those who don't feel guilty for doing something they have decided is right. 23 But if you have doubts about whether or not you should eat something, you are sinning if you go ahead and do it. For you are not following your convictions. If you do anything you believe is not right, you are sinning.

Living to Please Others

15 We who are strong must be considerate of those who are sensitive about things like this. We must not just please ourselves. 2 We should help others do what is right and build them up in the Lord. 3 For even Christ didn't live to please himself. As the Scriptures say, "The insults of those who insult you, O God, have fallen on me."* 4 Such things were written in the Scriptures long ago to teach us. And the Scriptures give us hope and encouragement as we wait patiently for God's promises to be fulfilled. 5 May God, who gives this patience and encouragement, help you live in complete harmony with each other, as is fitting for followers of Christ Jesus. 6 Then all of you can join together with one voice, giving praise and glory to God, the Father of our Lord Jesus Christ. 7 Therefore, accept each other just as Christ has accepted you so that God will be given glory. 8 Remember that Christ came as a servant to the Jews* to show that God is true to the promises he made to their ancestors. 9 He also came so that the Gentiles might give glory to God for his mercies to them. That is what the psalmist meant when he wrote: "For this, I will praise you among the Gentiles; I will sing praises to your name."* 10 And in another place it is written, "Rejoice with his people, you Gentiles."* 11 And yet again, "Praise the Lord, all you Gentiles. Praise him, all you people of the earth."* 12 And in another place Isaiah said, "The heir to David's throne* will come, and he will rule over the Gentiles. They will place their hope on him."* 13 I pray that God, the source of hope, will fill you completely with joy and peace because you trust in him. Then you will overflow with confident hope through the power of the Holy Spirit.

Paul's Reason for Writing

14 I am fully convinced, my dear brothers and sisters,* that you are full of goodness. You know these things so well you can teach each other all about them. 15 Even so, I have been bold enough to write about some of these points, knowing that all you need is this reminder. For by God's grace, 16 I am a special messenger from Christ Jesus to you Gentiles. I bring you the Good News so that I might present you as an acceptable offering to God, made holy by the Holy Spirit. 17 So I have reason to be enthusiastic about all Christ Jesus has done through me in my service to God. 18 Yet I dare not boast about anything except what Christ has done through me, bringing the Gentiles to God by my message and by the way I worked among them. 19 They were convinced by the power of miraculous signs and wonders and by the power of God's Spirit.* In this way, I have fully presented the Good News of Christ from Jerusalem all the way to Illyricum.* 20 My ambition has always been to preach the Good News where the name of Christ has never been heard, rather than where

a church has already been started by someone else. 21 I have been following the plan spoken of in the Scriptures, where it says, "Those who have never been told about him will see, and those who have never heard of him will understand."* 22 In fact, my visit to you has been delayed so long because I have been preaching in these places.

Paul's Travel Plans

23 But now I have finished my work in these regions, and after all these long years of waiting, I am eager to visit you. 24 I am planning to go to Spain, and when I do, I will stop off in Rome. And after I have enjoyed your fellowship for a little while, you can provide for my journey. 25 But before I come, I must go to Jerusalem to take a gift to the believers there. 26 For you see, the believers in Macedonia and Achaia* have eagerly taken up an offering for the poor among the believers in Jerusalem. 27 They were glad to do this because they feel they owe a real debt to them. Since the Gentiles received the spiritual blessings of the Good News from the believers in Jerusalem, they feel the least they can do in return is to help them financially. 28 As soon as I have delivered this money and completed this good deed of theirs, I will come to see you on my way to Spain. 29 And I am sure that when I come, Christ will richly bless our time together. 30 Dear brothers and sisters, I urge you in the name of our Lord Jesus Christ to join in my struggle by praying to God for me. Do this because of your love for me, given to you by the Holy Spirit. 31 Pray that I will be rescued from those in Judea who refuse to obey God. Pray also that the believers there will be willing to accept the donation* I am taking to Jerusalem. 32 Then, by the will of God, I will be able to come to you with a joyful heart, and we will be an encouragement to each other. 33 And now may God, who gives us his peace, be with you all. Amen.*

Paul Greets His Friends

16 I commend to you our sister Phoebe, who is a deacon in the church in Cenchrea. 2 Welcome her in the Lord as one who is worthy of honor among God's people. Help her in whatever she needs, for she has been helpful to many, and especially to me. 3 Give my greetings to Priscilla and Aquila, my co-workers in the ministry of Christ Jesus. 4 In fact, they once risked their lives for me. I am thankful to them, and so are all the Gentile churches. 5 Also give my greetings to the church that meets in their home. Greet my dear friend Epenetus. He was the first person from the province of Asia to become a follower of Christ. 6 Give my greetings to Mary, who has worked so hard for your benefit. 7 Greet Andronicus and Junia,* my fellow Jews,* who were in prison with me. They are highly respected among the apostles and became followers of Christ before I did. 8 Greet Ampliatus, my dear friend in the Lord. 9 Greet Urbanus, our co-worker in Christ, and my dear friend Stachys. 10 Greet Apelles, a good man whom Christ approves. And give my greetings to the believers from the household of Aristobulus. 11 Greet Herodion, my fellow Jew.* Greet the Lord's people from the household of Narcissus. 12 Give my greetings to Tryphena and Tryphosa, the Lord's workers, and to dear Persis, who has worked so hard for the Lord. 13 Greet Rufus, whom the Lord picked out to be his very own; and also his dear mother, who has been a mother to me. 14 Give my greetings to Asyncritus, Phlegon, Hermes, Patrobas, Hermas, and the brothers and sisters* who meet with them. 15 Give my greetings to Philologus, Julia, Nereus and his sister, and to Olympas and all the believers who meet with them. 16 Greet each other in Christian love.* All the churches of Christ send you their greetings.

Paul's Final Instructions

17 And now I make one more appeal, my dear brothers and sisters. Watch out for people who cause divisions and upset people's faith by teaching things contrary to what you have been taught. Stay away from them. 18 Such people are not serving Christ our Lord; they are serving their own personal interests. By smooth talk and glowing words they deceive innocent people. 19 But everyone knows that you are obedient to the Lord. This makes me

very happy. I want you to be wise in doing right and to stay innocent of any wrong. 20 The God of peace will soon crush Satan under your feet. May the grace of our Lord Jesus* be with you. 21 Timothy, my fellow worker, sends you his greetings, as do Lucius, Jason, and Sosipater, my fellow Jews. 22 I, Tertius, the one writing this letter for Paul, send my greetings, too, as one of the Lord's followers. 23 Gaius says hello to you. He is my host and also serves as host to the whole church. Erastus, the city treasurer, sends you his greetings, and so does our brother Quartus.* 25 Now all glory to God, who is able to make you strong, just as my Good News says. This message about Jesus Christ has revealed his plan for you Gentiles, a plan kept secret from the beginning of time. 26 But now as the prophets* foretold and as the eternal God has commanded, this message is made known to all Gentiles everywhere, so that they too might believe and obey him. 27 All glory to the only wise God, through Jesus Christ, forever. Amen. Holy Bible, New Living Translation ®, copyright © 1996, 2004 by Tyndale Charitable Trust. Used by permission of Tyndale House Publishers. All rights reserved.

CHAPTER 5
(27) Matthew 20:18-19 KJV
18 Behold, we go up to Jerusalem; and the Son of man shall be betrayed unto the chief priests and unto the scribes, and they shall condemn him to death, 19 and shall deliver him to the Gentiles to mock, and to scourge, and to crucify him: and the third day he shall rise again. KJV

(28; 29) Matthew 20:20-23 KJV
20 Then came to him the mother of Zebedee's children with her sons, worshipping him, and desiring a certain thing of him. 21 And he said unto her, "What wilt thou?" She saith unto him, "Grant that these my two sons may sit, the one on thy right hand, and the other on the left, in thy kingdom. 22 But Jesus answered and said, "Ye know not what ye ask. Are ye able to drink of the cup that I shall drink of, and to be baptized with the baptism that I am baptized with?" They say unto him, "We are able." 23 And he saith unto them, "Ye shall drink indeed of my cup, and be baptized with the baptism that I am baptized with: but to sit on my right hand, and on my left, is not mine to give, but it shall be given to them for whom it is prepared of my Father." KJV

(30) Ecclesiastes 3:1-22 KJV
1 To everything there is a season, and a time to every purpose under the heaven: 2 A time to be born, and a time to die; a time to plant, and a time to pluck up that which is planted; 3 A time to kill, and a time to heal; a time to break down, and a time to build up; 4 A time to weep, and a time to laugh; a time to mourn, and a time to dance; 5 time to cast away stones, and a time to gather stones together; a time to embrace, and a time to refrain from embracing; 6 A time to get, and a time to lose; a time to keep, and a time to cast away; 7 A time to rend, and a time to sew; a time to keep silence, and a time to speak; 8 A time to love, and a time to hate; a time of war, and a time of peace. 9 What profit hath he that worketh in that wherein he laboureth? 10 I have seen the travail, which God hath given to the sons of men to be exercised in it. 11 He hath made everything beautiful in his time: also he hath set the world in their heart, so that no man can find out the work that God maketh from the beginning to the end. 12 I know that there is no good in them, but for a man to rejoice, and to do good in his life. 13 And also that every man should eat and drink, and enjoy the good of all his labour, it is the gift of God. 14 I know that, whatsoever God doeth, it shall be forever: nothing can be put to it, nor any thing taken from it: and God doeth it, that men should fear before him. 15 That which hath been is now; and that which is to be hath already been; and God requireth that which is past. 16 And moreover I saw under the

sun the place of judgment, that wickedness was there; and the place of righteousness, that iniquity was there. 17 I said in mine heart, God shall judge the righteous and the wicked: for there is a time there for every purpose and for every work. 18 I said in mine heart concerning the estate of the sons of men, that God might manifest them, and that they might see that they themselves are beasts. 19 For that which befalleth the sons of men befalleth beasts; even one thing befalleth them: as the one dieth, so dieth the other; yea, they have all one breath; so that a man hath no preeminence above a beast: for all is vanity. 20 All go unto one place; all are of the dust, and all turn to dust again. 21 Who knoweth the spirit of man that goeth upward, and the spirit of the beast that goeth downward to the earth? 22 Wherefore I perceive that there is nothing better, than that a man should rejoice in his own works; for that is his portion: for who shall bring him to see what shall be after him? KJV

CHAPTER 6
(31) Revelation 13:8 KJV
And all that dwell upon the earth shall worship him, whose names are not written in the book of life of the Lamb slain from the foundation of the world. KJV

(32) Matthew 2:1-23 KJV
1 Now when Jesus was born in Bethlehem of Judaea in the days of Herod the king, behold, there came wise men from the east to Jerusalem, 2 Saying, Where is he that is born King of the Jews? for we have seen his star in the east, and are come to worship him. 3 When Herod the king had heard these things, he was troubled, and all Jerusalem with him. 4 And when he had gathered all the chief priests and scribes of the people together, he demanded of them where Christ should be born. 5 And they said unto him, In Bethlehem of Judaea: for thus it is written by the prophet, 6 And thou Bethlehem, in the land of Juda, art not the least among the princes of Juda: for out of thee shall come a Governor, that shall rule my people Israel. 7 Then Herod, when he had privily called the wise men, inquired of them diligently what time the star appeared. And he sent them to Bethlehem, and said, Go and search diligently for the young child; and when ye have found him, bring me word again, that I may come and worship him also. 9 When they had heard the king, they departed; and, lo, the star, which they saw in the east, went before them, till it came and stood over where the young child was. 10 When they saw the star, they rejoiced with exceeding great joy. 11 And when they were come into the house, they saw the young child with Mary his mother, and fell down, and worshipped him: and when they had opened their treasures, they presented unto him gifts; gold, and frankincense, and myrrh. 12 And being warned of God in a dream that they should not return to Herod, they departed into their own country another way. 13 And when they were departed, behold, the angel of the Lord appeareth to Joseph in a dream, saying, Arise, and take the young child and his mother, and flee into Egypt, and be thou there until I bring thee word: for Herod will seek the young child to destroy him. 14 When he arose, he took the young child and his mother by night, and departed into Egypt: 15 And was there until the death of Herod: that it might be fulfilled which was spoken of the Lord by the prophet, saying, Out of Egypt have I called my son. 16 Then Herod, when he saw that he was mocked of the wise men, was exceeding wroth, and sent forth, and slew all the children that were in Bethlehem, and in all the coasts thereof, from two years old and under, according to the time which he had diligently inquired of the wise men. 17 Then was fulfilled that which was spoken by Jeremy the prophet, saying, 18 In Rama was there a voice heard, lamentation, and weeping, and great mourning, Rachel weeping for her children, and would not be comforted, because they are not. 19 But when Herod was dead, behold, an angel of the Lord appeareth in a dream to Joseph in Egypt, 20 Saying, Arise, and take the young child and his mother, and go into the land of Israel: for they are dead which sought the young child's life. 21 And he arose, and took the young

child and his mother, and came into the land of Israel. 22 But when he heard that Archelaus did reign in Judaea in the room of his father Herod, he was afraid to go thither: notwithstanding, being warned of God in a dream, he turned aside into the parts of Galilee: 23 And he came and dwelt in a city called Nazareth: that it might be fulfilled which was spoken by the prophets, He shall be called a Nazarene. KJV

(33) John 8:44-52 KJV
44 Ye are of your father the devil, and the lusts of your father ye will do. He was a murderer from the beginning, and abode not in the truth, because there is no truth in him. When he speaketh a lie, he speaketh of his own: for he is a liar, and the father of it. 45 And because I tell you the truth, ye believe me not. 46 Which of you convinceth me of sin? And if I say the truth, why do ye not believe me? 47 He that is of God heareth God's words: ye therefore hear them not, because ye are not of God. 48 Then answered the Jews, and said unto him, Say we not well that thou art a Samaritan, and hast a devil? Jesus answered, I have not a devil; but I honour my Father, and ye do dishonour me. 50 And I seek not mine own glory: there is one that seeketh and judgeth. 51 Verily, verily, I say unto you, If a man keep my saying, he shall never see death. 52 Then said the Jews unto him, Now we know that thou hast a devil. Abraham is dead, and the prophets; and thou sayest, If a man keep my saying, he shall never taste of death. KJV

(34) John 1:1-14 KJV
1 In the beginning was the Word, and the Word was with God, and the Word was God. 2 The same was in the beginning with God. 3 All things were made by him; and without him was not anything made that was made. 4 In him was life; and the life was the light of men. 5 And the light shineth in darkness; and the darkness comprehended it not. 6 There was a man sent from God, whose name was John. 7 The same came for a witness, to bear witness of the Light, that all men through him might believe. 8 He was not that Light, but was sent to bear witness of that Light. 9 That was the true Light, which lighteth every man that cometh into the world. 10 He was in the world, and the world was made by him, and the world knew him not. 11 He came unto his own, and his own received him not. 12 But as many as received him, to them gave he power to become the sons of God, even to them that believe on his name: 13 Which were born, not of blood, nor of the will of the flesh, nor of the will of man, but of God. 14 And the Word was made flesh, and dwelt among us, (and we beheld his glory, the glory as of the only begotten of the Father,) full of grace and truth. KJV

(35) 2 Timothy 4:1-4 KJV
1 I charge thee therefore before God, and the Lord Jesus Christ, who shall judge the quick and the dead at his appearing and his kingdom; 2 Preach the word; be instant in season, out of season; reprove, rebuke, exhort with all longsuffering and doctrine. 3 For the time will come when they will not endure sound doctrine; but after their own lusts shall they heap to themselves teachers, having itching ears; 4 And they shall turn away their ears from the truth, and shall be turned unto fables. KJV

(36) Hebrews 12:3-4 KJV
3 For consider him that endured such contradiction of sinners against himself, lest ye be wearied and faint in your minds. 4 Ye have not yet resisted unto blood, striving against sin. KJV

(37) Revelation 12:7-9 NKJV

7 And war broke out in heaven: Michael and his angels fought with the dragon; and the dragon and his angels fought, 8 but they did not prevail, nor was a place found for them in heaven any longer. 9 So the great dragon was cast out, that serpent of old, called the Devil and Satan, who deceives the whole world; he was cast to the earth, and his angels were cast out with him. NKJV

(38) 1 John 3:1-10 NLT
1 See how very much our Father loves us, for he calls us his children, and that is what we are! But the people who belong to this world don't recognize that we are God's children because they don't know him. 2 Dear friends, we are already God's children, but he has not yet shown us what we will be like when Christ appears. But we do know that we will be like him, for we will see him as he really is. 3 And all who have this eager expectation will keep themselves pure, just as he is pure. 4 Everyone who sins is breaking God's law, for all sin is contrary to the law of God. 5 And you know that Jesus came to take away our sins, and there is no sin in him. 6 Anyone who continues to live in him will not sin. But anyone who keeps on sinning does not know him or understand who he is. 7 Dear children, don't let anyone deceive you about this: When people do what is right, it shows that they are righteous, even as Christ is righteous. 8 But when people keep on sinning, it shows that they belong to the devil, who has been sinning since the beginning. But the Son of God came to destroy the works of the devil. 9 Those who have been born into God's family do not make a practice of sinning, because God's life is in them. So they can't keep on sinning, because they are children of God. 10 So now we can tell who are children of God and who are children of the devil. Anyone who does not live righteously and does not love other believers does not belong to God. (Holy Bible, New Living Translation ®, copyright © 1996, 2004 by Tyndale Charitable Trust. Used by permission of Tyndale House Publishers. All rights reserved).

CHAPTER 7
(39) Hebrews 4:14-16 NLT
14 So then, since we have a great High Priest who has entered heaven, Jesus the Son of God, let us hold firmly to what we believe. 15 This High Priest of ours understands our weaknesses, for he faced all of the same testings we do, yet he did not sin. 16 So let us come boldly to the throne of our gracious God. There we will receive his mercy, and we will find grace to help us when we need it most. (Holy Bible, New Living Translation ®, copyright © 1996, 2004 by Tyndale Charitable Trust. Used by permission of Tyndale House Publishers. All rights reserved).

(40) James 1:12-18 NLT
12 God blesses those who patiently endure testing and temptation. Afterward they will receive the crown of life that God has promised to those who love him. 13 And remember, when you are being tempted, do not say, "God is tempting me." God is never tempted to do wrong, and he never tempts anyone else. 14 Temptation comes from our own desires, which entice us and drag us away. 15 These desires give birth to sinful actions. And when sin is allowed to grow, it gives birth to death. 16 So don't be misled, my dear brothers and sisters. 17 Whatever is good and perfect comes down to us from God our Father, who created all the lights in the heavens. He never changes or casts a shifting shadow. 18 He chose to give birth to us by giving us his true word. And we, out of all creation, became his prized possession. (Holy Bible, New Living Translation ®, copyright © 1996, 2004 by Tyndale Charitable Trust. Used by permission of Tyndale House Publishers. All rights reserved).

(41) Genesis 3:6-13 KJV

6 And when the woman saw that the tree was good for food, and that it was pleasant to the eyes, and a tree to be desired to make one wise, she took of the fruit thereof, and did eat, and gave also unto her husband with her; and he did eat. 7 And the eyes of them both were opened, and they knew that they were naked; and they sewed fig leaves together, and made themselves aprons. 8 And they heard the voice of the Lord God walking in the garden in the cool of the day: and Adam and his wife hid themselves from the presence of the Lord God amongst the trees of the garden. 9 And the Lord God called unto Adam, and said unto him, Where art thou? 10 And he said, I heard thy voice in the garden, and I was afraid, because I was naked; and I hid myself. 11 And he said, Who told thee that thou wast naked? Hast thou eaten of the tree, whereof I commanded thee that thou shouldest not eat? 12 And the man said, The woman whom thou gavest to be with me, she gave me of the tree, and I did eat. 13 And the Lord God said unto the woman, What is this that thou hast done? And the woman said, The serpent beguiled me, and I did eat. KJV

(42) Job 1:9-13 NKJV

9 So Satan answered the Lord and said, "Does Job fear God for nothing? 10 Have You not made a hedge around him, around his household, and around all that he has on every side? You have blessed the work of his hands, and his possessions have increased in the land. 11 But now, stretch out Your hand and touch all that he has, and he will surely curse You to Your face!" 12 And the Lord said to Satan, "Behold, all that he has *is* in your power; only do not lay a hand on his *person.*" So Satan went out from the presence of the Lord. NKJV

(43) Job 42:12-17 NLT

12 So the Lord blessed Job in the second half of his life even more than in the beginning. For now he had 14,000 sheep, 6,000 camels, 1,000 teams of oxen, and 1,000 female donkeys. 13 He also gave Job seven more sons and three more daughters. 14 He named his first daughter Jemimah, the second Keziah, and the third Keren-happuch. 15 In all the land no women were as lovely as the daughters of Job. And their father put them into his will along with their brothers. 16 Job lived 140 years after that, living to see four generations of his children and grandchildren. 17 Then he died, an old man who had lived a long, full life. (Holy Bible, New Living Translation ®, copyright © 1996, 2004 by Tyndale Charitable Trust. Used by permission of Tyndale House Publishers. All rights reserved).

(44) Hebrews 4:15 KJV

For we have not an high priest which cannot be touched with the feeling of our infirmities; but was in all points tempted like as we are, yet without sin. KJV

(45; 46; 47; 48; 49) Luke 4:1-13 NLT

1 Then Jesus, full of the Holy Spirit, returned from the Jordan River. He was led by the Spirit in the wilderness, 2 where he was tempted by the devil for forty days. Jesus ate nothing all that time and became very hungry. 3 Then the devil said to him, "If you are the Son of God, change this stone into a loaf of bread." 4 But Jesus told him, "No! The Scriptures say, 'People do not live by bread alone.'" 5 Then the devil took him up and revealed to him all the kingdoms of the world in a moment of time. 6 "I will give you the glory of these kingdoms and authority over them," the devil said, "because they are mine to give to anyone I please. 7 I will give it all to you if you will worship me." 8 Jesus replied, "The Scriptures say, 'You must worship the LORD your God and serve only him.'" 9 Then the devil took him to Jerusalem, to the highest point of the Temple, and said, "If you are the Son of God, jump off! 10 For the Scriptures say, 'He will order his angels to protect and guard you. 11 And they will hold you up with their hands so you won't even hurt your

foot on a stone.'" 12 Jesus responded, "The Scriptures also say, 'You must not test the LORD your God.'" 13 When the devil had finished tempting Jesus, he left him until the next opportunity came. (Holy Bible, New Living Translation ®, copyright © 1996, 2004 by Tyndale Charitable Trust. Used by permission of Tyndale House Publishers. All rights reserved).

(50) Romans 8:1-5 ESV
1 There is therefore now no condemnation for those who are in Christ Jesus. 2 For the law of the Spirit of life has set you free in Christ Jesus from the law of sin and death. 3 For God has done what the law, weakened by the flesh, could not do. By sending his own Son in the likeness of sinful flesh and for sin, he condemned sin in the flesh, 4 in order that the righteous requirement of the law might be fulfilled in us, who walk not according to the flesh but according to the Spirit. 5 For those who live according to the flesh set their minds on the things of the flesh, but those who live according to the Spirit set their minds on the things of the Spirit. ESV

(51) 1 John 3:19-21 KJV
19 And hereby we know that we are of the truth, and shall assure our hearts before him. 20 For if our heart condemn us, God is greater than our heart, and knoweth all things. 21 Beloved, if our heart condemn us not, then have we confidence toward God. KJV

(52) 1 Corinthians 14:33 KJV
For God is not the author of confusion, but of peace, as in all churches of the saints. KJV

(53) James 3:16-18 KJV
16 For where envying and strife is, there is confusion and every evil work. 17 But the wisdom that is from above is first pure, then peaceable, gentle, and easy to be intreated, full of mercy and good fruits, without partiality, and without hypocrisy. 18 And the fruit of righteousness is sown in peace of them that make peace. KJV

(54) Hebrews 11:6 KJV
But without faith it is impossible to please him: for he that cometh to God must believe that he is, and that he is a rewarder of them that diligently seek him. KJV

(55) 2 Tim 1:7-12 KJV
7 For God hath not given us the spirit of fear; but of power, and of love, and of a sound mind. 8 Be not thou therefore ashamed of the testimony of our Lord, nor of me his prisoner: but be thou partaker of the afflictions of the gospel according to the power of God; 9 Who hath saved us, and called us with an holy calling, not according to our works, but according to his own purpose and grace, which was given us in Christ Jesus before the world began, 10 But is now made manifest by the appearing of our Saviour Jesus Christ, who hath abolished death, and hath brought life and immortality to light through the gospel: 11 Whereunto I am appointed a preacher, and an apostle, and a teacher of the Gentiles. 12 For the which cause I also suffer these things: nevertheless I am not ashamed: for I know whom I have believed, and am persuaded that he is able to keep that which I have committed unto him against that day. KJV

(56) 1 John 4:18 KJV
There is no fear in love; but perfect love casteth out fear: because fear hath torment. He that feareth is not made perfect in love. KJV

(57) Proverbs 9:10-11 KJV
10 The fear of the Lord is the beginning of wisdom: and the knowledge of the holy is understanding. 11 For by me thy days shall be multiplied, and the years of thy life shall be increased. KJV

(58) 2 Corinthians 7:1 KJV
Having therefore these promises, dearly beloved, let us cleanse ourselves from all filthiness of the flesh and spirit, perfecting holiness in the fear of God. KJV

(59) Ephesians 6:10-12 NLT
10 A final word: Be strong in the Lord and in his mighty power. 11 Put on all of God's armor so that you will be able to stand firm against all strategies of the devil. 12 For we are not fighting against flesh-and-blood enemies, but against evil rulers and authorities of the unseen world, against mighty powers in this dark world, and against evil spirits in the heavenly places. (Holy Bible, New Living Translation ®, copyright © 1996, 2004 by Tyndale Charitable Trust. Used by permission of Tyndale House Publishers. All rights reserved).

CHAPTER 8
(60) James 1:19-21 NLT
19 Understand this, my dear brothers and sisters: You must all be quick to listen, slow to speak, and slow to get angry. 20 Human anger* does not produce the righteousness* God desires. 21 So get rid of all the filth and evil in your lives, and humbly accept the word God has planted in your hearts, for it has the power to save your souls. Holy Bible, New Living Translation ®, copyright © 1996, 2004 by Tyndale Charitable Trust. Used by permission of Tyndale House Publishers. All rights reserved.

(61) James 5:13-18 NLT
13 Are any of you suffering hardships? You should pray. Are any of you happy? You should sing praises. 14 Are any of you sick? You should call for the elders of the church to come and pray over you, anointing you with oil in the name of the Lord. 15 Such a prayer offered in faith will heal the sick, and the Lord will make you well. And if you have committed any sins, you will be forgiven. 16 Confess your sins to each other and pray for each other so that you may be healed. The earnest prayer of a righteous person has great power and produces wonderful results. 17 Elijah was as human as we are, and yet when he prayed earnestly that no rain would fall, none fell for three and a half years! 18 Then, when he prayed again, the sky sent down rain and the earth began to yield its crops. Holy Bible, New Living Translation ®, copyright © 1996, 2004 by Tyndale Charitable Trust. Used by permission of Tyndale House Publishers. All rights reserved.

(62) Philippians 4:6-7 NLT
6 Don't worry about anything; instead, pray about everything. Tell God what you need, and thank him for all he has done. 7 Then you will experience God's peace, which exceeds anything we can understand. His peace will guard your hearts and minds as you live in Christ Jesus. Holy Bible, New Living Translation ®, copyright © 1996, 2004 by Tyndale Charitable Trust. Used by permission of Tyndale House Publishers. All rights reserved.

(63) 1 Peter 4:7-8 NLT
7 The end of the world is coming soon. Therefore, be earnest and disciplined in your prayers. 8 Most important of all, continue to show deep love for each other, for love covers a multitude of sins. Holy Bible, New Living Translation ®, copyright © 1996, 2004 by

(64) Luke 11:1 KJV
11 And it came to pass, that, as he was praying in a certain place, when he ceased, one of his disciples said unto him, Lord, teach us to pray, as John also taught his disciples. KJV

(65) Luke 11:2-4 KJV
2 And he said unto them, When ye pray, say, Our Father which art in heaven, Hallowed be thy name. Thy kingdom come. Thy will be done, as in heaven, so in earth. 3 Give us day by day our daily bread. 4 And forgive us our sins; for we also forgive every one that is indebted to us. And lead us not into temptation; but deliver us from evil. KJV

(66) Psalms 46 KJV
46 God is our refuge and strength, a very present help in trouble. 2 Therefore will not we fear, though the earth be removed, and though the mountains be carried into the midst of the sea; 3 Though the waters thereof roar and be troubled, though the mountains shake with the swelling thereof. Selah. 4 There is a river, the streams whereof shall make glad the city of God, the holy place of the tabernacles of the most High. 5 God is in the midst of her; she shall not be moved: God shall help her, and that right early. 6 The heathen raged, the kingdoms were moved: he uttered his voice, the earth melted. 7 The Lord of hosts is with us; the God of Jacob is our refuge. Selah. 8 Come, behold the works of the Lord , what desolations he hath made in the earth. 9 He maketh wars to cease unto the end of the earth; he breaketh the bow, and cutteth the spear in sunder; he burneth the chariot in the fire. 10 Be still, and know that I am God: I will be exalted among the heathen, I will be exalted in the earth. 11 The Lord of hosts is with us; the God of Jacob is our refuge. Selah. KJV

(67) Colossians 1:11-22 NLT
11 We also pray that you will be strengthened with all his glorious power so you will have all the endurance and patience you need. May you be filled with joy,* 12 always thanking the Father. He has enabled you to share in the inheritance that belongs to his people, who live in the light. 13 For he has rescued us from the kingdom of darkness and transferred us into the Kingdom of his dear Son, 14 who purchased our freedom* and forgave our sins.
Christ Is Supreme
15 Christ is the visible image of the invisible God. He existed before anything was created and is supreme over all creation,* 16 for through him God created everything in the heavenly realms and on earth. He made the things we can see and the things we can't see— such as thrones, kingdoms, rulers, and authorities in the unseen world. Everything was created through him and for him. 17 He existed before anything else, and he holds all creation together. 18 Christ is also the head of the church, which is his body. He is the beginning, supreme over all who rise from the dead.* So he is first in everything. 19 For God in all his fullness was pleased to live in Christ, 20 and through him God reconciled everything to himself. He made peace with everything in heaven and on earth by means of Christ's blood on the cross. 21 This includes you who were once far away from God. You were his enemies, separated from him by your evil thoughts and actions. 22 Yet now he has reconciled you to himself through the death of Christ in his physical body. As a result, he has brought you into his own presence, and you are holy and blameless as you stand before him without a single fault.

(68) 1 John 5:14-15 NKJV
14 Now this is the confidence that we have in Him, that if we ask anything according to His will, He hears us. 15 And if we know that He hears us, whatever we ask, we know that we have the petitions that we have asked of Him. NKJV

(69) James 4:2-3 NLT
2 You want what you don't have, so you scheme and kill to get it. You are jealous of what others have, but you can't get it, so you fight and wage war to take it away from them. Yet you don't have what you want because you don't ask God for it. 3 And even when you ask, you don't get it because your motives are all wrong—you want only what will give you pleasure. Holy Bible, New Living Translation ®, copyright © 1996, 2004 by Tyndale Charitable Trust. Used by permission of Tyndale House Publishers. All rights reserved.

(70) Genesis 1:1-5 KJV
1 In the beginning God created the Heaven and the earth. 2 And the earth was without form, and void; and darkness was upon the face of the deep. And the Spirit of God moved upon the face of the waters. 3 And God said, Let there be light: and there was light. 4 And God saw the light, that it was good: and God divided the light from the darkness. 5 And God called the light Day, and the darkness he called Night. And the evening and the morning were the first day. KJV

(71) John 8:12 KJV
12 Then spake Jesus again unto them, saying, I am the light of the world: he that followeth me shall not walk in darkness, but shall have the light of life. KJV

(72) John 9:4-5 KJV
4 I must work the works of him that sent me, while it is day: the night cometh, when no man can work. 5 As long as I am in the world, I am the light of the world. KJV

(73) John 1:1-5 NLT
1 1 In the beginning the Word already existed. The Word was with God, and the Word was God. 2 He existed in the beginning with God. 3 God created everything through him, and nothing was created except through him. 4 The Word gave life to everything that was created,* and his life brought light to everyone. 5 The light shines in the darkness, and the darkness can never extinguish it.* Holy Bible, New Living Translation ®, copyright © 1996, 2004 by Tyndale Charitable Trust. Used by permission of Tyndale House Publishers. All rights reserved.

(74) John 1:6-13 NLT
6 God sent a man, John the Baptist,* 7 to tell about the light so that everyone might believe because of his testimony. 8 John himself was not the light; he was simply a witness to tell about the light. 9 The one who is the true light, who gives light to everyone, was coming into the world. 10 He came into the very world he created, but the world didn't recognize him. 11 He came to his own people, and even they rejected him. 12 But to all who believed him and accepted him, he gave the right to become children of God. 13 They are reborn— not with a physical birth resulting from human passion or plan, but a birth that comes from God. Holy Bible, New Living Translation ®, copyright © 1996, 2004 by Tyndale Charitable Trust. Used by permission of Tyndale House Publishers. All rights reserved.

(75) John 1:14-18 NLT

14 So the Word became human* and made his home among us. He was full of unfailing love and faithfulness.* And we have seen his glory, the glory of the Father's one and only Son. 15 John testified about him when he shouted to the crowds, "This is the one I was talking about when I said, 'Someone is coming after me who is far greater than I am, for he existed long before me.'" 16 From his abundance we have all received one gracious blessing after another.* 17 For the law was given through Moses, but God's unfailing love and faithfulness came through Jesus Christ. 18 No one has ever seen God. But the one and only Son is himself God and* is near to the Father's heart. He has revealed God to us. Holy Bible, New Living Translation ®, copyright © 1996, 2004 by Tyndale Charitable Trust. Used by permission of Tyndale House Publishers. All rights reserved.

(76) Luke 12:22-32 NKJV
22 Then He said to His disciples, "Therefore I say to you, do not worry about your life, what you will eat; nor about the body, what you will put on. 23 Life is more than food, and the body *is more* than clothing. 24 Consider the ravens, for they neither sow nor reap, which have neither storehouse nor barn; and God feeds them. Of how much more value are you than the birds? 25 And which of you by worrying can add one cubit to his stature? 26 If you then are not able to do *the* least, why are you anxious for the rest? 27 Consider the lilies, how they grow: they neither toil nor spin; and yet I say to you, even Solomon in all his glory was not arrayed like one of these. 28 If then God so clothes the grass, which today is in the field and tomorrow is thrown into the oven, how much more *will He clothe* you, O *you* of little faith? 29 "And do not seek what you should eat or what you should drink, nor have an anxious mind. 30 For all these things the nations of the world seek after, and your Father knows that you need these things. 31 But seek the kingdom of God, and all these things* shall be added to you. 32 "Do not fear, little flock, for it is your Father's good pleasure to give you the kingdom. NKJV

(77) 1 John 1:8-2:2 NLT
8 If we claim we have no sin, we are only fooling ourselves and not living in the truth. 9 But if we confess our sins to him, he is faithful and just to forgive us our sins and to cleanse us from all wickedness. 10 If we claim we have not sinned, we are calling God a liar and showing that his word has no place in our hearts. 2 My dear children, I am writing this to you so that you will not sin. But if anyone does sin, we have an advocate who pleads our case before the Father. He is Jesus Christ, the one who is truly righteous. 2 He himself is the sacrifice that atones for our sins—and not only our sins but the sins of all the world. Holy Bible, New Living Translation ®, copyright © 1996, 2004 by Tyndale Charitable Trust. Used by permission of Tyndale House Publishers. All rights reserved.

(78) Mark 2:1-12 NLT
2 When Jesus returned to Capernaum several days later, the news spread quickly that he was back home. 2 Soon the house where he was staying was so packed with visitors that there was no more room, even outside the door. While he was preaching God's word to them, 3 four men arrived carrying a paralyzed man on a mat. 4 They couldn't bring him to Jesus because of the crowd, so they dug a hole through the roof above his head. Then they lowered the man on his mat, right down in front of Jesus. 5 Seeing their faith, Jesus said to the paralyzed man, "My child, your sins are forgiven." 6 But some of the teachers of religious law who were sitting there thought to themselves, 7 "What is he saying? This is blasphemy! Only God can forgive sins!" 8 Jesus knew immediately what they were thinking, so he asked them, "Why do you question this in your hearts? 9 Is it easier to say to the paralyzed man 'Your sins are forgiven,' or 'Stand up, pick up your mat, and walk'? 10 So I will prove to you that the Son of Man* has the authority on earth to forgive sins."

Then Jesus turned to the paralyzed man and said, 11 "Stand up, pick up your mat, and go home!" 12 And the man jumped up, grabbed his mat, and walked out through the stunned onlookers. They were all amazed and praised God, exclaiming, "We've never seen anything like this before!" Holy Bible, New Living Translation ®, copyright © 1996, 2004 by Tyndale Charitable Trust. Used by permission of Tyndale House Publishers. All rights reserved.

(79) Matthew 5:21-24 CEV
21 You know that our ancestors were told, "Do not murder" and "A murderer must be brought to trial." 22 But I promise you that if you are angry with someone,v you will have to stand trial. If you call someone a fool, you will be taken to court. And if you say that someone is worthless, you will be in danger of the fires of hell. 23 So if you are about to place your gift on the altar and remember that someone is angry with you, 24 leave your gift there in front of the altar. Make peace with that person, then come back and offer your gift to God. CEV

(80) Luke 17:3-4 KJV
3 Take heed to yourselves: If thy brother trespass against thee, rebuke him; and if he repent, forgive him. 4 And if he trespass against thee seven times in a day, and seven times in a day turn again to thee, saying, I repent; thou shalt forgive him. KJV

(81) 2 Corinthians 2:5-11 NLT
5 I am not overstating it when I say that the man who caused all the trouble hurt all of you more than he hurt me. 6 Most of you opposed him, and that was punishment enough. 7 Now, however, it is time to forgive and comfort him. Otherwise he may be overcome by discouragement. 8 So I urge you now to reaffirm your love for him. 9 I wrote to you as I did to test you and see if you would fully comply with my instructions. 10 When you forgive this man, I forgive him, too. And when I forgive whatever needs to be forgiven, I do so with Christ's authority for your benefit, 11 so that Satan will not outsmart us. For we are familiar with his evil schemes. Holy Bible, New Living Translation ®, copyright © 1996, 2004 by Tyndale Charitable Trust. Used by permission of Tyndale House Publishers. All rights reserved.

(82) James 1:13 KJV
13 Let no man say when he is tempted, I am tempted of God: for God cannot be tempted with evil, neither tempteth he any man: KJV

(83) James 1:12-15 NLT
12 God blesses those who patiently endure testing and temptation. Afterward they will receive the crown of life that God has promised to those who love him. 13 And remember, when you are being tempted, do not say, "God is tempting me." God is never tempted to do wrong,* and he never tempts anyone else. 14 Temptation comes from our own desires, which entice us and drag us away. 15 These desires give birth to sinful actions. And when sin is allowed to grow, it gives birth to death. Holy Bible, New Living Translation ®, copyright © 1996, 2004 by Tyndale Charitable Trust. Used by permission of Tyndale House Publishers. All rights reserved.

(84) 2 Timothy 3:13-14 NLT
13 But evil people and impostors will flourish. They will deceive others and will themselves be deceived. 14 But you must remain faithful to the things you have been taught. You know they are true, for you know you can trust those who taught you. Holy

(85) John 3:19-21 KJV
19 And this is the condemnation, that light is come into the world, and men loved darkness rather than light, because their deeds were evil. 20 For every one that doeth evil hateth the light, neither cometh to the light, lest his deeds should be reproved. 21 But he that doeth truth cometh to the light, that his deeds may be made manifest, that they are wrought in God. KJV

(86) 3 John 11 KJV
11 Beloved, follow not that which is evil, but that which is good. He that doeth good is of God: but he that doeth evil hath not seen God. KJV

CHAPTER 9
(87) Matthew 26:36-46 NLT
36 Then Jesus went with them to the olive grove called Gethsemane, and he said, "Sit here while I go over there to pray." 37 He took Peter and Zebedee's two sons, James and John, and he became anguished and distressed. 38 He told them, "My soul is crushed with grief to the point of death. Stay here and keep watch with me." 39 He went on a little farther and bowed with his face to the ground, praying, "My Father! If it is possible, let this cup of suffering be taken away from me. Yet I want your will to be done, not mine." 40 Then he returned to the disciples and found them asleep. He said to Peter, "Couldn't you watch with me even one hour? 41 Keep watch and pray, so that you will not give in to temptation. For the spirit is willing, but the body is weak!" 42 Then Jesus left them a second time and prayed, "My Father! If this cup cannot be taken away* unless I drink it, your will be done." 43 When he returned to them again, he found them sleeping, for they couldn't keep their eyes open.44 So he went to pray a third time, saying the same things again. 45 Then he came to the disciples and said, "Go ahead and sleep. Have your rest. But look—the time has come. The Son of Man is betrayed into the hands of sinners. 46 Up, let's be going. Look, my betrayer is here!" Holy Bible, New Living Translation ®, copyright © 1996, 2004 by Tyndale Charitable Trust. Used by permission of Tyndale House Publishers. All rights reserved.

(88) Matthew 26:47-56 NLT
47 And even as Jesus said this, Judas, one of the twelve disciples, arrived with a crowd of men armed with swords and clubs. They had been sent by the leading priests and elders of the people. 48 The traitor, Judas, had given them a prearranged signal: "You will know which one to arrest when I greet him with a kiss." 49 So Judas came straight to Jesus. "Greetings, Rabbi!" he exclaimed and gave him the kiss. 50 Jesus said, "My friend, go ahead and do what you have come for." Then the others grabbed Jesus and arrested him. 51 But one of the men with Jesus pulled out his sword and struck the high priest's slave, slashing off his ear. 52 "Put away your sword," Jesus told him. "Those who use the sword will die by the sword. 53 Don't you realize that I could ask my Father for thousands* of angels to protect us, and he would send them instantly? 54 But if I did, how would the Scriptures be fulfilled that describe what must happen now?" 55 Then Jesus said to the crowd, "Am I some dangerous revolutionary, that you come with swords and clubs to arrest me? Why didn't you arrest me in the Temple? I was there teaching every day. 56 But this is all happening to fulfill the words of the prophets as recorded in the Scriptures." At that point, all the disciples deserted him and fled. Holy Bible, New Living Translation ®,

(89) Luke 15:3-10 NLT
3 So Jesus told them this story: 4 "If a man has a hundred sheep and one of them gets lost, what will he do? Won't he leave the ninety-nine others in the wilderness and go to search for the one that is lost until he finds it? 5 And when he has found it, he will joyfully carry it home on his shoulders. 6 When he arrives, he will call together his friends and neighbors, saying, 'Rejoice with me because I have found my lost sheep.' 7 In the same way, there is more joy in heaven over one lost sinner who repents and returns to God than over ninety-nine others who are righteous and haven't strayed away!

Parable of the Lost Coin
8 "Or suppose a woman has ten silver coins* and loses one. Won't she light a lamp and sweep the entire house and search carefully until she finds it? 9 And when she finds it, she will call in her friends and neighbors and say, 'Rejoice with me because I have found my lost coin.' 10 In the same way, there is joy in the presence of God's angels when even one sinner repents."

CHAPTER 10
(90) John 11:44-54 NLT
44 And the dead man came out, his hands and feet bound in graveclothes, his face wrapped in a headcloth. Jesus told them, "Unwrap him and let him go!"

The Plot to Kill Jesus
45 Many of the people who were with Mary believed in Jesus when they saw this happen. 46 But some went to the Pharisees and told them what Jesus had done. 47 Then the leading priests and Pharisees called the high council* together. "What are we going to do?" they asked each other. "This man certainly performs many miraculous signs. 48 If we allow him to go on like this, soon everyone will believe in him. Then the Roman army will come and destroy both our Temple* and our nation." 49 Caiaphas, who was high priest at that time,* said, "You don't know what you're talking about! 50 You don't realize that it's better for you that one man should die for the people than for the whole nation to be destroyed." 51 He did not say this on his own; as high priest at that time he was led to prophesy that Jesus would die for the entire nation. 52 And not only for that nation, but to bring together and unite all the children of God scattered around the world. 53 So from that time on, the Jewish leaders began to plot Jesus' death. 54 As a result, Jesus stopped his public ministry among the people and left Jerusalem. He went to a place near the wilderness, to the village of Ephraim, and stayed there with his disciples.

(91) John 18:1-3 NLT
18 After saying these things, Jesus crossed the Kidron Valley with his disciples and entered a grove of olive trees. 2 Judas, the betrayer, knew this place, because Jesus had often gone there with his disciples. 3 The leading priests and Pharisees had given Judas a contingent of Roman soldiers and Temple guards to accompany him. Now with blazing torches, lanterns, and weapons, they arrived at the olive grove.

(92) 2 Kings 1:2-15 NLT

2 One day Israel's new king, Ahaziah, fell through the latticework of an upper room at his palace in Samaria and was seriously injured. So he sent messengers to the temple of Baal-zebub, the god of Ekron, to ask whether he would recover. 3 But the angel of the Lord told Elijah, who was from Tishbe, "Go and confront the messengers of the king of Samaria and ask them, 'Is there no God in Israel? Why are you going to Baal-zebub, the god of Ekron, to ask whether the king will recover? 4 Now, therefore, this is what the Lord says: You will never leave the bed you are lying on; you will surely die.'" So Elijah went to deliver the message. 5 When the messengers returned to the king, he asked them, "Why have you returned so soon?" 6 They replied, "A man came up to us and told us to go back to the king and give him this message. 'This is what the Lord says: Is there no God in Israel? Why are you sending men to Baal-zebub, the god of Ekron, to ask whether you will recover? Therefore, because you have done this, you will never leave the bed you are lying on; you will surely die.'" 7 "What sort of man was he?" the king demanded. "What did he look like?" 8 They replied, "He was a hairy man,* and he wore a leather belt around his waist." "Elijah from Tishbe!" the king exclaimed. 9 Then he sent an army captain with fifty soldiers to arrest him. They found him sitting on top of a hill. The captain said to him, "Man of God, the king has commanded you to come down with us." 10 But Elijah replied to the captain, "If I am a man of God, let fire come down from heaven and destroy you and your fifty men!" Then fire fell from heaven and killed them all. 11 So the king sent another captain with fifty men. The captain said to him, "Man of God, the king demands that you come down at once." 12 Elijah replied, "If I am a man of God, let fire come down from heaven and destroy you and your fifty men!" And again the fire of God fell from heaven and killed them all. 13 Once more the king sent a third captain with fifty men. But this time the captain went up the hill and fell to his knees before Elijah. He pleaded with him, "O man of God, please spare my life and the lives of these, your fifty servants. 14 See how the fire from heaven came down and destroyed the first two groups. But now please spare my life!" 15 Then the angel of the Lord said to Elijah, "Go down with him, and don't be afraid of him." So Elijah got up and went with him to the king. Holy Bible, New Living Translation ®, copyright © 1996, 2004 by Tyndale Charitable Trust. Used by permission of Tyndale House Publishers. All rights reserved.

(93) John 18:4-9 NLT

4 Jesus fully realized all that was going to happen to him, so he stepped forward to meet them. "Who are you looking for?" he asked. 5 "Jesus the Nazarene,"* they replied. "I AM he,"* Jesus said. (Judas, who betrayed him, was standing with them.) 6 As Jesus said "I AM he," they all drew back and fell to the ground! 7 Once more he asked them, "Who are you looking for?" And again they replied, "Jesus the Nazarene." 8 "I told you that I AM he," Jesus said. "And since I am the one you want, let these others go." 9 He did this to fulfill his own statement: "I did not lose a single one of those you have given me."* Holy Bible, New Living Translation ®, copyright © 1996, 2004 by Tyndale Charitable Trust. Used by permission of Tyndale House Publishers. All rights reserved.

(94) John 18:12-14 NLT

12 So the soldiers, their commanding officer, and the Temple guards arrested Jesus and tied him up. 13 First they took him to Annas, the father-in-law of Caiaphas, the high priest at that time.* 14 Caiaphas was the one who had told the other Jewish leaders, "It's better that one man should die for the people." Holy Bible, New Living Translation ®, copyright © 1996, 2004 by Tyndale Charitable Trust. Used by permission of Tyndale House Publishers. All rights reserved.

(95) John 18:19-24 NLT
19 Inside, the high priest began asking Jesus about his followers and what he had been teaching them. 20 Jesus replied, "Everyone knows what I teach. I have preached regularly in the synagogues and the Temple, where the people* gather. I have not spoken in secret. 21 Why are you asking me this question? Ask those who heard me. They know what I said." 22 Then one of the Temple guards standing nearby slapped Jesus across the face. "Is that the way to answer the high priest?" he demanded. 23 Jesus replied, "If I said anything wrong, you must prove it. But if I'm speaking the truth, why are you beating me?" 24 Then Annas bound Jesus and sent him to Caiaphas, the high priest.Holy Bible, New Living Translation ®, copyright © 1996, 2004 by Tyndale Charitable Trust. Used by permission of Tyndale House Publishers. All rights reserved.

(96) John 18:15-18 NLT
15 Simon Peter followed Jesus, as did another of the disciples. That other disciple was acquainted with the high priest, so he was allowed to enter the high priest's courtyard with Jesus. 16 Peter had to stay outside the gate. Then the disciple who knew the high priest spoke to the woman watching at the gate, and she let Peter in. 17 The woman asked Peter, "You're not one of that man's disciples, are you?" "No," he said, "I am not." 18 Because it was cold, the household servants and the guards had made a charcoal fire. They stood around it, warming themselves, and Peter stood with them, warming himself. Holy Bible, New Living Translation ®, copyright © 1996, 2004 by Tyndale Charitable Trust. Used by permission of Tyndale House Publishers. All rights reserved.

(97) John 18:25-27 NLT
25 Meanwhile, as Simon Peter was standing by the fire, they asked him again, "You're not one of his disciples, are you?" He denied it, saying, "No, I am not." 26 But one of the household slaves of the high priest, a relative of the man whose ear Peter had cut off, asked, "Didn't I see you out there in the olive grove with Jesus?" 27 Again Peter denied it. And immediately a rooster crowed. Holy Bible, New Living Translation ®, copyright © 1996, 2004 by Tyndale Charitable Trust. Used by permission of Tyndale House Publishers. All rights reserved.

CHAPTER 11
(98) Matthew 26:57, 59-60 NKJV
57 And those who had laid hold of Jesus led *Him* away to Caiaphas the high priest, where the scribes and the elders were assembled. 59 Now the chief priests, the elders,* and all the council sought false testimony against Jesus to put Him to death, 60 but found none. Even though many false witnesses came forward, they found none.* But at last two false witnesses* came forward NKJV

(99) Matthew 26:60-61 NKJV
Even though many false witnesses came forward, they found none.* But at last two false witnesses* came forward 61 and said, "This *fellow* said, 'I am able to destroy the temple of God and to build it in three days.'" NKJV

(100) Matthew 26:62-63 NKJV
62 And the high priest arose and said to Him, "Do You answer nothing? What *is it* these men testify against You?" 63 But Jesus kept silent. And the high priest answered and said to Him, "I put You under oath by the living God: Tell us if You are the Christ, the Son of God!" NKJV

(101) Matthew 26:64-68 NKJV

64 Jesus said to him, "*It is as* you said. Nevertheless, I say to you, hereafter you will see the Son of Man sitting at the right hand of the Power, and coming on the clouds of heaven." 65 Then the high priest tore his clothes, saying, "He has spoken blasphemy! What further need do we have of witnesses? Look, now you have heard His blasphemy! 66 What do you think?" They answered and said, "He is deserving of death." 67 Then they spat in His face and beat Him; and others struck *Him* with the palms of their hands, 68 saying, "Prophesy to us, Christ! Who is the one who struck You?" NKJV

(102; 103; 104; 105; 106; 107; 108; 109; 110; 111; 112; 113) John 18:28 NLT

28 Jesus' trial before Caiaphas ended in the early hours of the morning. Then he was taken to the headquarters of the Roman governor.* His accusers didn't go inside because it would defile them, and they wouldn't be allowed to celebrate the Passover. 29 So Pilate, the governor, went out to them and asked, "What is your charge against this man?" 30 "We wouldn't have handed him over to you if he weren't a criminal!" they retorted. 31 "Then take him away and judge him by your own law," Pilate told them. "Only the Romans are permitted to execute someone," the Jewish leaders replied. 32 (This fulfilled Jesus' prediction about the way he would die.*) 33 Then Pilate went back into his headquarters and called for Jesus to be brought to him. "Are you the king of the Jews?" he asked him. 34 Jesus replied, "Is this your own question, or did others tell you about me?" 35 "Am I a Jew?" Pilate retorted. "Your own people and their leading priests brought you to me for trial. Why? What have you done?" 36 Jesus answered, "My Kingdom is not an earthly kingdom. If it were, my followers would fight to keep me from being handed over to the Jewish leaders. But my Kingdom is not of this world." 37 Pilate said, "So you are a king?" Jesus responded, "You say I am a king. Actually, I was born and came into the world to testify to the truth. All who love the truth recognize that what I say is true." 38 "What is truth?" Pilate asked. Then he went out again to the people and told them, "He is not guilty of any crime. 39 But you have a custom of asking me to release one prisoner each year at Passover. Would you like me to release this 'King of the Jews'?" 40 But they shouted back, "No! Not this man. We want Barabbas!" (Barabbas was a revolutionary.)

Jesus Sentenced to Death

19 Then Pilate had Jesus flogged with a lead-tipped whip. 2 The soldiers wove a crown of thorns and put it on his head, and they put a purple robe on him. 3 "Hail! King of the Jews!" they mocked, as they slapped him across the face. 4 Pilate went outside again and said to the people, "I am going to bring him out to you now, but understand clearly that I find him not guilty." 5 Then Jesus came out wearing the crown of thorns and the purple robe. And Pilate said, "Look, here is the man!" 6 When they saw him, the leading priests and Temple guards began shouting, "Crucify him! Crucify him!" "Take him yourselves and crucify him," Pilate said. "I find him not guilty." 7 The Jewish leaders replied, "By our law he ought to die because he called himself the Son of God." 8 When Pilate heard this, he was more frightened than ever. 9 He took Jesus back into the headquarters* again and asked him, "Where are you from?" But Jesus gave no answer. 10 "Why don't you talk to me?" Pilate demanded. "Don't you realize that I have the power to release you or crucify you?" 11 Then Jesus said, "You would have no power over me at all unless it were given to you from above. So the one who handed me over to you has the greater sin." 12 Then Pilate tried to release him, but the Jewish leaders shouted, "If you release this man, you are no 'friend of Caesar.'* Anyone who declares himself a king is a rebel against Caesar." 13 When they said this, Pilate brought Jesus out to them again. Then Pilate sat down on the judgment seat on the platform that is called the Stone Pavement (in Hebrew, *Gabbatha*). 14 It was now about noon on the day of preparation for the Passover. And Pilate said to the people,* "Look, here is your king!" 15 "Away with him," they yelled.

"Away with him! Crucify him!" "What? Crucify your king?" Pilate asked. "We have no king but Caesar," the leading priests shouted back. 16 Then Pilate turned Jesus over to them to be crucified. Holy Bible, New Living Translation ®, copyright © 1996, 2004 by Tyndale Charitable Trust. Used by permission of Tyndale House Publishers. All rights reserved.

CHAPTER 12
(114) Hebrews 12:1-3 KJV
12 Wherefore seeing we also are compassed about with so great a cloud of witnesses, let us lay aside every weight, and the sin which doth so easily beset us, and let us run with patience the race that is set before us, 2 Looking unto Jesus the author and finisher of our faith; who for the joy that was set before him endured the cross, despising the shame, and is set down at the right hand of the throne of God. 3 For consider him that endured such contradiction of sinners against himself, lest ye be wearied and faint in your minds. KJV

(115) Matthew 16:21 CEV
21 From then on, Jesus began telling his disciples what would happen to him. He said, "I must go to Jerusalem. There the nation's leaders, the chief priests, and the teachers of the Law of Moses will make me suffer terribly. I will be killed, but three days later I will rise to life." CEV

(116) Matthew 17:22-23 CEV
22 While Jesus and his disciples were going from place to place in Galilee, he told them, "The Son of Man will be handed over to people 23 who will kill him. But three days later he will rise to life." All of this made the disciples very sad. CEV

(117) Matthew 20:17-19 CEV
17 As Jesus was on his way to Jerusalem, he took his twelve disciples aside and told them in private: 18 We are now on our way to Jerusalem, where the Son of Man will be handed over to the chief priests and the teachers of the Law of Moses. They will sentence him to death, 19 and then they will hand him over to foreignerst who will make fun of him. They will beat him and nail him to a cross. But on the third day he will rise from death. CEV

(118) John 19:16-37 NIV
16 Finally Pilate handed him over to them to be crucified. So the soldiers took charge of Jesus. 17 Carrying his own cross, he went out to the place of the Skull (which in Aramaic is called Golgotha). 18 Here they crucified him, and with him two others — one on each side and Jesus in the middle. 19 Pilate had a notice prepared and fastened to the cross. It read: JESUS OF NAZARETH, THE KING OF THE JEWS. 20 Many of the Jews read this sign, for the place where Jesus was crucified was near the city, and the sign was written in Aramaic, Latin and Greek. 21 The chief priests of the Jews protested to Pilate, "Do not write 'The King of the Jews,' but that this man claimed to be king of the Jews." 22 Pilate answered, "What I have written, I have written." 23 When the soldiers crucified Jesus, they took his clothes, dividing them into four shares, one for each of them, with the undergarment remaining. This garment was seamless, woven in one piece from top to bottom. 24 "Let's not tear it," they said to one another. "Let's decide by lot who will get it." "This happened that the scripture might be fulfilled which said, "They divided my garments among them and cast lots for my clothing." a So this is what the soldiers did. 25 Near the cross of Jesus stood his mother, his mother's sister, Mary the wife of Clopas, and Mary Magdalene. 26 When Jesus saw his mother there, and the disciple whom he loved standing nearby, he said to his mother, "Dear woman, here is your son," 27 and to the disciple, "Here is your mother." From that time on, this disciple took her into his home. 28 Later, knowing

that all was now completed, and so that the Scripture would be fulfilled, Jesus said, "I am thirsty." 29 A jar of wine vinegar was there, so they soaked a sponge in it, put the sponge on a stalk of the hyssop plant, and lifted it to Jesus' lips. 30 When he had received the drink, Jesus said, "It is finished." With that, he bowed his head and gave up his spirit. 31 Now it was the day of Preparation, and the next day was to be a special Sabbath. Because the Jews did not want the bodies left on the crosses during the Sabbath, they asked Pilate to have the legs broken and the bodies taken down. 32 The soldiers therefore came and broke the legs of the first man who had been crucified with Jesus, and then those of the other. 33 But when they came to Jesus and found that he was already dead, they did not break his legs. 34 Instead, one of the soldiers pierced Jesus' side with a spear, bringing a sudden flow of blood and water. 35 The man who saw it has given testimony, and his testimony is true. He knows that he tells the truth, and he testifies so that you also may believe. 36 These things happened so that the scripture would be fulfilled: "Not one of his bones will be broken," b 37 and, as another scripture says, "They will look on the one they have pierced." c NIV

(119) Zechariah 12:10 NKJV
10 "And I will pour on the house of David and on the inhabitants of Jerusalem the Spirit of grace and supplication; then they will look on Me whom they pierced. Yes, they will mourn for Him as one mourns for *his* only *son,* and grieve for Him as one grieves for a firstborn. NKJV

(120) Psalms 22:1-31 NLT
22 1 My God, my God, why have you abandoned me? Why are you so far away when I groan for help? 2 Every day I call to you, my God, but you do not answer. Every night you hear my voice, but I find no relief. 3 Yet you are holy, enthroned on the praises of Israel. 4 Our ancestors trusted in you, and you rescued them. 5 They cried out to you and were saved. They trusted in you and were never disgraced. 6 But I am a worm and not a man. I am scorned and despised by all! 7 Everyone who sees me mocks me. They sneer and shake their heads, saying, 8 "Is this the one who relies on the Lord? Then let the Lord save him! If the Lord loves him so much, let the Lord rescue him!" 9 Yet you brought me safely from my mother's womb and led me to trust you at my mother's breast. 10 I was thrust into your arms at my birth. You have been my God from the moment I was born. 11 Do not stay so far from me, for trouble is near, and no one else can help me. 12 My enemies surround me like a herd of bulls; fierce bulls of Bashan have hemmed me in! 13 Like lions they open their jaws against me, roaring and tearing into their prey. 14 My life is poured out like water, and all my bones are out of joint. My heart is like wax, melting within me. 15 My strength has dried up like sunbaked clay. My tongue sticks to the roof of my mouth. You have laid me in the dust and left me for dead. 16 My enemies surround me like a pack of dogs; an evil gang closes in on me. They have pierced my hands and feet. 17 I can count all my bones. My enemies stare at me and gloat. 18 They divide my garments among themselves and throw dice* for my clothing. 19 O Lord, do not stay far away! You are my strength; come quickly to my aid! 20 Save me from the sword; spare my precious life from these dogs. 21 Snatch me from the lion's jaws and from the horns of these wild oxen. 22 I will proclaim your name to my brothers and sisters.* I will praise you among your assembled people. 23 Praise the Lord, all you who fear him! Honor him, all you descendants of Jacob! Show him reverence, all you descendants of Israel! 24 For he has not ignored or belittled the suffering of the needy. He has not turned his back on them, but has listened to their cries for help. 25 I will praise you in the great assembly. I will fulfill my vows in the presence of those who worship you. 26 The poor will eat and be satisfied. All who seek the Lord will praise him. Their hearts will rejoice with everlasting joy. 27

The whole earth will acknowledge the Lord and return to him. All the families of the nations will bow down before him. 28 For royal power belongs to the Lord. He rules all the nations. 29 Let the rich of the earth feast and worship. Bow before him, all who are mortal, all whose lives will end as dust. 30 Our children will also serve him. Future generations will hear about the wonders of the Lord. 31 His righteous acts will be told to those not yet born. They will hear about everything he has done. Holy Bible, New Living Translation ®, copyright © 1996, 2004 by Tyndale Charitable Trust. Used by permission of Tyndale House Publishers. All rights reserved.

(121) Isaiah 52:13-53:12 NLT
13 See, my servant will prosper; he will be highly exalted. 14 But many were amazed when they saw him.* His face was so disfigured he seemed hardly human, and from his appearance, one would scarcely know he was a man. 15 And he will startle* many nations. Kings will stand speechless in his presence. For they will see what they had not been told; they will understand what they had not heard about.* 53 1 Who has believed our message? To whom has the Lord revealed his powerful arm? 2 My servant grew up in the Lord's presence like a tender green shoot, like a root in dry ground. There was nothing beautiful or majestic about his appearance, nothing to attract us to him. 3 He was despised and rejected—a man of sorrows, acquainted with deepest grief. We turned our backs on him and looked the other way. He was despised, and we did not care. 4 Yet it was our weaknesses he carried; it was our sorrows* that weighed him down. And we thought his troubles were a punishment from God, a punishment for his own sins! 5 But he was pierced for our rebellion, crushed for our sins. He was beaten so we could be whole. He was whipped so we could be healed. 6 All of us, like sheep, have strayed away. We have left God's paths to follow our own. Yet the Lord laid on him the sins of us all. 7 He was oppressed and treated harshly, yet he never said a word. He was led like a lamb to the slaughter. And as a sheep is silent before the shearers, he did not open his mouth. 8 Unjustly condemned, he was led away.* No one cared that he died without descendants, that his life was cut short in midstream.* But he was struck down for the rebellion of my people. 9 He had done no wrong and had never deceived anyone. But he was buried like a criminal; he was put in a rich man's grave. 10 But it was the Lord's good plan to crush him and cause him grief. Yet when his life is made an offering for sin, he will have many descendants. He will enjoy a long life, and the Lord's good plan will prosper in his hands. 11 When he sees all that is accomplished by his anguish, he will be satisfied. And because of his experience, my righteous servant will make it possible for many to be counted righteous, for he will bear all their sins. 12 I will give him the honors of a victorious soldier, because he exposed himself to death. He was counted among the rebels. He bore the sins of many and interceded for rebels. F Holy Bible, New Living Translation ®, copyright © 1996, 2004 by Tyndale Charitable Trust. Used by permission of Tyndale House Publishers. All rights reserved.

CHAPTER 13
(122) John 19:38-42 NIV
38 Later, Joseph of Arimathea asked Pilate for the body of Jesus. Now Joseph was a disciple of Jesus, but secretly because he feared the Jews. With Pilate's permission, he came and took the body away. 39 He was accompanied by Nicodemus, the man who earlier had visited Jesus at night. Nicodemus brought a mixture of myrrh and aloes, about seventy-five pounds. d 40 Taking Jesus' body, the two of them wrapped it, with the spices, in strips of linen. This was in accordance with Jewish burial customs. 41 At the place where Jesus was crucified, there was a garden, and in the garden a new tomb, in which no one had ever been

laid. 42 Because it was the Jewish day of Preparation and since the tomb was nearby, they laid Jesus there. NIV

(123) John 3:2-21 NLT
2 After dark one evening, he came to speak with Jesus. "Rabbi," he said, "we all know that God has sent you to teach us. Your miraculous signs are evidence that God is with you." 3 Jesus replied, "I tell you the truth, unless you are born again,* you cannot see the Kingdom of God." 4 "What do you mean?" exclaimed Nicodemus. "How can an old man go back into his mother's womb and be born again?" 5 Jesus replied, "I assure you, no one can enter the Kingdom of God without being born of water and the Spirit.* 6 Humans can reproduce only human life, but the Holy Spirit gives birth to spiritual life.* 7 So don't be surprised when I say, 'You* must be born again.' 8 The wind blows wherever it wants. Just as you can hear the wind but can't tell where it comes from or where it is going, so you can't explain how people are born of the Spirit." 9 "How are these things possible?" Nicodemus asked. 10 Jesus replied, "You are a respected Jewish teacher, and yet you don't understand these things? 11 I assure you, we tell you what we know and have seen, and yet you won't believe our testimony. 12 But if you don't believe me when I tell you about earthly things, how can you possibly believe if I tell you about heavenly things? 13 No one has ever gone to heaven and returned. But the Son of Man* has come down from heaven. 14 And as Moses lifted up the bronze snake on a pole in the wilderness, so the Son of Man must be lifted up, 15 so that everyone who believes in him will have eternal life.* 16 "For God loved the world so much that he gave his one and only Son, so that everyone who believes in him will not perish but have eternal life. 17 God sent his Son into the world not to judge the world, but to save the world through him. 18 "There is no judgment against anyone who believes in him. But anyone who does not believe in him has already been judged for not believing in God's one and only Son. 19 And the judgment is based on this fact: God's light came into the world, but people loved the darkness more than the light, for their actions were evil. 20 All who do evil hate the light and refuse to go near it for fear their sins will be exposed. 21 But those who do what is right come to the light so others can see that they are doing what God wants.*" Holy Bible, New Living Translation ®, copyright © 1996, 2004 by Tyndale Charitable Trust. Used by permission of Tyndale House Publishers. All rights reserved.

(124) Romans 5:6-11 NKJV
6 For when we were still without strength, in due time Christ died for the ungodly. 7 For scarcely for a righteous man will one die; yet perhaps for a good man someone would even dare to die. 8 But God demonstrates His own love toward us, in that while we were still sinners, Christ died for us. 9 Much more then, having now been justified by His blood, we shall be saved from wrath through Him. 10 For if when we were enemies we were reconciled to God through the death of His Son, much more, having been reconciled, we shall be saved by His life. 11 And not only *that,* but we also rejoice in God through our Lord Jesus Christ, through whom we have now received the reconciliation. NKJV

(125) Ephesians 4:7-16 NKJV
7 But to each one of us grace was given according to the measure of Christ's gift. 8 Therefore He says: "*When He ascended on high, He led captivity captive, And gave gifts to men.*"* 9 (Now this, *"He ascended"* — what does it mean but that He also first* descended into the lower parts of the earth? 10 He who descended is also the One who ascended far above all the heavens, that He might fill all things.) 11 And He Himself gave some *to be* apostles, some prophets, some evangelists, and some pastors and teachers, 12 for the equipping of the saints for the work of ministry, for the edifying of the body of

Christ, 13 till we all come to the unity of the faith and of the knowledge of the Son of God, to a perfect man, to the measure of the stature of the fullness of Christ; 14 that we should no longer be children, tossed to and fro and carried about with every wind of doctrine, by the trickery of men, in the cunning craftiness of deceitful plotting, 15 but, speaking the truth in love, may grow up in all things into Him who is the head — Christ — 16 from whom the whole body, joined and knit together by what every joint supplies, according to the effective working by which every part does its share, causes growth of the body for the edifying of itself in love. NKJV

(126) 1 Corinthians 12:12-27 NKJV
12 For as the body is one and has many members, but all the members of that one body, being many, are one body, so also *is* Christ. 13 For by one Spirit we were all baptized into one body — whether Jews or Greeks, whether slaves or free — and have all been made to drink into* one Spirit. 14 For in fact the body is not one member but many. 15 If the foot should say, "Because I am not a hand, I am not of the body," is it therefore not of the body? 16 And if the ear should say, "Because I am not an eye, I am not of the body," is it therefore not of the body? 17 If the whole body *were* an eye, where *would be* the hearing? If the whole *were* hearing, where *would be* the smelling? 18 But now God has set the members, each one of them, in the body just as He pleased. 19 And if they *were* all one member, where *would* the body *be?* 20 But now indeed *there are* many members, yet one body. 21 And the eye cannot say to the hand, "I have no need of you"; nor again the head to the feet, "I have no need of you." 22 No, much rather, those members of the body which seem to be weaker are necessary. 23 And those *members* of the body which we think to be less honorable, on these we bestow greater honor; and our unpresentable *parts* have greater modesty, 24 but our presentable *parts* have no need. But God composed the body, having given greater honor to that *part* which lacks it, 25 that there should be no schism in the body, but *that* the members should have the same care for one another. 26 And if one member suffers, all the members suffer with *it;* or if one member is honored, all the members rejoice with *it.* 27 Now you are the body of Christ, and members individually. NKJV

CHAPTER 14
(127) John 19:25-27 NKJV
25 Now there stood by the cross of Jesus His mother, and His mother's sister, Mary the *wife* of Clopas, and Mary Magdalene. 26 When Jesus therefore saw His mother, and the disciple whom He loved standing by, He said to His mother, "Woman, behold your son!" 27 Then He said to the disciple, "Behold your mother!" And from that hour that disciple took her to his own *home.* NKJV

(128) Matthew 28:2-10 NLT
2 Suddenly there was a great earthquake! For an angel of the Lord came down from heaven, rolled aside the stone, and sat on it. 3 His face shone like lightning, and his clothing was as white as snow. 4 The guards shook with fear when they saw him, and they fell into a dead faint. 5 Then the angel spoke to the women. "Don't be afraid!" he said. "I know you are looking for Jesus, who was crucified. 6 He isn't here! He is risen from the dead, just as he said would happen. Come, see where his body was lying. 7 And now, go quickly and tell his disciples that he has risen from the dead, and he is going ahead of you to Galilee. You will see him there. Remember what I have told you." 8 The women ran quickly from the tomb. They were very frightened but also filled with great joy, and they rushed to give the disciples the angel's message. 9 And as they went, Jesus met them and greeted them. And they ran to him, grasped his feet, and worshiped him. 10 Then Jesus said to them, "Don't

be afraid! Go tell my brothers to leave for Galilee, and they will see me there." Holy Bible, New Living Translation ®, copyright © 1996, 2004 by Tyndale Charitable Trust. Used by permission of Tyndale House Publishers. All rights reserved.

(129) Deuteronomy 30:11-20 CEV
11 You know God's laws, and it isn't impossible to obey them. 12 His commands aren't in heaven, so you can't excuse yourselves by saying, "How can we obey the Lord's commands? They are in heaven, and no one can go up to get them, then bring them down and explain them to us." 13 And you can't say, "How can we obey the Lord's commands? They are across the sea, and someone must go across, then bring them back and explain them to us." 14 No, these commands are nearby and you know them by heart. All you have to do is obey! 15 Today I am giving you a choice. You can choose life and success or death and disaster. 16-18 I am commanding you to be loyal to the Lord, to live the way he has told you, and to obey his laws and teachings. You are about to cross the Jordan River and take the land that he is giving you. If you obey him, you will live and become successful and powerful. On the other hand, you might choose to disobey the Lord and reject him. So I'm warning you that if you bow down and worship other gods, you won't have long to live. 19 Right now I call the sky and the earth to be witnesses that I am offering you this choice. Will you choose for the Lord to make you prosperous and give you a long life? Or will he put you under a curse and kill you? Choose life! 20 Be completely faithful to the Lord your God, love him, and do whatever he tells you. The Lord is the only one who can give life, and he will let you live a long time in the land that he promised to your ancestors Abraham, Isaac, and Jacob. CEV

(130) Revelation 3:14-22 NLT
14 "Write this letter to the angel of the church in Laodicea. This is the message from the one who is the Amen—the faithful and true witness, the beginning* of God's new creation: 15 "I know all the things you do, that you are neither hot nor cold. I wish that you were one or the other! 16 But since you are like lukewarm water, neither hot nor cold, I will spit you out of my mouth! 17 You say, 'I am rich. I have everything I want. I don't need a thing!' And you don't realize that you are wretched and miserable and poor and blind and naked. 18 So I advise you to buy gold from me—gold that has been purified by fire. Then you will be rich. Also buy white garments from me so you will not be shamed by your nakedness, and ointment for your eyes so you will be able to see. 19 I correct and discipline everyone I love. So be diligent and turn from your indifference. 20 "Look! I stand at the door and knock. If you hear my voice and open the door, I will come in, and we will share a meal together as friends. 21 Those who are victorious will sit with me on my throne, just as I was victorious and sat with my Father on his throne. 22 "Anyone with ears to hear must listen to the Spirit and understand what he is saying to the churches." Holy Bible, New Living Translation ®, copyright © 1996, 2004 by Tyndale Charitable Trust. Used by permission of Tyndale House Publishers. All rights reserved.

(131) 1 Peter 4:17-19 NKJV
17 For the time *has come* for judgment to begin at the house of God; and if *it begins* with us first, what will *be* the end of those who do not obey the gospel of God? 18 Now "*If the righteous one is scarcely saved, Where will the ungodly and the sinner appear?*"* 19 Therefore let those who suffer according to the will of God commit their souls *to Him* in doing good, as to a faithful Creator. NKJV

(132) Revelation 12:7-12 NKJV

7 And war broke out in heaven: Michael and his angels fought with the dragon; and the dragon and his angels fought, 8 but they did not prevail, nor was a place found for them* in heaven any longer. 9 So the great dragon was cast out, that serpent of old, called the Devil and Satan, who deceives the whole world; he was cast to the earth, and his angels were cast out with him. 10 Then I heard a loud voice saying in heaven, "Now salvation, and strength, and the kingdom of our God, and the power of His Christ have come, for the accuser of our brethren, who accused them before our God day and night, has been cast down. 11 And they overcame him by the blood of the Lamb and by the word of their testimony, and they did not love their lives to the death. 12 Therefore rejoice, O heavens, and you who dwell in them! Woe to the inhabitants of the earth and the sea! For the devil has come down to you, having great wrath, because he knows that he has a short time." *T* NKJV

CHAPTER 15
(133) Hebrews 11:1-12:29 NKJV
11 Now faith is the substance of things hoped for, the evidence of things not seen. 2 For by it the elders obtained a *good* testimony. 3 By faith we understand that the worlds were framed by the word of God, so that the things which are seen were not made of things which are visible.
Faith at the Dawn of History
4 By faith Abel offered to God a more excellent sacrifice than Cain, through which he obtained witness that he was righteous, God testifying of his gifts; and through it he being dead still speaks. 5 By faith Enoch was taken away so that he did not see death, *"and was not found, because God had taken him"*;* for before he was taken he had this testimony, that he pleased God. 6 But without faith *it is* impossible to please *Him*, for he who comes to God must believe that He is, and *that* He is a rewarder of those who diligently seek Him. 7 By faith Noah, being divinely warned of things not yet seen, moved with godly fear, prepared an ark for the saving of his household, by which he condemned the world and became heir of the righteousness which is according to faith.
Faithful Abraham
8 By faith Abraham obeyed when he was called to go out to the place which he would receive as an inheritance. And he went out, not knowing where he was going. 9 By faith he dwelt in the land of promise as *in* a foreign country, dwelling in tents with Isaac and Jacob, the heirs with him of the same promise; 10 for he waited for the city which has foundations, whose builder and maker *is* God. 11 By faith Sarah herself also received strength to conceive seed, and she bore a child* when she was past the age, because she judged Him faithful who had promised. 12 Therefore from one man, and him as good as dead, were born *as many* as the stars of the sky in multitude — innumerable as the sand which is by the seashore.
The Heavenly Hope
13 These all died in faith, not having received the promises, but having seen them afar off were assured of them,* embraced *them* and confessed that they were strangers and pilgrims on the earth. 14 For those who say such things declare plainly that they seek a homeland. 15 And truly if they had called to mind that *country* from which they had come out, they would have had opportunity to return. 16 But now they desire a better, that is, a heavenly *country.* Therefore God is not ashamed to be called their God, for He has prepared a city for them.
The Faith of the Patriarchs
17 By faith Abraham, when he was tested, offered up Isaac, and he who had received the promises offered up his only begotten *son,* 18 of whom it was said, *"In Isaac your seed shall be called,"** 19 concluding that God *was* able to raise *him* up, even from the dead,

from which he also received him in a figurative sense. 20 By faith Isaac blessed Jacob and Esau concerning things to come. 21 By faith Jacob, when he was dying, blessed each of the sons of Joseph, and worshiped, *leaning* on the top of his staff. 22 By faith Joseph, when he was dying, made mention of the departure of the children of Israel, and gave instructions concerning his bones.

The Faith of Moses

23 By faith Moses, when he was born, was hidden three months by his parents, because they saw *he was* a beautiful child; and they were not afraid of the king's command. 24 By faith Moses, when he became of age, refused to be called the son of Pharaoh's daughter, 25 choosing rather to suffer affliction with the people of God than to enjoy the passing pleasures of sin, 26 esteeming the reproach of Christ greater riches than the treasures in* Egypt; for he looked to the reward. 27 By faith he forsook Egypt, not fearing the wrath of the king; for he endured as seeing Him who is invisible. 28 By faith he kept the Passover and the sprinkling of blood, lest he who destroyed the firstborn should touch them. 29 By faith they passed through the Red Sea as by dry *land, whereas* the Egyptians, attempting *to do* so, were drowned.

By Faith They Overcame

30 By faith the walls of Jericho fell down after they were encircled for seven days. 31 By faith the harlot Rahab did not perish with those who did not believe, when she had received the spies with peace. 32 And what more shall I say? For the time would fail me to tell of Gideon and Barak and Samson and Jephthah, also *of* David and Samuel and the prophets: 33 who through faith subdued kingdoms, worked righteousness, obtained promises, stopped the mouths of lions, 34 quenched the violence of fire, escaped the edge of the sword, out of weakness were made strong, became valiant in battle, turned to flight the armies of the aliens. 35 Women received their dead raised to life again.

Others were tortured, not accepting deliverance, that they might obtain a better resurrection. 36 Still others had trial of mockings and scourgings, yes, and of chains and imprisonment. 37 They were stoned, they were sawn in two, were tempted,* were slain with the sword. They wandered about in sheepskins and goatskins, being destitute, afflicted, tormented — 38 of whom the world was not worthy. They wandered in deserts and mountains, *in* dens and caves of the earth. 39 And all these, having obtained a good testimony through faith, did not receive the promise, 40 God having provided something better for us, that they should not be made perfect apart from us.

The Race of Faith

12 Therefore we also, since we are surrounded by so great a cloud of witnesses, let us lay aside every weight, and the sin which so easily ensnares *us,* and let us run with endurance the race that is set before us, 2 looking unto Jesus, the author and finisher of *our* faith, who for the joy that was set before Him endured the cross, despising the shame, and has sat down at the right hand of the throne of God.

The Discipline of God

3 For consider Him who endured such hostility from sinners against Himself, lest you become weary and discouraged in your souls. 4 You have not yet resisted to bloodshed, striving against sin. 5 And you have forgotten the exhortation which speaks to you as to sons: "*My son, do not despise the chastening of the* Lord, *Nor be discouraged when you are rebuked by Him;* 6 *For whom the* Lord *loves He chastens, And scourges every son whom He receives.*"* 7 If* you endure chastening, God deals with you as with sons; for what son is there whom a father does not chasten? 8 But if you are without chastening, of which all have become partakers, then you are illegitimate and not sons. 9 Furthermore, we have had human fathers who corrected *us,* and we paid *them* respect. Shall we not much more readily be in subjection to the Father of spirits and live? 10 For they indeed for a few days chastened *us* as seemed *best* to them, but He for *our* profit, that *we* may be partakers

of His holiness. 11 Now no chastening seems to be joyful for the present, but painful; nevertheless, afterward it yields the peaceable fruit of righteousness to those who have been trained by it.

Renew Your Spiritual Vitality
12 Therefore strengthen the hands which hang down, and the feeble knees, 13 and make straight paths for your feet, so that what is lame may not be *dislocated,* but rather be healed. 14 Pursue peace with all *people,* and holiness, without which no one will see the Lord: 15 looking carefully lest anyone fall short of the grace of God; lest any root of bitterness springing up cause trouble, and by this many become defiled; 16 lest there *be* any fornicator or profane person like Esau, who for one morsel of food sold his birthright. 17 For you know that afterward, when he wanted to inherit the blessing, he was rejected, for he found no place for repentance, though he sought it diligently with tears.

The Glorious Company
18 For you have not come to the mountain that* may be touched and that burned with fire, and to blackness and darkness* and tempest, 19 and the sound of a trumpet and the voice of words, so that those who heard *it* begged that the word should not be spoken to them anymore. 20 (For they could not endure what was commanded: *"And if so much as a beast touches the mountain, it shall be stoned* or shot with an arrow."** 21 And so terrifying was the sight *that* Moses said, *"I am exceedingly afraid and trembling."**) 22 But you have come to Mount Zion and to the city of the living God, the heavenly Jerusalem, to an innumerable company of angels, 23 to the general assembly and church of the firstborn *who are* registered in heaven, to God the Judge of all, to the spirits of just men made perfect, 24 to Jesus the Mediator of the new covenant, and to the blood of sprinkling that speaks better things than *that of* Abel.

Hear the Heavenly Voice
25 See that you do not refuse Him who speaks. For if they did not escape who refused Him who spoke on earth, much more *shall we not escape* if we turn away from Him who *speaks* from heaven, 26 whose voice then shook the earth; but now He has promised, saying, *"Yet once more I shake* not only the earth, but also heaven."** 27 Now this, *"Yet once more,"* indicates the removal of those things that are being shaken, as of things that are made, that the things which cannot be shaken may remain. 28 Therefore, since we are receiving a kingdom which cannot be shaken, let us have grace, by which we may* serve God acceptably with reverence and godly fear. 29 For our God *is* a consuming fire. *C* NKJV

(134) John 14:1-7 CEV
14 Jesus said to his disciples, "Don't be worried! Have faith in God and have faith in me. 2 There are many rooms in my Father's house. I wouldn't tell you this, unless it was true. I am going there to prepare a place for each of you. 3 After I have done this, I will come back and take you with me. Then we will be together. 4 You know the way to where I am going." 5 Thomas said, "Lord, we don't even know where you are going! How can we know the way?" 6 "I am the way, the truth, and the life!" Jesus answered. "Without me, no one can go to the Father. 7 If you had known me, you would have known the Father. But from now on, you do know him, and you have seen him." CEV

(135) 1 Corinthians 2:1-16 CEV
2 Friends, when I came and told you the mystery that God had shared with us, I didn't use big words or try to sound wise. 2 In fact, while I was with you, I made up my mind to speak only about Jesus Christ, who had been nailed to a cross. 3 At first, I was weak and trembling with fear. 4 When I talked with you or preached, I didn't try to prove anything by sounding wise. I simply let God's Spirit show his power. 5 That way you would have faith because of God's power and not because of human wisdom. 6 We do use wisdom when speaking

to people who are mature in their faith. But it isn't the wisdom of this world or of its rulers, who will soon disappear. 7 We speak of God's hidden and mysterious wisdom that God decided to use for our glory long before the world began. 8 The rulers of this world didn't know anything about this wisdom. If they had known about it, they would not have nailed the glorious Lord to a cross. 9 But it is just as the Scriptures say, "What God has planned for people who love him is more than eyes have seen or ears have heard. It has never even entered our minds!" 10 God's Spirit has shown you everything. His Spirit finds out everything, even what is deep in the mind of God. 11 You are the only one who knows what is in your own mind, and God's Spirit is the only one who knows what is in God's mind. 12 But God has given us his Spirit. That's why we don't think the same way that the people of this world think. That's also why we can recognize the blessings that God has given us. 13 Every word we speak was taught to us by God's Spirit, not by human wisdom. And this same Spirit helps us teach spiritual things to spiritual people. 14 That's why only someone who has God's Spirit can understand spiritual blessings. Anyone who doesn't have God's Spirit thinks these blessings are foolish. 15 People who are guided by the Spirit can make all kinds of judgments, but they cannot be judged by others. 16 The Scriptures ask, "Has anyone ever known the thoughts of the Lord or given him advice?" But we understand what Christ is thinking. CEV

(136) Acts 1:1-14 NKJV

1 The former account I made, O Theophilus, of all that Jesus began both to do and teach, 2 until the day in which He was taken up, after He through the Holy Spirit had given commandments to the apostles whom He had chosen, 3 to whom He also presented Himself alive after His suffering by many infallible proofs, being seen by them during forty days and speaking of the things pertaining to the kingdom of God.

The Holy Spirit Promised

4 And being assembled together with *them,* He commanded them not to depart from Jerusalem, but to wait for the Promise of the Father, "which," *He said,* "you have heard from Me; 5 for John truly baptized with water, but you shall be baptized with the Holy Spirit not many days from now." 6 Therefore, when they had come together, they asked Him, saying, "Lord, will You at this time restore the kingdom to Israel?" 7 And He said to them, "It is not for you to know times or seasons which the Father has put in His own authority. 8 But you shall receive power when the Holy Spirit has come upon you; and you shall be witnesses to Me* in Jerusalem, and in all Judea and Samaria, and to the end of the earth."

Jesus Ascends to Heaven

9 Now when He had spoken these things, while they watched, He was taken up, and a cloud received Him out of their sight. 10 And while they looked steadfastly toward heaven as He went up, behold, two men stood by them in white apparel, 11 who also said, "Men of Galilee, why do you stand gazing up into heaven? This *same* Jesus, who was taken up from you into heaven, will so come in like manner as you saw Him go into heaven."

The Upper Room Prayer Meeting

12 Then they returned to Jerusalem from the mount called Olivet, which is near Jerusalem, a Sabbath day's journey. 13 And when they had entered, they went up into the upper room where they were staying: Peter, James, John, and Andrew; Philip and Thomas; Bartholomew and Matthew; James *the son* of Alphaeus and Simon the Zealot; and Judas *the son* of James. 14 These all continued with one accord in prayer and supplication,* with the women and Mary the mother of Jesus, and with His brothers. NKJV

(137) Jeremiah 50:6-7 NKJV

6 "My people have been lost sheep. Their shepherds have led them astray; They have turned them away *on* the mountains. They have gone from mountain to hill; They have forgotten their resting place. 7 All who found them have devoured them; And their adversaries said,'We have not offended, Because they have sinned against the Lord, the habitation of justice, The Lord, the hope of their fathers.' NKJV

(138) Jeremiah 25:32-38 NIV
32 This is what the Lord Almighty says: "Look! Disaster is spreading from nation to nation; a mighty storm is rising from the ends of the earth." 33 At that time those slain by the Lord will be everywhere — from one end of the earth to the other. They will not be mourned or gathered up or buried, but will be like refuse lying on the ground. 34 Weep and wail, you shepherds; roll in the dust, you leaders of the flock. For your time to be slaughtered has come; you will fall and be shattered like fine pottery. 35 The shepherds will have nowhere to flee, the leaders of the flock no place to escape. 36 Hear the cry of the shepherds, the wailing of the leaders of the flock, for the Lord is destroying their pasture. 37 The peaceful meadows will be laid waste because of the fierce anger of the Lord. 38 Like a lion he will leave his lair, and their land will become desolate because of the sword of the oppressor and because of the Lord's fierce anger. NIV

(139) Jeremiah 23:1-12 CEV
23 You leaders of my people are like shepherds that kill and scatter the sheep. 2 You were supposed to take care of my people, but instead you chased them away. So now I'll really take care of you, and believe me, you will pay for your crimes! 3 I will bring the rest of my people home from the lands where I have scattered them, and they will grow into a mighty nation. 4 I promise to choose leaders who will care for them like real shepherds. All of my people will be there, and they will never again be frightened. 5 Someday I will appoint an honest king from the family of David, a king who will be wise and rule with justice. 6 As long as he is king, Israel will have peace, and Judah will be safe. The name of this king will be "The Lord Gives Justice." 7 A time will come when you will again worship me. But you will no longer call me the Living God who rescued Israel from Egypt. 8 Instead, you will call me the Living God who rescued you from the land in the north and from all the other countries where I had forced you to go. And you will once again live in your own land.
Jeremiah Thinks about Unfaithful Prophets
9 When I think of the prophets, I am shocked, and I tremble like someone drunk, because of the Lord and his sacred words. 10 Those unfaithful prophets misuse their power all over the country. So God turned the pasturelands into scorching deserts.
The Lord *Will Punish Unfaithful Prophets*
11 The Lord told me to say: You prophets and priests think so little of me, the Lord, that you even sin in my own temple! 12 Now I will punish you with disaster, and you will slip and fall in the darkness. I, the Lord, have spoken. CEV

(140) Ephesians 4:11-16 NLT
11 Now these are the gifts Christ gave to the church: the apostles, the prophets, the evangelists, and the pastors and teachers. 12 Their responsibility is to equip God's people to do his work and build up the church, the body of Christ. 13 This will continue until we all come to such unity in our faith and knowledge of God's Son that we will be mature in the Lord, measuring up to the full and complete standard of Christ. 14 Then we will no longer be immature like children. We won't be tossed and blown about by every wind of new teaching. We will not be influenced when people try to trick us with lies so clever they sound like the truth. 15 Instead, we will speak the truth in love, growing in every way more

and more like Christ, who is the head of his body, the church. 16 He makes the whole body fit together perfectly. As each part does its own special work, it helps the other parts grow, so that the whole body is healthy and growing and full of love. Holy Bible, New Living Translation ®, copyright © 1996, 2004 by Tyndale Charitable Trust. Used by permission of Tyndale House Publishers. All rights reserved.

(141) Acts 2:1-21 NLT

2 On the day of Pentecost* all the believers were meeting together in one place. 2 Suddenly, there was a sound from heaven like the roaring of a mighty windstorm, and it filled the house where they were sitting. 3 Then, what looked like flames or tongues of fire appeared and settled on each of them. 4 And everyone present was filled with the Holy Spirit and began speaking in other languages,* as the Holy Spirit gave them this ability. 5 At that time there were devout Jews from every nation living in Jerusalem. 6 When they heard the loud noise, everyone came running, and they were bewildered to hear their own languages being spoken by the believers. 7 They were completely amazed. "How can this be?" they exclaimed. "These people are all from Galilee, 8 and yet we hear them speaking in our own native languages! 9 Here we are—Parthians, Medes, Elamites, people from Mesopotamia, Judea, Cappadocia, Pontus, the province of Asia, 10 Phrygia, Pamphylia, Egypt, and the areas of Libya around Cyrene, visitors from Rome (both Jews and converts to Judaism), 11 Cretans, and Arabs. And we all hear these people speaking in our own languages about the wonderful things God has done!" 12 They stood there amazed and perplexed. "What can this mean?" they asked each other. 13 But others in the crowd ridiculed them, saying, "They're just drunk, that's all!"

Peter Preaches to the Crowd

14 Then Peter stepped forward with the eleven other apostles and shouted to the crowd, "Listen carefully, all of you, fellow Jews and residents of Jerusalem! Make no mistake about this. 15 These people are not drunk, as some of you are assuming. Nine o'clock in the morning is much too early for that. 16 No, what you see was predicted long ago by the prophet Joel: 17 'In the last days,' God says, 'I will pour out my Spirit upon all people. Your sons and daughters will prophesy. Your young men will see visions, and your old men will dream dreams. 18 In those days I will pour out my Spirit even on my servants—men and women alike—and they will prophesy. 19 And I will cause wonders in the heavens above and signs on the earth below—blood and fire and clouds of smoke. 20 The sun will become dark, and the moon will turn blood red before that great and glorious day of the Lord arrives. 21 But everyone who calls on the name of the Lord will be saved.'* Holy Bible, New Living Translation ®, copyright © 1996, 2004 by Tyndale Charitable Trust. Used by permission of Tyndale House Publishers. All rights reserved.

CHAPTER 16

(142) Revelation 1:4-8 NKJV

4 John, to the seven churches which are in Asia: Grace to you and peace from Him who is and who was and who is to come, and from the seven Spirits who are before His throne, 5 and from Jesus Christ, the faithful witness, the firstborn from the dead, and the ruler over the kings of the earth. To Him who loved us and washed* us from our sins in His own blood, 6 and has made us kings* and priests to His God and Father, to Him *be* glory and dominion forever and ever. Amen. 7 Behold, He is coming with clouds, and every eye will see Him, even they who pierced Him. And all the tribes of the earth will mourn because of Him. Even so, Amen. 8 "I am the Alpha and the Omega, *the* Beginning and *the* End,"* says the Lord,* "who is and who was and who is to come, the Almighty." NKJV

(143) Hebrews 4:12-13 NKJV

12 For the word of God *is* living and powerful, and sharper than any two-edged sword, piercing even to the division of soul and spirit, and of joints and marrow, and is a discerner of the thoughts and intents of the heart. 13 And there is no creature hidden from His sight, but all things *are* naked and open to the eyes of Him to whom we *must give* account. NKJV

(144) Revelation 6:15-17 CEV
15 The kings of the earth, its famous people, and its military leaders hid in caves or behind rocks on the mountains. They hid there together with the rich and the powerful and with all the slaves and free people. 16 Then they shouted to the mountains and the rocks, "Fall on us! Hide us from the one who sits on the throne and from the anger of the Lamb. 17 That terrible day has come! God and the Lamb will show their anger, and who can face it?" CEV

(145) James 1:21-25 NKJV
21 Therefore lay aside all filthiness and overflow of wickedness, and receive with meekness the implanted word, which is able to save your souls. 22 But be doers of the word, and not hearers only, deceiving yourselves. 23 For if anyone is a hearer of the word and not a doer, he is like a man observing his natural face in a mirror; 24 for he observes himself, goes away, and immediately forgets what kind of man he was. 25 But he who looks into the perfect law of liberty and continues *in it,* and is not a forgetful hearer but a doer of the work, this one will be blessed in what he does. NKJV

(146) Joel 2:11-13 KJV
11 And the Lord shall utter his voice before his army: for his camp is very great: for he is strong that executeth his word: for the day of the Lord is great and very terrible; and who can abide it? 12 Therefore also now, saith the Lord, turn ye even to me with all your heart, and with fasting, and with weeping, and with mourning: 13 And rend your heart, and not your garments, and turn unto the Lord your God: for he is gracious and merciful, slow to anger, and of great kindness, and repenteth him of the evil. KJV

(147) Joel 2:28-32 NLT
28 *"Then, after doing all those things, I will pour out my Spirit upon all people. Your sons and daughters will prophesy. Your old men will dream dreams, and your young men will see visions. 29 In those days I will pour out my Spirit even on servants—men and women alike. 30 And I will cause wonders in the heavens and on the earth—blood and fire and columns of smoke. 31 The sun will become dark, and the moon will turn blood red before that great and terrible* day of the Lord arrives. 32 But everyone who calls on the name of the Lord will be saved, for some on Mount Zion in Jerusalem will escape, just as the Lord has said. These will be among the survivors whom the Lord has called. Holy Bible, New Living Translation ®, copyright © 1996, 2004 by Tyndale Charitable Trust. Used by permission of Tyndale House Publishers. All rights reserved.

(148) 1 John 3:1-3 NKJV
3 Behold what manner of love the Father has bestowed on us, that we should be called children of God!* Therefore the world does not know us,* because it did not know Him. 2 Beloved, now we are children of God; and it has not yet been revealed what we shall be, but we know that when He is revealed, we shall be like Him, for we shall see Him as He is. 3 And everyone who has this hope in Him purifies himself, just as He is pure. NKJV